Praise for *Creative People Must Be Stopped*

"Read *Creative People Must Be Stopped* only if you are serious about making stuff, and making stuff happen. This is a survival guide for navigating a world that is dangerous for good ideas. And it is required reading for the creative people who love them!"

—Peter Durand, founder, The Center for Graphic Facilitation, and creative director, Alphachimp Studio Inc.

"This is no rarefied academic treatment on innovation as an abstract ideal, but a nuts-and-bolts handbook to dissecting our thought patterns about innovation. Owens dispels the myth that innovation is a binary trait that either exists or does not in a given product, process, or business model. *Creative People Must Be Stopped* addresses the myriad ways that novel ideas can fail in the marketplace. Working through a combination of thought experiments and real-world examples, the book demonstrates how failures in understanding the context for innovation can prove every bit as deadly to progress as failures of imagination."

—Mark Rowan, president, Griffin Technology Inc., maker of iPod, iPhone, and iPad accessories

"*Creative People Must Be Stopped* is among the best books ever written about human imagination in the workplace. David Owens is a master innovator, having practiced his craft as a product designer, researcher, teacher, creativity coach, and executive. The breadth and depth of his experience fills every page of this little gem, which is chock-full of hundreds of big and little steps that you can take right now to do more creative work and to lead more innovative teams and organizations."

—Robert Sutton, professor, Stanford University, and author of the *New York Times* bestseller *Good Boss, Bad Boss*

Creative People Must Be Stopped

Six Ways We Kill Innovation (Without Even Trying)

David A. Owens

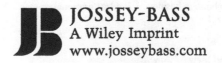
JOSSEY-BASS
A Wiley Imprint
www.josseybass.com

Published by Jossey-Bass
A Wiley Imprint
989 Market Street, San Francisco, CA 94103-1741—www.josseybass.com

Readers should be aware that Internet Web sites offered as citations and/or sources for
further information may have changed or disappeared between the time this was written
and when it is read.

Limit of Liability/Disclaimer of Warranty: While the publisher and author have used their
best efforts in preparing this book, they make no representations or warranties with respect
to the accuracy or completeness of the contents of this book and specifically disclaim any
implied warranties of merchantability or fitness for a particular purpose. No warranty may
be created or extended by sales representatives or written sales materials. The advice and
strategies contained herein may not be suitable for your situation. You should consult
with a professional where appropriate. Neither the publisher nor author shall be liable for
any loss of profit or any other commercial damages, including but not limited to special,
incidental, consequential, or other damages.

Jossey-Bass books and products are available through most bookstores. To contact Jossey-
Bass directly call our Customer Care Department within the U.S. at 800-956-7739, outside
the U.S. at 317-572-3986, or fax 317-572-4002.

Jossey-Bass also publishes its books in a variety of electronic formats. Some content that
appears in print may not be available in electronic books.

Library of Congress Cataloging-in-Publication Data
Owens, David A.
   Creative people must be stopped: six ways we kill innovation (without even trying) /
David A. Owens.—1st ed.
       p. cm.
   Includes bibliographical references and index.
   ISBN 978-1-118-00290-2 (hardback); ISBN 978-1-118-12900-5 (ebk);
   ISBN 978-1-118-12901-2 (ebk); ISBN 978-1-118-12902-9 (ebk)
      1. Creative ability in business.   2. Organizational change.   I. Title.
   HD53.O94   2012
   658.4'063—dc23   2011032504

Printed in the United States of America
FIRST EDITION
HB Printing   SKY10034426_051722

Contents

This book is dedicated to my lovely ladies,
Jennifer, Charlotte, and Adelaide

Introduction

Creative People Must Be Stopped!

Given that a search on the term "innovation" returns more than forty thousand book entries on Amazon.com, does the world really need another book on the topic? Maybe the better question is *Why do so many organizations continue to kill good ideas and fail in their innovation attempts despite this wealth of research and advice?*

Innovation is a natural and desirable outcome of human interaction, yet it is systematically stopped in organizations, often by the very people who say they want it and who stand to benefit from it. I term these systematic stoppages *innovation constraints*.

Over the course of ten years of research, teaching, and consulting, I have identified the six dominant types of constraints that can keep creative new ideas from being formulated, developed into marketable products and services, or adopted by the intended users. This book organizes these innovation killers into a conceptual framework that demystifies what innovation is, how it happens, and how we stop it without even trying. In my executive programs, workshops, talks, and consulting engagements, thousands of managers, executives, and innovators have successfully used the framework to diagnose the primary causes of innovation failure in their organizations and to develop strategies for overcoming them. My goal in this book is to bring this power of understanding, diagnosing, and removing constraints on innovation to many, many more.

Although this book relies on academic research in a variety of disciplines to help explain why things happen the way they do, it is above all a practical guide to a new way of thinking about innovation, complete with diagnostic and other tools, as well as suggestions for action. It is not, however, a laundry list of "Do this, don't do that" advice. Rather, this book is aimed at giving aspiring innovators and managers of innovation the conceptual and practical basis they need to develop their own actionable insights and smart strategies for responding to the challenges of coming up with exciting new ideas and bringing them to fruition.

CHAPTER 1

The Context of Innovation

Why Everyone Wants Innovation but No One Wants to Change

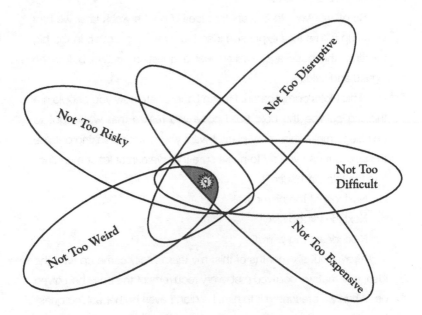

Figure 1.1

Our firm was in a bit of a slump. We had a hugely successful product a few years ago, but now we were facing increasing pressure to come up with the follow-up product, the next big thing. One day the big boss called the team into the office and said,

"People, this is serious. It has got to be big! Look, I really need you to think outside the box—don't constrain yourselves! Listen, I really want you to push the boundaries *way* out there on this one; remember, we're talking blue-sky this time—a real breakthrough!"

So the team and I ran off, excited, and "box be damned," we started thinking big. Just two sleepless weeks later, we had found it! We had come up with a *great* idea! So we set up a meeting to present it. In the meeting the boss listened for a while, asking a question or two. Then he let out a loud sigh and said,

"Hmm . . . this looks expensive . . . I mean, I appreciate how you people are thinking outside the box, but I hope you realize that we have a business to run here. Now remember that I *do* want you to keep thinking outside the box, but can you try to make sure that it's not quite so expensive?"

So off we went to find another idea. About a week later we had come up with a less expensive idea that was even better. In the big meeting, the boss again asked just a question or two before he sighed and said,

"This looks complicated. I mean I appreciate how you people are thinking outside the box, but I hope you realize that we've got to be able to make this in our plant. I want you to keep thinking outside the box, but can you try to make sure that we can at least manufacture the thing in-house?!"

Next idea: "Too disruptive!"

Next idea: "Too risky!"

Next idea: "Too weird!"

After about six months of this, my team finally came up with the idea, one that we believed met every requirement the boss had given us. When we presented it to him, he didn't even bother asking questions. Ten minutes into our spiel, he became agitated and said,

"This looks puny! I mean, I asked you people to think outside the box, and all you can bring me is this puny idea? What's wrong with you people? Don't you know how to be creative?"

———————

As the rate of product and service innovation speeds up, so does the need for a meaningful competitive response. For executives, managers, and employees in many organizations, this "innovation imperative" has been successfully met. Witness the many amazing innovations heaped upon us in the last ten years, from cell phones to smart phones, from MP3s to online television, from self-balancing scooters to private space travel.

This constant stream of newness left me curious about how executives and managers lead the aspiring innovators in their organizations on a path to successful innovation, so I started to ask them. In my executive programs, workshops, and consulting engagements, I began to ask people to tell me the stories of how innovation was managed and led in their organizations. Invariably they tell me surprising stories like the one you just read.

I have heard these tales of frustration again and again from people in organizations big and small across a wide swath of industries and in countries around the globe. To be fair, the story doesn't always point the finger at the boss as the lead knucklehead in torpedoing innovation efforts. Variations of the story implicate customers, clients, partners, suppliers, colleagues, and even the team itself.

Although I occasionally came across people who have more positive things to say, their stories tend to portray successful innovation in their organizations as isolated incidents or accidents of fate. So even though I had started out wondering how managers lead successful innovation, the impassioned frustration I had heard from thousands of people led me to a different set of questions, the ones at the heart of this book: *Why do people in organizations seem to work overtime ignoring, undermining, blocking, maiming, and killing the innocent, well-intentioned, and sometimes even great ideas in their organizations? Why do they so often act as if creative people must be stopped? And What can we do to change these behaviors so that innovation has a better chance to succeed?*

Why Does Innovation Fail?

There are countless variations on the familiar story of innovations being torpedoed even before they are launched, or of being launched with great fanfare only to sink without a trace once they hit the marketplace. Here are just a few from my personal experience:

- In an experiment aimed at improving its ability to innovate, a large consumer products company known for lean operations, low prices, and derivative products invents a breakthrough product that can launch it to the lead in a large and extremely competitive segment of the industry it serves. Before it can get the product through its development process, the firm lays off all of the people involved with the project, citing financial pressures. The project never regains momentum and is cancelled.

- Because they have an intimate understanding of their clients' businesses, the partners of an accounting consultancy agree to start an innovation practice aimed at helping clients grow their businesses. The new practice stalls when the partners, despite their earlier enthusiasm, refuse to refer their clients to the innovation consultants. The partners want proof that the innovation methods will work without creating any risk for their clients. Without clients to prove or improve their methods, the new practice languishes and eventually shuts down.

- A part-time inventor has the idea to invent a digital picture frame ten years before it becomes a household product. He starts working on the project until an expert from the electronics industry he meets tells him it's a dumb idea that will be too expensive and not even possible. The inventor gives up all interest in pursuing the project any further.

- A university seeking to increase the rate at which technologies are moved out of the lab and into commercial products undertakes a significant effort to build, house, and fund an organization for the purpose. Successful entrepreneurs avoid the place, saying that the university researchers have no idea what makes an idea a potential commercial success; the university researchers avoid the place, saying that the entrepreneurs have no imagination and care only about making money from their research.

- Consistent with its mission, a performing arts organization seeks to expand its ability to offer more modern and controversial works. After a multiyear capital campaign, it is able to build the larger and more flexible space it needed to support its goal. A few years after moving into the new space, the organization finds itself paying for the expansion by performing even more standards and commercial works than before out of a need to draw larger audiences than the modern, controversial pieces attracted.

On the surface, these stories have little in common beyond the theme of innovation failure. The contexts are very different from one another, the players are diverse, and in each case the causes of the failure seem to be distinctive if not difficult to pinpoint. Yet with the right conceptual tools, I believe we can analyze both failures and successes in innovation efforts. We can discover the common themes that run through stories like these, and in the process derive powerful lessons for how to increase our own chances of success.

Six Perspectives on Innovation

To understand why innovation fails so often, I began combing through the enormous quantity of books, articles, and cases devoted to innovation and creativity. I quickly found, as you may have also, that these writings seemed to be talking about innovation and related concepts from wildly divergent and often unrelated perspectives. Worse, the perspectives offered by one thinker or researcher conflicted with the insights of others. However, after years of initial confusion, a pattern emerged. There were, I discovered, six basic perspectives on innovation and what impedes it.

One set of books had as their ideology, or basic theory, the unsurprising idea that *the basic requirement for innovation is creative ideas*. Failures of innovation were therefore failures of *ideas*: individuals either did not generate good enough ideas or didn't recognize their good ideas for what they were and chose an inferior one. Intuitively this makes sense—without a good idea to base it on, innovation won't happen. To meet this challenge, you simply need to train people to use the tools and processes that help them "think different," and this will enable them to become better at generating and recognizing good ideas.

A second group of thinkers found this individual-centric view of innovation entirely unconvincing. For them, innovation fails because of a dysfunction in the emotional and cultural climate of the group undertaking an innovation initiative. Supported by experimental research and documented cases, they described precisely the emotional dynamics and social environments that reliably kill, among other things, the engagement, risk-taking, and creative expression necessary for innovation. This perspective could be summed up as *even if you have a roomful of da Vincis, the group's social climate will determine whether an innovation succeeds*. The prescription that follows from this diagnosis is equally clear: fix the group's climate, and you will fix innovation. At this point I had identified two compelling kinds of explanation for the failure of innovation. I probably should have quit while I was ahead. It turned out there were several more to come.

A third perspective came from writers who took an organization-centric approach. These authors convincingly showed how a firm's strategy, organizational structure, and access to resources were critical to successful innovation. If a firm doesn't have the intention of innovating and moving beyond its past laurels, or if it doesn't have a structure that allows for the free movement of new ideas, or if it doesn't have the human, monetary, or other resources to expend on developing an idea, then it's unlikely to be a fertile source of innovation. With an eye to big bureaucratic organizations like governments, educational institutions, and commodity producers in mature markets, the case seems easy to make: *the problem of innovation is the problem of organizing people in a way that won't kill it.*

A fourth set of writers widened the analytical lens even more and approached the problem of innovation from a market economics perspective. For them, innovation fails when a firm competing among a group of rivals in an industry fails to produce an innovation that the customers in that market are willing to adopt. In this perspective, *innovation fails when buyers do not adopt a new offering because they fail to see the utility and value of it.* If people don't adopt the idea, you may be able to call an idea "creative," but you cannot call it an innovation.

A fifth set of writers opened the lens still wider, emphasizing the social values of the individuals and groups for whom an innovation is intended. Their basic proposition is that *an innovation cannot succeed if a society does not see its ideals and aspirations embodied in it.* As we will discuss later, a good example of this argument is human cloning, or creating a human directly from the DNA of another human. Plants and animals have been successfully cloned in the past, so we might assume that human cloning is technologically possible and arguably would have certain benefits. However, most societies around the world ban the practice on the grounds that it is morally and ethically repugnant. Clearly, innovations that are discordant with societal values are unlikely to succeed.

Finally, a sixth perspective approached failures of innovation from a technological perspective. The premise was simple: some things are just hard to do. It is hard to keep the body alive during brain surgery, to derive energy from the splitting of uranium atoms in a controlled and safe way, or to plug an oil leak fifty miles offshore and one mile beneath the surface of the ocean. This perspective makes a strong case for the view that *for an innovation to succeed, it has to be technologically feasible.* In this view, the way to avoid failure is to advance our understanding and control of matter and energy through the use of science and technology. In other words, innovation is exactly what we already know as R&D.

Too Much of a Good Thing?

The table summarizes the six perspectives on innovation I have described. All six agree that there are interventions that can make innovation more likely to succeed. The only trouble is that each perspective assigns fault for failures in innovation to a different set of causes and therefore recommends a different set of "fixes."

Six Perspectives on Innovation		
Why Does Innovation Fail?	How Do We Fix Innovation?	Focus of Analysis
Individuals do not "think different"; they don't generate enough good ideas, the raw material of innovation.	The individual must improve his or her cognitive ability to recognize and generate relevant new ideas.	The individual
Groups allow negative emotions to derail the process of evaluating and implementing new ideas.	The group's processes and culture must be designed to support collaboration, open communication, and risk-taking.	The group
Organizations are designed to produce routine and consistent outputs, and innovation threatens this intended function.	The organization's strategy and structure must be changed in ways that support risk-taking and the development of new initiatives.	The organization

Six Perspectives on Innovation (Continued)		
Why Does Innovation Fail?	How Do We Fix Innovation?	Focus of Analysis
Industries are oriented toward the needs of today's markets and industry incumbents, and their customers are resistant to ideas that might alter the economic status quo.	The market served by an industry must be shown the utility and value of a new idea, and this is done through the creation of new products, markets, and industries.	The industry
Society rejects or regulates new ideas that are inconsistent with prevailing norms and ethics and members' sense of identity.	The society has to be shown how new ideas are legitimate, and this is best done in terms that it already accepts.	The society
New technologies take time, expertise, and resources to develop and will be adopted only once proven effective and reliable.	New technologies are best created by significant investment in research, development, and commercialization capabilities.	The technology

What emerges from this survey of work on innovation? First, as you look down the rows of the chart, your response to each perspective might well be "Of course!" *Of course* you need good ideas, *of course* you need a supportive group, *of course* you need the right organizational structure, and so on. Beyond intuition, each of these perspectives has been developed through a long history of thoughtful observation, research, and practice by a long list of reputable academics, writers, and managers. Yet each group thinks it has found *the* key to understanding innovation. They can't possibly all be misguided or wrong. Or can they?

A General Framework for Understanding Innovation

Let's agree that each of the perspectives offers an important insight into innovation. What are we to make of all of them, taken together? To answer this question, consider the work of designers and design consultants. In my experience working as a designer on many kinds of projects for many different clients, from laptops to luggage, from ski goggles to wine-in-a-box, I found that all designs had to meet some specific and detailed requirements. But these requirements were entirely different depending on the product, the client, the intended user, and sometimes even the design team itself. My job as designer was to tease out a deep and nuanced understanding of the particular requirements that would govern the problem I had been asked to solve. This is to say that the full set of requirements acted as a set of *constraints* on the solutions that might be possible and meaningful.

Here is an example of what I mean. A design consultancy I know well was hired in the mid-1990s to design a handheld personal digital assistant (PDA) device. Right off the bat there were clear requirements that would have to be met. Obviously, the cost of manufacturing the ultimate product would have to be less than the price customers were willing to pay for it. Success would also require that the design meet certain size requirements. While the PDA had to be large enough to accommodate the applications it was intended for, such as managing to-do lists, calendars, and a digital Rolodex of contact information, it couldn't be too large to fit in an average adult's hand. There were other requirements as well, governing such characteristics as screen size, weight, battery life, durability, and attractiveness. Another way to say this is that a successful solution—one that would be accepted by the client and welcomed by the ultimate users—had to satisfy a particular set of *constraints* if it was to be acceptable to the company that wanted to sell it and attractive to the customers who might buy it.

Using this same reasoning, look back at the chart summarizing the six perspectives on innovation. Each of these views can be seen as describing one of the general constraints that must be satisfied for an innovation effort to be successful. I can illustrate this point using the financial innovation called Keep the Change, a bank debit card program offered by Bank of America. The program works as follows: as an adopter of the innovation (that is, a member of the program), all of your debit card purchases that do not result in a round-dollar total amount are rounded up to the next whole dollar value, and the difference is transferred from your debit card account (usually your checking account) into your savings account. Thus if you purchase a cup of coffee and charge the resulting total of $5.51, the bank will round the amount deducted from your debit card account up to $6.00. Of that $6.00, $5.51 of it will go to the coffee shop, and the $0.49 remainder will be transferred into your savings account. Depending on how many purchases you make on the card, you can end up with a nice little treasure in your savings account at the end of the year.

Relating this innovation to the table, start in the first row, the individual-centric view. The truism of this view is that for successful innovation to take place, there must first of all be an individual with a good idea. Whether individuals act alone or in groups, in effect these authors were saying that innovating successfully requires meeting the *individual innovation constraint* of being able and willing to generate and recognize a new and relevant idea. When we apply that insight to the debit card innovation, it's clear that a person was able to generate this service product idea, probably on the basis of the insight that most people aren't able to (or don't like to) deposit large amounts of money in their savings accounts, but don't mind putting aside some "pocket change" now and again.

The second row of the table reflects the assumptions that innovation always involves the participation and cooperation of other people as contributors, collaborators, or supporters, and that group dynamics can therefore be critical to the fate of the idea. This means that success depends on satisfying some specific *group innovation constraints*. The Keep the Change innovation therefore required a group, most likely the design team, to understand and refine the original idea, probably first at a brainstorm meeting and then much later at an executive-level approval presentation. You can imagine that the project might generate controversy among bankers because it involves taking a *different* amount from the customer's account than he or she signed for at the point of purchase. As you can well imagine, this kind of small technical detail could easily have been a justification for killing the proposal at this stage.

The perspective described in the third row of the table emphasizes that an organization pursuing innovation must have the strategy, structure, and resources needed to carry an idea from conception all the way through implementation. In other words, to innovate successfully, we must satisfy some set of *organizational innovation constraints*. This means that Bank of America must possess the will, skills, and resources needed to implement the concept. The bank would need the resources for actually building and debugging the service, the ability to create awareness of it, and the ability to implement it using resources in its control.

Next are the *industry innovation constraints* inherent in the perspective that sees success as possible only when an innovation, be it product, process, or service, delivers a higher level of performance to customers at a cost that is as good as or better than current offerings. There is no requirement that cost be measured in dollars or performance in any particular units. For example, for some the cost of time may be significant, while performance might be measured in the pride that ownership brings. As a constraint this requires the bank to find a market of people for whom this is a valuable service. Given that Bank of America is among the largest in the country, finding potential adopters may not have been the hard part. It would also need to ensure that rival banks didn't steal or copy the idea and offer it at a lower price. It's probably also obvious that it needs to get more returns from the program than the costs it incurs, while still remaining price competitive in the personal bank account market.

Assuming that we've met all the requirements so far, society will test our proposed innovations against its moral, ethical, and legal standards. In effect, the fifth perspective is telling us that we'll also need to meet a set of *societal innovation constraints*. In order to protect vulnerable consumers, society will require that this banking innovation meet the spirit and the letter of the banking laws, both at the state and federal levels. For their part, participants in the program need to value the "savings" aspect of the program, while also not feeling that any downside to the program was unfair, as might occur if, for example, your account was overdrawn because more was transferred than you realized.

Finally, our sixth perspective makes the credible, if obvious, claim that to be successful, an innovation must actually exist in the world and that it must function in an intended and desirable way. In other words, a fundamental requirement of innovation is that we satisfy a particular set of *technological innovation constraints*. Here the bank must, for instance, be able to unequivocally identify members and nonmembers of the program in order to determine relevant fund transfer amounts. It must also be able to execute the funds transfers without errors and not, for example, transfer funds from an overdrawn account.

The Venn diagram in Figure 1.2 is a visual depiction of the overlapping requirements of the six constraints. Each constraint is represented by an oval with the area inside the oval representing when the condition is being met. Areas of overlap between any two or more ovals represent the conditions under which multiple

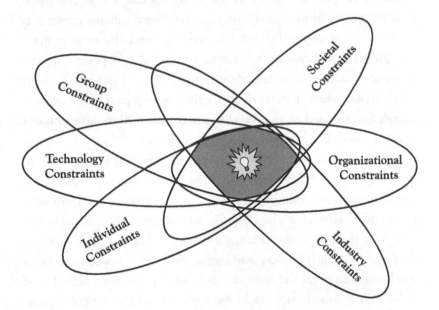

Figure 1.2

constraints are met. My proposition here is that *any* real, proposed, or even hypothetical innovation will have to satisfy all of the constraints presented by the context of that innovation. A quick trip to the Bank of America Web site proves that it was successful in meeting all six of the constraints.

Diagnosing Innovation Failures

By making the conditions of success clearer and more specific, the framework of six types of constraints can also illuminate the reasons why a particular innovation has failed. To see how, let's return to three of the brief examples I presented at the beginning of this chapter. In the case of the consumer products company with the breakthrough product that failed to move into production, *industry constraints* were apparent in the form of this organization's role within its industry as a "fast-follower" organization that waits for others to prove a market first; this made the company uncomfortable with competing on the basis of product innovation versus relying on its customary advantage of efficiency. The mention of "financial pressures" suggests that *organizational constraints* took the form of insufficient resources to fund the new project. Organizational innovation constraints are also apparent in the company's structure; it maintained its ability to manufacture its derivative products efficiently by sacrificing that part of the organization that focused on new products that were still in development and that were not currently producing revenue.

In the case of the part-time inventor, although he was able to come up with a promising idea, thus overcoming the *individual* constraints, he succumbed to *group* constraints in the form of a potential collaborator who ridiculed and dismissed his ideas. Rather than face the possibility of being embarrassed again, he decided to drop the project. It is also possible that the expert would have been vindicated if in fact the state of electronics at the time meant that *technological* constraints would have prevented the inventor from turning his idea into a viable product.

The arts organization appears to suffer from a combination of *organizational* and *societal* constraints. It has tied up immense resources in a building that has high value but comes with an even higher cost. Although the space is nice, the requirements of maintaining it create significant financial pressure on the organization. As a result, it finds itself forced to cater more than ever to the tastes and social values of potential audiences who are unwilling to pay to watch art being made when they just want to be entertained.

Identifying the "Showstopper" Constraint(s)

This framework of innovation constraints helps us understand more specifically why an attempt to innovate fails: it runs afoul of one or more of the six main types of constraints. But as you may have already started to see from the examples just discussed, in any given case the constraints are not all created equal. Instead, any given innovation is likely to satisfy several constraints (including the ones we intuitively see as important, and therefore pay attention to) but fail on one or more *critical* constraints (often ones we have failed to take into account). Identifying those showstopping constraints will further sharpen our understanding of why a particular innovation succeeds or fails.

One example of using the framework in this way concerns the early development of a product called Sow-N-Gro. The product comes in the form of a spongy black round mat about a half-inch thick and available in a variety of diameters ranging from about six to about twelve inches. This mat is made of organic materials and is intended for the inside bottom of pots that contain potted plants. According to the product packaging, the Sow-N-Gro material "retains moisture, promotes root growth, [and] releases nitrogen." The individually packaged mats were to be offered at a very economical price in the home and urban gardening enthusiast market.

At first glance, this innovative product, assuming it does what the packaging claims, would seem destined for immediate success, particularly in a segment of society that harbors increasing concerns about synthetic chemicals and excessive fertilizer use. Unfortunately, early success was elusive. A simple pass through the constraint analysis will show why.

At the individual level, someone had come up with a promising idea and recognized it as a good one, so it seems that individual constraints were met. Inasmuch as the innovation made it all the way from the "aha!" moment to production, we have to assume that it survived group constraints and won backing from people who helped fund and develop the idea. The Sow-N-Gro organization was created to commercialize the concept, and it possessed the skills and resources necessary to manufacture the material and get it in front of the retailers and distributors who would facilitate retail sale and adoption. This suggests that organizational constraints were met. The material was abundant, and the processes for matting and packaging it were relatively inexpensive. Because it had never been used in this industry before, it had no direct competitor in the "no chemicals" home gardener market, thus satisfying the industry constraints. The fiber was easily sterilized and therefore met all health code requirements that might impede importing it into the United States, thereby meeting a key societal constraint.

Despite all this, Sow-N-Gro didn't fly off the shelves. The product exists, meets a real need, is priced right, and can't be faulted for failing to do what it promised. The problem is with the last step—adoption by the intended users. But where exactly had the innovator and the organization gone wrong?

Clues to the answer may lie in the negative reaction Sow-N-Gro elicits from people when I pass samples around in seminars and workshops. At first, when I pass the disk around the room and people look at it, sniff it, and feel it, they are mostly sold. Where can they buy some of these organic plant disks? they ask. Then I show them the product packaging. As that gets passed around, there is invariably a gasp as someone reads the statement of what the product contains. It proudly states, "Sow-N-Gro is 100% Recycled Human Hair." Suddenly the enthusiasm for the product vaporizes. The poor person holding the material at the moment involuntarily flings the mat onto the floor in disgust. No one seems to want anything more to do with it after that (except to make jokes about one of the bald men in attendance).

These admittedly unscientific samplings of potential customers' reactions point to the showstopping constraint that the makers of Sow-N-Gro failed to anticipate. We clearly have a problem when an innovation's intended customers say "Yuck!" and fling the product to the floor when they are told what it is made of. Fundamentally, Sow-N-Gro, an economically and technologically sound product, fails at the *societal* level—at least in our culture— by clashing with the values of the people it was designed for. So oblivious to this constraint were the manufacturers of the product that they actually boasted about Sow-N-Gro's fatal flaw.

Beyond casting light on what exactly went wrong with Sow-N-Gro, this diagnosis suggests what we need to do to give the innovation a better chance of success. We need to somehow "enlarge" the societal-level constraint in a way that allows it to enter the full overlap—that is, the area where the constraints can *all* be satisfied (see Figure 1.3).

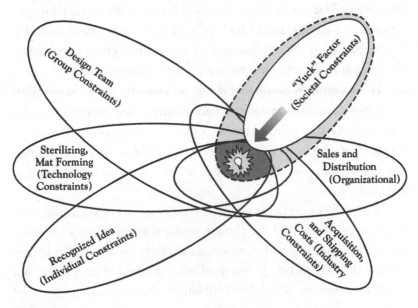

Figure 1.3

At this point I ask people how they might go about fixing the innovation problem in this way. With this little bit of coaxing, the ideas come pouring out. First, use a different material—anything but human hair. Another common piece of advice is to prevaricate about the contents: disclose the truth, but not too much of the truth. Simply call it "organic material" or "natural keratin" or, as human hair is described scientifically, "filamentous biomaterial." Clearly the company received and acted on similar advice; the latest iterations of the product describe it as "all-natural organic plant-growth supplement."

A later version of the product shows several other ways that an enlarged overlap was pursued. The name Sow-N-Gro is confusing. When heard aurally it is not clear which meaning of the sound "so" is intended: So? Sew? Sow? Changing the name to SmartGrow alleviated that confusion. The new name SmartGrow also served to enlarge the constraint by enacting a basic strategy of marketing: change the basis of comparison. The consumer is led to conclude, *Since this stuff is the smart grow, that other stuff on the shelf next to it must be "dumb grow"*! Another tactic was to change the color of the packaging. The original packaging was bright yellow, which brought to my mind the last time I had spilled a large quantity of Roundup herbicide on my lawn. Changing to a "healthy" green color makes for a much more coherent presentation to the consumer.

This example suggests that if we can identify the key constraints for a particular innovation, we can usually come up with ideas for interventions that increase the odds that our innovation will succeed. Quite often the knowledge we need is already at hand. We already know the things we need to know; we just need to remember that we know them.

With the benefit of hindsight, identifying the key constraint may seem quite simple. Yet the showstopping constraint on what came to be known as SmartGrow managed to elude the smart people who invented, manufactured, and packaged it. And their case is not at all uncommon. Why? The problem is that we tend to interpret situations using only our "favored" constraint perspectives, the ones that we are most comfortable with, based on our experience, training, area of expertise, and so on. As a result, we may spend a great deal of time and energy on the wrong set of problems. For example, the makers of Sow-N-Gro may have initially congratulated themselves on having come up with a new idea and conquering every technological challenge in producing it. At that point they might have felt that their key problem was "industry economics." In that case they might have devoted their attention to the question, *How can we cut our costs so that we can price our product more competitively?* Now this may have been wise, in that price might well have been a significant constraint, one that could sink their product if it were not met. However, there was an even more binding constraint that became evident only after the product was already on the market.

What we need is the kind of vision correction that will enable us to see *in advance* the vital factors that determine our chances for success when we embark on an innovation. This is just what the constraints framework is designed to provide.

How to Use This Book

I have found this innovation constraints framework to be applicable to every type of innovation in all of the hundreds of organizations that I have worked with. I have been using the framework (along with appropriate tools) on a daily basis in my teaching, workshops, and consulting to give individuals and organizations the analytical and practical knowledge they need to identify, understand, and overcome the particular constraints they face.

To put the constraints framework to work in your own situation, you need several things:

- An overview of innovation constraints that you reliably apply so that you are sure not to overlook a potential source of disaster

- A clear understanding of each of the six main types of innovation constraints

- A way to diagnose which of the constraints is particularly critical for the case at hand (there may be more than one) so that you can direct your attention and corrective action appropriately

- Ideas for how to satisfy or overcome those key constraints

Over the next six chapters, I will explore each type of constraint in detail, showing how it operates and why, with plentiful examples drawn from real-world cases. The analysis is followed by a discussion of ways that the particular constraints can be overcome. Toward the end of each chapter, you will find a "constraints diagnostic survey" that you and your colleagues can fill out and score. The surveys are based on my research and consulting work and will serve as a pointer to the most urgent and potentially limiting constraints you are facing. (An electronic version can be found on the book's Web site.) Appendix A, Using the Assessment Results, presents a process for analyzing your diagnostic results to help you pinpoint the steps you can take to overcome the constraints you have identified in each chapter. The appendix also contains additional exercises to help you move toward action. In the last chapter of the book, I will consider how the constraints model might be applied to your potential customers, explore the big-picture issues in leading an innovation team, and discuss the steps you might take to help your organization become more strategic about innovation.

Taken together, the analysis, stories, recommendations, and tools in this book provide a springboard for effective action, not a fail-safe recipe for success. No one can give you that recipe, especially when it comes to innovation, which by definition is constantly new. Only you can devise the specific solutions that will work for your particular situation. But if you engage with the analysis in the chapters to come, and follow through with the diagnostic surveys and exercises, you will be able to identify and come to grips with innovation killers with a deeper and sharper understanding of what they are and how you can overcome them.

Summary

It is puzzling when people say that they want innovation, then seem to do everything they can to stop it; but this is bound to happen when we rely on our vague intuitions and don't have a clear idea of what innovation is or how it really works. This mystery is compounded by the thousands upon thousands of authors and thinkers who use differing definitions of innovation and who diverge completely in their prescriptions about how to make it work. However, there is one assumption they all have in common—that there are specific conditions or constraints that have to be met in order for innovation to be successful—that serves as the key for bringing the six perspectives into a single framework.

The innovation constraints framework described in this book allows you to gain deeper and more specific insights about the constraint or set of constraints that were critical for a particular innovation. By learning to analyze these constraints in advance, turning from retrospective analysis to proactive strategy development, you can dramatically improve your chances of innovation success.

CHAPTER

2

Why Most of Us Are More Creative Than We Think

Individual Innovation Constraints

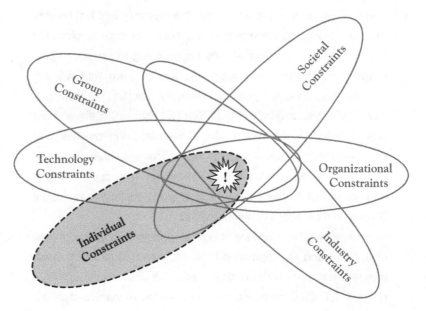

Figure 2.1

In 1966, after finishing his PhD in chemistry, young Spence Silver joined the R&D division of a diverse and entrepreneurial products company. Then, in 1968, while working in one of the labs, essentially "fooling around" with some of the company's established technology, Silver developed what should have been a high-end version of one of its core products. Unfortunately, the product he had invented simply could not compete against the firm's current product lineup. Still he thought it might be interesting to play with.

Instead of throwing the experiment away and starting over, Silver insisted on showing the thing to his colleagues. He characterizes the reception as "not stellar." Still he continued to play with it and show it around.

Over the next five years, Silver kept working on his pet idea without the faintest idea of what it might actually be useful for. Unwilling to take no for an answer, he continued to hold seminars for people throughout the company, hoping that maybe they would have a better idea for how to use his technology. Unfortunately, they didn't.

Some time later, Art Fry, another employee of the firm, realized that he had a problem that Silver's invention might just be able to solve: organizing the music for his hobby of choir singing. Fry met with Silver, and together they began trying to develop a prototype. Over the next two years, the two of them kept working on their "unauthorized" project, eventually resorting to building a prototype-manufacturing setup in Silver's basement. Several more years passed by the time a stable manufacturing process was developed. As this was happening, Fry had taken to giving away the invention to a few people inside the company. They started using it and began to tell other colleagues; the users couldn't get enough! So maybe there was a demand, after all.

Armed with this evidence about the potential popularity of their idea, Silver and Fry approached the marketing department. There they received "an unenthusiastic reception." It was only through Fry's appeals for the intervention of more senior managers that the marketing group begrudgingly agreed to help market the invention.

In the first market trials, conducted in four major cities, customers failed to see the value of the product and didn't bite. The marketing department was clear that the project should now be put to rest. Fry rejected these findings, believing that people loved the product once they used it, but that no amount of advertising could convey its true value. He appealed to the chairman and CEO for help. Only after this high level of intervention did the marketing group agree to conduct a final trial, a very expensive "product sampling" strategy in the Boise, Idaho, test market.

In that test, they found that more than 90 percent of the people who tried the product wanted to buy it, so it was finally given the official go-ahead. In 1980, twelve long years after Sliver's accidental invention of an "inferior adhesive," the product they invented for 3M, the Post-it, finally launched.

There are a number of questions that may come to mind in this story of the travails of a creative individual in a bureaucratic organization. For example, what motivates a person like Silver to keep working on a failed and unauthorized project for over five years? What enabled him to perceive the makings of a successful invention where others saw only a failed experiment? Why do some people continue to push hard and long while others give up at the first sign of rejection or resistance? Was 3M just lucky to find Silver, or did he possess some secret qualities that the company identified in its recruiting process? Were Silver's creative abilities genetic and unique only to him, or are they ones everyone has but that they just don't express? And, finally, why on earth wasn't he fired!?

Are Innovators Born or Made?

You may have heard the Post-it saga before and wondered why 3M didn't see the immense value of Silver's product much earlier. That is the thought that occupied me the first time I heard it. But after considering the story more carefully over the years, I came to understand it to be less about how organizations recognize a brilliant idea and more about how they make innovation immensely difficult because they don't understand what creativity is or how to foster it.

Despite one hundred years of study, there is still a great deal of contention about what creativity is and where it comes from. The one thing that does seem certain, however, may surprise you: *there is no such thing as a creative personality* (Taggar, 2002). At least, creativity is not a fundamental attribute of "personality" in the technical sense that psychologists reserve for those core behavioral tendencies that are relatively stable over time, such as how introverted or extroverted we are.

But if personality is not what determines how creative we are, then what is? Research suggests that our habits of perception and thinking drive creativity more than some mysterious genetic trait— and habits are things we can do something about. Specifically, the power to be creative largely relies on three core components:

- Perception
- Intellection (thinking)
- Expression

But if these three components are the heart of individual creativity, it is also just as true that limitations, or constraints, found within each of these three components can squash creativity flat. We can all learn to be more creative by overcoming the constraints associated with perception, intellection, and expression. By the same token, an understanding of these constraints can help organizations do a better job of supporting individuals' efforts to be innovative. Let's look at some of these constraints in detail.

Perception Constraints: Looking Without Seeing

The first step in the creative process is to get raw data (perceptions) into your brain, where they can serve as the basis of new ideas.

Although this may seem as simple as looking around you, you often look without seeing, certainly without seeing clearly what really matters to your problem.

Selective Perception and Stereotyping

Let's start by considering how our perceptual apparatus actually gathers data we use in everyday life. Most of us are "naive realists," which is a fancy way of saying that we take for granted that the world outside our bodies is just as we experience it through our senses. In fact, however, perception even at a very physical level, is always selective, limited, and, in a sense, biased.

Figure 2.2 shows the human body with the parts shown in a size proportional to the number of touch-sensitive nerves that connect that part to the brain. Notice that your big toes have an enormous amount of neural representation, which means that they are constantly sending immense amounts of data to your brain. Yet

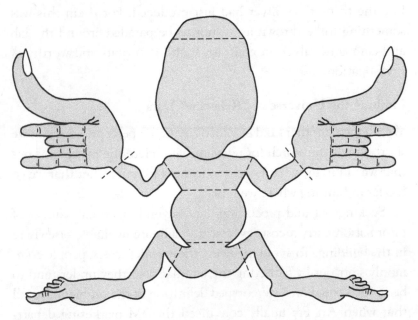

Figure 2.2
Source: Adapted from Knapp, 1978.

when was the last time you actually paid close attention to all that "big-toe" data? (Probably it was the last time you stubbed your toe.)

This simple example illustrates a larger truth: we're constantly bombarded by vast amounts of information that we routinely ignore because of the cognitive limits of the human brain. One strategy the brain uses to deal with the onslaught of input coming from the senses is to look for patterns that simplify the data. For example, when you enter a room and experience certain visual sensations, your brain looks for a close-enough match to a set of familiar patterns and very quickly labels its perceptions as "chair" or "regrettably tasteless table lamp."

Pattern finding, or stereotyping, is of course both necessary and ordinarily quite beneficial. We literally couldn't get through the day without it. But stereotypes and patterns can also obscure a great deal of potentially relevant data that might open our minds if only we were aware of them. Silver's colleagues at 3M probably had a clear stereotype of what a "bad adhesive" looked like: like the thing that Silver had just produced. For them this was something to be thrown away, not to be paraded around the lab and company. Silver, in contrast, found it curious and worthy of investigation.

Limiting the Universe of "Relevant" Data

We exercise another kind of selectivity in our perceptions when we short-circuit the search for relevant data. Here the problem is not that we fail to see what is right in front of us, but rather that we go too far in limiting where we look.

Seeking out and processing data beyond our usual sources of information carry a cost, even if the data are available elsewhere in the building. To avoid incurring these search costs, people commonly start out by gathering the familiar data they understand to be needed based on a stereotyped definition of the problem. Recall that when Art Fry finally convinced the 3M marketing department to gather market data for the Post-it, it set up the market test the way it always sets up market tests. This was efficient, as the department already had test markets established and already knew how to interpret the data. Unfortunately, because this product needed to be tried before people would be convinced of its value, these were the wrong kind of data to answer the question. Only by insisting on an alternative data-gathering method was Fry able to generate the insights he needed to understand the value of the product in the consumer's mind and to go about convincing the consumer of that value.

The kind of data we have access to may also be limited by organizational policy or even organizational culture. For instance, we may arbitrarily or unconsciously limit data gathering to data that are already available inside our organization, perhaps because of organizational policies that discourage revealing ideas to the public or to competitors. Even Fry confined early "market testing" inside 3M by providing samples to colleagues. In addition, some kinds of information may be tightly guarded and inaccessible to the innovator, such as information on financial performance, market size, clientele, and product failures. Organizations may also limit the types of outside data you can buy or subscribe to. In one consumer products company, the marketing director had to go to her local university to gain access to important market-share information because her company "was too cheap to buy it." Only after proving the value of insights she had gleaned from the data was she able to convince the company of the wisdom of purchasing a legitimate subscription.

Not Getting Close to the Data

Your physical environment also affects the perceptions you have and the data you gather. Look around your work environment and think about the things you've used as inspiration or as sources of information. I recently gained insight into my own reliance on my environment for data. Instead of using my small office to meet with student project teams for a course I teach, I tried conducting the meetings in a nearby conference room. The conference room was larger and had a bigger whiteboard, more comfortable seating, and better climate control; yet the meetings in the conference room felt oddly unsatisfactory. I couldn't figure out why. Then, because of a scheduling glitch, I was forced to move the meetings back into my office. It was then that I realized that I relied heavily on the many books on my shelves for inspiration and as memory aids. Simply glancing at them on the shelves was enough to give me ideas to help the teams during discussions and to remind me of what I know. Also, when my own words failed at conveying what I meant, I could pull down a book with an example and show them.

Firms intent on creating an air of professionalism can inadvertently constrain perception by controlling your working habits as well as your environment. In many organizations, even ones with avowed objectives of supporting innovation, being "professional" means only doing work while seated at your neatly arranged desk. Being outside the office, even if you are working hard on a project, may not be considered a legitimate use of time. Informing a supervisor or colleague that you are going to a library to look for relevant information or to a busy café so you can do your best creative thinking generates the immediate query, "OK, but when are you getting back to work?"

Overcoming Perception Constraints

You may or may not be able to influence the ways your organization limits your ability to gather and assimilate enough relevant data. But you can do a great deal to loosen the most binding constraints on perception, the ones that come from within. If we want to improve the quality and quantity of the input that goes into our efforts to think creatively, we need to become sensitive to the biases that are built into our perceptions and work hard to overcome them.

Broaden Your Sources of Data

One easy way to reduce the constraints on perception is to develop a list of the sources of data you know could apply to your problem before you actually begin gathering information. You aren't gathering the data at this point, only noting potential sources of data. For example, a team in an arts organization seeking to increase the number of season subscribers might start with the following: current subscriber list (with addresses), government census maps of the area showing family income, data on events attended by subscribers, list of competitive organizations, list of upcoming events, historical subscriber numbers, and a few other relevant sources or types of information that the team thinks could have value. The information doesn't even have to exist yet; it just needs to be potentially relevant to the problem at hand.

Creating the data source list will help in several ways. First, you are less likely to overlook obvious sources of data; with a list in hand, you can go over it carefully or with others. Someone looking at it might suggest, "What about lapsed subscribers? What do you know about them?" If you missed it, then add it to the list. Another advantage is that you can come back to the list during later phases in the project. Circle back at strategic points to see if the team is overlooking some important data you already know about that would help move the project forward. For instance, while the team is trying to generate insights about how to price new subscriptions, a review of the data source list might remind them about the possibility of using census data to map where lapsed subscribers lived. Of course you won't do that if it doesn't make sense, but at least you raised the question and can discuss it with the team. Finally, you can use the list to serve as input to future projects. It is appalling when organizations, especially ones with scarce resources, don't know what they know. You may spend weeks compiling a big list of addresses, only to have someone say, "Why are you doing that? Janis made a list like that six months ago."

Use Practiced Empathy

Being open to fresh perceptions requires practice. Our powers of stereotyping are extremely strong, and without effort we are unlikely to overcome them. One technique that can help is what I call "practiced empathy." The idea is to give yourself permission to open up and work at vividly imagining how people unlike you experience the world.

A young playwright once told me how she worked on developing this kind of openness to other ways of perceiving. She would go to newsstands and look through copies of what she considered to be "weird" magazines, imagining what it was like to be a member of that core readership. For her, the exercise served as practice for seeing the world through their eyes, especially looking at the photos and ads the way *they* might see them. As a person gifted with words, she was adept at hearing what her plays' characters would say, but she used this practice to see what they would see.

I found this method useful in work with designers at a company looking to redesign a product to appeal to younger audiences. We spent time browsing copies of *MAD* magazine, *Skateboarding*, *Game Pro*, *American Cheerleader*, *PC Gamer*, and *BMXer*, among others. Thinking and talking about how the readers of these magazines saw the world forced us to challenge our stereotypes, enabling us to be more specific and insightful about what might actually matter to them. In turn, these enriched perceptions became the input that allowed fresh ideas for the product's packaging, for new use scenarios, and for its positioning against products already in the market.

Change Your Perspective

In meetings and classes, I notice how rarely people change where they sit. They seem to find their way to exactly the same seat, class after class and meeting after meeting. To prove the point during classes I teach on innovation, I require students to move to a different quadrant of the classroom every few weeks. As much as they protest, you'd think I'd asked them to show up to class at 5:00 A.M. However, it doesn't take long for them to realize that this simple change in perspective allows them to notice things about the classroom, the instructor, and their colleagues that they had never noticed before. Not everything they notice is profound; some have observed, for example, that the glare on the whiteboard is worse over here than over there, or that they can hear much better from this part of the room. But sometimes people report seeing the class-room in a wholly new light—for example, realizing that sitting in the front or middle of the room causes people to participate a lot, whereas sitting in the back or on the sides has the opposite effect.

You can take this kind of perspective change to an even higher level by *literally* changing your perspective. If you are accustomed to using quantitative sales data to manage the products in your com-pany's lineup, go see those products actually displayed in a store. If you are used to looking for only the latest technology to incorpo-rate in your product, take some steps back by visiting a museum or junkyard. Certainly there is no guarantee that this approach will yield immediate, tangible results. But looking at a problem in the same way that you always have does come with a guarantee: that you'll end up exactly where you started.

Enrich the Input

Organizations sometimes put strict limits on changes employees can make to their working environment. In a former Hughes Aircraft Company building where I once worked in San Bruno, California, employees in the 1950s—all of them men—were allowed only one decoration in their office: a single desk photograph of their wife. Although this example may seem a little extreme, there are plenty of work settings today with rules only slightly less restrictive.

Contrast the practice at Hughes with what I found when I worked at IDEO, a product design consulting firm about twenty minutes away in Palo Alto. At IDEO the buildings are open plan, and employees build their own workspace, even down to the walls, tables, desks, shelves, and computer stands. All manner of personal effects are proudly displayed, primarily collections of parts, models, and prototypes from past projects, but also those eclectic things designers find interesting or "cool." A walk through one of the buildings is more likely to leave you with the impression of a high-tech Goodwill store than of a world-class design and engineering firm.

The result isn't just something more informal and, dare I say, human, but a richer flow of sensation—that is, data. The environment gives the visual thinkers at IDEO, who work in the world of product development and 3-D problem solving, immediate access to new perceptions about problems they may be working on—for example, inventing a new way to gear a motor, gaining insight on how to paint on rubber, or understanding the process used to mold a bowling ball. Not only is the imagery at hand, but so are the colleagues who actually worked on the projects and who are enthusiastic about sharing the trials and tribulations of their own innovation efforts. Although your innovation work may not take form as gadgets and widgets as at IDEO, encouraging and legitimizing even simple items, such as mounted photos of implemented solutions, team photos, company innovation certificates, or other mementos of projects, allows people to proudly display their accomplishments, while providing clues to others about what they know and giving others an excuse to engage them about it.

Intellection Constraints:
Old Thought Patterns for New Problems

Once we have data in sufficient quantity and quality, the next step is to work through the data in ways that can reveal new connections and relationships, which in turn may lead us to innovative solutions. This cognitive process, *intellection*, is what we normally call thinking. As is true of perception, several significant constraints can bias our thought processes, including the way we frame the problem, the approach we take to solving it, and the persistence with which we pursue an optimal solution.

Becoming Captive to the Way You Frame the Problem

When we face a problem to be solved, the first step of defining or *framing* the problem is critical. The way we frame a problem reflects explicit or implicit notions about the goals we are trying to achieve, and it directly affects the choice of strategies for gathering data, analyzing the data, and determining the validity and pertinence of our insights. Not examining the assumptions that are built into our framing can make the problem more difficult to solve or, worse, lead us to solve the wrong problem.

A common error in problem framing is defining the problem at the wrong level of analysis. Much of this book is about exactly this mistake in the case of innovation—for example, framing our innovation problem as "our miserable lack of creative thinkers" instead of "how to overcome the institutional constraints (group, cultural, and so on) that prevent even our best people from thinking in more creative ways."

We may be tempted to operate at the wrong level of analysis partly because of the information we happen to have at hand. For example, we might lack information about the larger context of the problem or, in the other direction, about the minute details of it, and so attend only to the aspect of the problem that our data address.

Besides forgetting that shifting our perspective to other levels of analysis is an option, we may also lack enthusiasm for changing our framing. To a big-picture thinker, looking at a situation from a vantage point deep down in the details may make ideas for innovation efforts seem disappointingly puny. For a master of detail, viewing the same situation from a high vista that takes in cultural and market forces may lead to the conclusion that the problem is too complex to solve.

Being Seduced by Your Problem-Solving Strategies

After deciding on a way of framing the problem, the next step is to choose a strategy or set of strategies for analyzing and solving the problem. Although it might seem obvious that we should choose the solution strategies that best suit our particular problem, intellection constraints often keep us from doing so.

One basic constraint is that instead of consciously considering what strategy to adopt, we tend to revert to approaches that have worked for us in the past. As a financial analyst, you may start by opening a spreadsheet; as a marketing manager, you begin by constructing a survey; as a designer, you reach for your sketchpad. Up to a point, this tendency is perfectly rational—after all, the strategies have worked for us before. The problem with falling back on them too quickly is twofold. First, our "proven" strategies may not be optimal for the new problem we are facing. Second, settling too easily on a strategy, even a good one, may cause us to overlook the insights we would gain if we tried alternative approaches.

To illustrate the first difficulty, imagine a very large sheet of paper about the thickness of a standard sheet of copy paper or a page in this book. Now imagine folding that piece of paper in half, leaving you with two layers. Now fold it in half again, and you will have a stack that is four layers thick. Keep imagining folding that paper on itself in the same way fifty times. Now estimate how thick the stack of paper will be. Before reading any further, note your answer.

If you are like most people, your tendency will be to answer this kind of question using a visual problem-solving approach. Not only is our visual imagination easily available, but I've formulated the question in a manner that suggests that you can solve it that way ("imagine a very large sheet of paper . . ."). Common answers I get to this question range from three inches to fifty feet, though occasionally someone will suggest one or two miles. However, a significantly better estimate is arrived at by using mathematical reasoning and a calculator as your problem-solving tools. The better answer is found by multiplying the thickness of a single piece of paper, about 0.1 millimeters, times the number of layers you will end up with (2 raised to the power of 50)—in equation form: thickness $= 0.1$ mm $\times 2^{50}$.

Many people don't believe the answer: 113,000,000 kilometers, or 70,000,000 miles—about three-quarters of the way to the sun! At this point you may feel that there must be some mistake in the way the problem was presented or in the way I calculated the solution. But there isn't. The mistake lies in our not consciously choosing a problem-solving strategy that fits the type of problem we are facing.

Even when we are deliberate about choosing a strategy that fits the problem, we may constrain our ability to generate solutions by failing to consider alternative approaches. Unlike the paper-folding problem, many problems have multiple possible answers, some of which are more powerful or cost-effective than others. Unless we try alternative problem-solving strategies, we may never discover or invent the optimal solutions we are seeking.

The recent turmoil in the music industry illustrates the point. In response to widespread music sharing that was enabled by Napster starting in 1999, record companies came to rely on law enforcement as their one solution to the problem of a free-for-all of music copying. Their approach was to threaten and then sue those they felt they could prove to be illegally sharing. By mid-2006 they had sued more than twenty thousand music fans, many who were their most loyal customers and who were otherwise law-abiding citizens (Electronic Frontier Foundation, 2006). Their failure to consider other approaches to the problem gave Steve Jobs the opening he needed to step in with his own solution and to found (and own) the iTunes Store.

Prematurely Narrowing the Range of Possible Solutions

As I've just noted, we often have powerful incentives (cognitive and otherwise) to settle prematurely on a problem-solving strategy. A similar constraint can constrict the depth and range of possible solutions that make it to the assessment phase of our project.

During workshops, I ask people how many ideas a team in their organization might expect to generate in response to an important problem. The usual response is on the order of "five or ten good ones." You can imagine the silence that ensues when I insist they should work with a *minimum* of seventy-five relevant ideas and ideally one hundred—*per person.*

At that point someone is likely to say something like "Look, we don't need such a huge number of ideas—we just need one really good one. After all, we can really only implement one idea, anyway." True enough, but limiting the solution space in order to get to that one good idea is self-defeating. If you restrict your effort to coming up with only ten possible ideas, the chances are good that number eleven (or number twenty, or number ninety-nine) is the one you're looking for. Sometimes we think it is too costly to invest time generating and critiquing so many ideas early in the process. What we forget is how much more expensive it is to try to implement ideas that aren't the best we could possibly have generated.

Overcoming Intellection Constraints

Innovation problems, almost by definition, require fresh ways of thinking. To solve these kinds of problems, we need conscious strategies for keeping our cognitive habits from becoming a crippling constraint.

Reformulate the Problem

Problems are rarely given to us in a way that makes them easy to solve; that's why we call them problems. There can be hard work in reworking the problem into a form that does make it easier to solve. One strategy is to seek other perspectives on our problem, ones that might not view it as a problem at all or that might even consider it an asset. Another is to consider the problem as simply a clue that points the way to a better solution.

Consider the Walters Art Museum in Baltimore, which was founded on an eclectic group of artifacts, at first collected more because the objects were interesting than because of their academic curatorial value. In making the transition from being a gallery to becoming known as a world-class museum, the curatorial staff arrived at the point where the most beautiful and important artifacts they might have liked to acquire were simply too expensive.

In most organizations, this problem would be defined as "how to increase the budget so that the museum could compete with other world-class museums for those rare, 'crowd-drawing' items." However, the board and staff of the Walters ended up on a different course that began with looking at the problem differently. With a mission that has them striving "to create a place where people of every background can be touched by art" (http://thewalters.org /museum_art_baltimore/themuseum_mission.aspx), they reformulated the problem to one of seeking relevance for their clientele consisting of "people of every background," rather than one of increasing the budget to acquire the rarest items. Seeing the problem in this way, they decline to take part in bidding wars for rare, expensive, and "most important" treasures. Instead, they focus on those "unimportant" artifacts overlooked by big museums with large budgets. So, rather than blow the total annual acquisitions budget on a single jewel-encrusted goblet from the Middle Ages, they might buy a decidedly average goblet, then an average knife and fork, an average plate, and an average table and chair. The result, something that other museums can't match: one of the few *complete* place settings from the Middle Ages. From it we can learn a lot more about the experience of day-to-day life of ordinary people far in the past than we can from one king's fabulous cup.

Think of Spence Silver's behavior in this light. Rather than seeing his adhesive as a failure, he turned the problem on its head: the task wasn't how to avoid making a bad adhesive, but rather how to make a "bad" adhesive insanely useful.

Use Multiple Problem-Solving Approaches

The technique of varying your problem-solving methods is well known. In fact, there are a number of tools available online and in bookstores that can help you change your approach to a problem. As one example, Roger von Oech's *Creative Whack Pack*, is a deck of sixty-four cards that will "whack you out of habitual thought patterns" by suggesting different ways of looking at your problem and ultimately solving it. When you find yourself in a place where you are not sure how to proceed, you simply pull a card from the deck, read it, and try to do what it tells you: "Magnify," for instance, or "Turn it upside down." (The Whack Pack is available at www .creativethink.com/products.html.)

More recently, the design firm IDEO released a set of fifty-one "method cards" organized in four categories of problem-solving methods: Ask, Watch, Learn, and Try. A Try card might say "Scenarios" and offer a few sentences about how to implement the scenario process and why it works. The cards can serve as a handy master list to which you can refer to ensure that you have explored a wide range of possible methods.

This is not to say that the product is the solution. The goal is to help us overcome the brain's tendency to do things in the easiest, most habitual, and least resource-intensive way possible. One senior design manager at Newell Rubbermaid even made his own deck of cards from printed images that he found interesting or even jarring. Anything that helps you try different problem-solving strategies will serve the need just fine.

Set an Ideation Goal

One easily avoidable constraint is limiting our idea generation to the first five or ten ideas we come up with. Although your best idea is probably not going to be the 101st one you generate, it is not usually going to be the first or second one either. (Besides, unless you generate lots more, how would you know?) Setting an aggressive ideation goal ensures that you explore the search space sufficiently and increases the chances that you will arrive at an idea or combination of ideas that can work.

Keep your idea production up by remembering that ideas are (relatively) cheap and easy to generate. A few hours spent in the early stages of a project finding a truly workable idea can save hundreds of hours near the end. Try doing a brain dump (or cleansing) by writing down every idea you think of in a thirty-minute period of time or for as long as it takes you to come up with 101 ideas. Don't assess the ideas as you do this—save that for a later phase.

When you reach your time limit or the target number of ideas, look through the ideas and see if any themes or categories emerge. (A spreadsheet can make this part of the task easier.) For example, your ideas on increasing the profit of one of your company's products might fall into rough categories of *reducing its cost, increasing its price,* and *increasing its value,* among others. There may be other themes that cross the categories, such as *physical changes to the product, changes of perception of the product, changes in distribution channels,* and more. Then, looking at the groupings of categories and themes, determine which have lots of ideas and which are light on ideas. Make an effort to explore those areas with few ideas and create new categories as they occur to you. If you have the benefit of working with colleagues, compare your lists to see whether the ideas indicate that you all understand the problem the same way. Likewise, look for similarities or differences in your schemes for chunking. This kind of meta-level thinking will always lead to a productive conversation yielding insights to guide the evolving innovation strategy.

Apart from increasing the odds of generating a killer idea, there is another critically important value in generating and recording as many possibilities as you can. Your master list of ideas is your documentation of the thoroughness of your search of the solution space. Besides serving as a basis for determining whether potentially critical areas were missed, the list provides valuable ammunition during the approval process. As you are presenting the proposal, some obstructionist will invariably ask, "But did you consider x?" Your ready answer: "Yes we did. We thought of it (and the related y and z) during our idea generation process, and here's why those ideas did not make it through our subsequent assessment process." Case closed.

Explore, Don't Search

The goal in early stages of the process should not be to "find the best idea." Taking that approach suggests that there is some right answer out there, and all you have to do is locate it. Thinking this way will set you up for stopping the search once you run across an idea that you think might solve the problem—which it may, but only if you're lucky, and even then it's unlikely to be the optimal solution. Your goal should be to develop a reliable process for generating innovative solutions that doesn't depend on luck to work.

Instead of doing a "search" for the right answer, *explore* the solution space thoroughly, taking in even unlikely ideas. In this way, you will gain a much better sense of multiple solutions that may bear on your problem. By comparing them, combining them, and looking for missed areas of exploration, you'll be better able to develop the best approach during your assessment phase.

I experienced this firsthand in work I did with a pottery collective. The group's artists, administrators, patrons, and audience all felt that as an arts organization, the collective should reduce its carbon footprint in order to work in the most environmentally sustainable way possible. Our brainstorm uncovered many possible steps that could be taken, such as to install solar panels, turn down the heat, or even buy a windmill generator (remember, even wild ideas are welcome at this stage). After playing with these notions and a few hundred others, the team came to realize that some of their ideas for carbon reduction centered on the administration of the collective, while others centered on the art itself. This insight spawned a second look at the solutions they had gathered, and ultimately gave rise to a two-step approach to the problem. They decided that they could work to reduce the collective's administrative power needs, with the ultimate goal of getting those functions fully off the grid. At that point any queries about footprint could be met with the statement, "All the nonsustainable energy resources we use go directly into the art." Then, with the clear understanding that this would be a long-term project, they could focus more of their efforts on sponsoring, supporting, and promoting those pottery practices that reduce environmental impact, such as using low-temperature electric kilns and low-impact glazes and colorings.

Expression Constraints: Difficulty Articulating Your Ideas

The third critical constraint on individual creativity is the need for accurate, articulate expression of our ideas and insights. Being able to express our ideas clearly and persuasively is key to winning support for them—and without support, all the work we've done at earlier stages may come to naught. Although the ideas may feel resolved in our own heads, the process of getting them out in the open where they can be tested and shared is not as easy as it may seem.

Clear and accurate expression is also central to the creative process itself. Without the tools or willingness to express our ideas in the most definitive way possible, we let ourselves be captivated by gauzy notions we haven't really pinned down—as we invariably find out when we try to work with them later. Once an idea is expressed in an articulate way, you can store it, refer back to it, analyze it, and get feedback on it from others. You can generate additional ideas without worry that you will forget the one you just had. And after you compare it to other ideas that you have generated and expressed, you can give it a full and fair assessment before deciding with confidence whether you intend it to live or to die.

Having Only One Language for Exploring and Expressing Ideas

It's only natural to want to communicate in the modes we feel most comfortable with. But limiting ourselves to our current ways of expressing ideas impairs our ability to articulate new ideas in ways that will make them clear, precise, and persuasive.

Verbally inclined people tend to assume that expressing an idea means putting it into words. But can all our ideas and insights be articulately expressed in this way? Most of us recognize the truth in the saying "A picture is worth a thousand words," yet we may rarely try to express ourselves in visual terms. I sometimes find astounding examples of this resistance, such as the team in one organization that wanted to reconfigure the lobby but didn't want to draw a picture of it. How else could they know whether their ideas could possibly work? (The same constraint, by the way, can operate in the other direction. One book designer had a habit of frustrating the editors she worked with by demanding that they draw pictures to express what they wanted. "I'm a designer, not a word person," she would say.)

Similarly, many people are intimidated by numbers and won't try to work with them. But having others "do the math" for us is risky emotionally, because the analysis might show that our idea was a dumb one after all. More important, without being able to play with the numbers ourselves, we will find it very difficult to understand how to turn a dumb idea into a brilliant one.

Insufficient Vocabularies

Using the language that best suits our ideas won't get us far if our "vocabulary" in that language is too impoverished to express our ideas accurately. Ironically, while the store of business ideas is becoming richer and more creative by the day, many people's vocabularies are getting thinner as they overuse buzzwords, clichés, and business-speak terms. Talking about the *bottom line*, the *net*

net, the *expected synergies*, and being *leveraged* may make us feel as though we're part of the club, but often these kinds of expressions are used poorly in vague ways that fail to express clear, definite ideas.

A similar point applies to using technical language outside the context in which it has a precisely defined meaning. Terms like *profit margin*, *value*, and *return on investment* have specific, precise definitions and uses in the field of accounting, but in more general use their meaning tends to be watered down and generalized. To be sure, expanding our technical vocabularies can increase our power to express ideas precisely—but only if we use the terms to articulate specific meanings. Otherwise, even in our internal monologues, it's easy for this kind of shorthand to obscure the vagueness of the underlying idea. Here's an easy test: Can we restate our point concretely and specifically, without using the "technical" terms?

Although you may be able to express simple ideas through storytelling, playacting, or taking snapshots, communicating more masterfully through these ways takes work you are not always willing to do. For example, if you've ever taken a picture of a famous landmark, you may have noticed that your pictures do not look quite as compelling as those you see in travel books, on Web sites, or on postcards. It is not a matter of the equipment; many classic photographs were taken with equipment far inferior to today's digital wizardry. Instead it is a matter of those photographers' being articulate in their art. They don't settle for the clichéd photo you will get by shooting standing in front of the tourist shop. Rather, they look at the scene from all angles, at all times of day, and in all types of light, all the while taking pictures, in an effort to find the best way to express what they have learned from all this looking and seeing.

Failures of Communication

The goal of expression is to represent our ideas accurately to ourselves and to others. Even though you may be articulate in expressing your ideas, there is a potential for them to be misinterpreted on the receiving side. For example, you may use different terms than the listener would to express the same concepts, use the same terms to express different concepts, or possibly even have no overlap in terms or concepts. The constraint takes different forms depending on which communication error takes place.

Correspondence is caused when different words are used for the same basic concept. You may have observed this "violent agreement" as two people failed to realize they were saying the same thing. *Conflict* results when the same words describe different concepts. This often occurs when communicators use technical terms in imprecise ways, especially across different areas of expertise. The word *efficient* means something very different to an industrial engineer (more output for less input) than it does to a general manager (done more easily). Imprecisely using words like *value*, *profit margin*, or *bottom line*, to name a few, can reliably create this error. *Contrast* occurs when there is no overlap in words or concepts, which makes communication all but impossible (Shaw and Gaines, 1989).

In your effort to convey your ideas to others, these constraints can pose significant challenges. They can make it impossible to get meaningful feedback that might help you improve your ideas; they make the path toward implementation more difficult as people don't know how to help; and they endanger the adoption of your ideas, because people don't want to adopt what they can't understand.

Overcoming Expression Constraints

Expression need not be a constraint on our ability to work with ideas, by ourselves or with others. By nurturing your innate ability to communicate in different modes, and by putting effort into using those languages articulately and precisely, you can improve your ability to generate and evaluate the ideas and insights that will be needed to make the innovation process a success.

Stay Mindful of Your Favored Ways of Talking (and Thinking)

Many years ago my wife (and best friend) gave me some candid feedback about the clichés I had begun to sprinkle liberally into my conversations: "That's the way the cookie crumbles!" I'd say. "That's the net net." "It is what it is!" I felt down-home and folksy using these kinds of expressions, but she pointed out that I wasn't really communicating any definite meaning when I used them.

All of us fall into these kinds of communication habits, and the first step to recovery is to notice them. This small act of mindfulness can bring you important insights about the subtle differences between what you are trying to say and what you are actually communicating. Try recording yourself in meetings and conversations and listening carefully afterward for your pet ways of talking. Or try asking a friendly colleague to wave a hand when you use an expression without clear and definite meaning. Reread your own memos and ruthlessly highlight every cliché or vague expression you can find. Better yet, ask someone else to read your memo and hunt down all the expressions that aren't doing useful work.

Once you begin noticing your verbal shorthand, with a little practice you can consciously reach a little deeper for the precise ideas you are trying to convey. When you hear yourself say "Think outside the box!" did you mean "With our established reputation and customer base, what we're looking for is a slightly more novel version of this product than our competitors offer" or "Unless we come up with something truly radical, we have no chance to compete with the gorillas in this market"? Were you even clear in your own mind about which of these you were trying to say?

Get Out the Crayons

Drawing and other visual techniques can open up a wide range of expressive possibilities. Many of us, though, believe we simply can't draw and don't have either the talent or the time to learn how. But the goal here isn't to become a master artist. There are many forms of visual communication that we already know or that are easy to pick up.

If you ever get a chance to peek inside the notebook that most designers and architects use to record their personal thoughts and problem-solving records, chances are you won't see Michelangelo-like productions suitable for framing. You'll see stick figures and crooked lines along with bad perspective and all sorts of other errors you might make yourself. The difference is that designers and architects aren't embarrassed by these "flaws"; they know they were "just thinking" when they made those sketches. Their focus was on visually articulating an idea just well enough to be able to play with it, test it, combine it with other ideas, and share it with others. In fact, the more time we spend making really good drawings of an idea, the more likely we are to become attached to that particular expression of the concept, and the less willing we'll be to let it go.

The book *Rapid Viz*, by Kurt Hanks and Larry Belliston (2006), offers a concise lesson in creating the kind of quick, lean, throwaway "thought experiment" sketches that I'm advocating. Their method involves developing a personalized vocabulary consisting of the visual symbols you are likely to use the most. After a little practice, you'll be able to effortlessly do sketches that include persons, chairs, products, arrows, lettering, and other symbols that help get your idea across. There are also a number of programs available online and as packaged software that offer ways of drawing and mapping relationships among ideas using a computer. Although your new drawing abilities will seem impressive to some, what will be even more impressive is your improved ability to articulate your ideas.

Sell Your Ideas

Many would-be innovators make an assumption that causes them no end of frustration as it torpedoes their efforts and leads straight to rejection of their ideas. The assumption is that their task is done when they have come up with an innovation they are sure will work, and that the people around them are somehow obligated to accept it as soon as it is presented to them. The reality is that the work of innovation isn't done until you've *sold* the idea to others.

By selling, I don't mean making a "hard sell." Consider that at one time you needed to be sold on the idea, too. When you first came up with it, it might have been well down the list of possibilities you were considering. But eventually it grew on you, and you came to see its advantages over other solutions. Now take a step back and look at the idea from the perspective of other people. If you can articulate the idea in a way that makes its merits clear, others can sell themselves on it, too.

Sweat the Presentation

Edward Tufte, rock-star statistician and author of *The Visual Display of Quantitative Information*, put it best: "Power corrupts. PowerPoint corrupts absolutely." In his article "PowerPoint Is Evil," he rightly argues that "slideware" tools like PowerPoint have a peculiar built-in logic that tends to favor making slides easy to produce, rather than making them communicate better (Tufte, 2003). For example, think about the last time you put together a slideware presentation and found yourself editing sentences to get them short enough to fit a bulleted list. You may also remember struggling to get a photo to fit on a slide with text, make a table of information display at a readable size, or, god forbid, get a video to play reliably. This also applies to spreadsheet programs and clipart the same way it applies to all languages: the tool favors expression of one kind over others.

How do you fight this? Simple: first think about what you want to say and then think about the best way to say it. When choosing the best way, pay attention to the following three considerations. First, consider the best way of expressing the idea on its own terms. If your idea is based on an insight about large amounts of categorical data, then a chart, table, or spreadsheet is probably your best bet. If your ideas are about a process, then a process flow chart, storyboard, or timeline might be better suited. If your idea involves artifacts in the physical world, then a physical prototype would make sense.

The second consideration is to decide what kind of interaction your material is meant to support. For instance, if you are intending to provide input for a free-ranging discussion or a kick-off brainstorm, maybe video, photos, and terse headlines of text are enough to inform and excite the group; you probably don't want the details of a spreadsheet or the formal structure of a bulleted list. To present the results of your analysis with the goal of getting a decision made, you will want to put all the detailed data, analyses, and supporting information in a handout, allowing people to parse the information at a rate and in an order that works best for them. In that case, use the slideware to help manage time and to provide landmarks for navigating the information you've provided. Are you facilitating an interactive collaboration that requires you to document the insights? Maybe preprint a set of easel pad sheets, tape them to the whiteboard, and provide markers for everyone present.

I am not at all naïve about the difficulty of deciding how to weight these considerations, nor about the significant amount of work it takes to learn a new form of expression. It is a tremendous amount of work. But I see it as a simple trade-off: you can do the work up front to try to ensure clear communication and speed the process of the group during the meeting, or you can try to get everyone else to do the work in the meeting itself, a process sure to take longer, result in errors, be more frustrating, and leave no time for doing the work that prompted the meeting in the first place.

Putting the Framework to Work: Individual Constraints

To aid you in assessing the constraints at this level, use the following diagnostic survey. It is intended to help you assess the extent to which the constraints described in this chapter may be unintentional hindrances to innovation in your organization.

Individual Constraints Diagnostic Survey

The survey lists eighteen statements describing symptoms that can be caused by the constraints discussed in this chapter. As you read each statement, consider how closely it describes your behavior in your current working group or project team. Assess yourself in terms of the behavior you are most likely to exhibit while working on projects in your organization. Record your assessment by putting a checkmark in the box that indicates how accurately the statement describes your situation.

1 = Highly Descriptive; this occurs often or on a routine basis

2 = Moderately Descriptive; this occurs sometimes or occasionally

3 = Not Descriptive; this occurs rarely or not at all

Constraint Level	Constraint Type	Diagnostic Statement
Perception		
1 ☐ 2 ☐ 3 ☐	Selective Perception	I know what the solution will look like beforehand, even for new problems
1 ☐ 2 ☐ 3 ☐		I classify the problems I face as being only of one or two types
1 ☐ 2 ☐ 3 ☐	Limiting Data	I classify problems early so that I'll know exactly what data to gather
1 ☐ 2 ☐ 3 ☐		I don't spend time looking at problems from different angles early in a project
1 ☐ 2 ☐ 3 ☐	Distance from Data	I gather all the information I use sitting at my desk
1 ☐ 2 ☐ 3 ☐		I use one reputable information source rather than several less authoritative ones
Intellection		
1 ☐ 2 ☐ 3 ☐	Problem Framing	The problems I am assigned are well formulated, and I get started right away
1 ☐ 2 ☐ 3 ☐		I don't ask why; I just solve the problem I am assigned

(Survey continued on next page)

(Survey continued from previous page)

Constraint Level	Constraint Type	Diagnostic Statement
Intellection		
1☐ 2☐ 3☐	Problem-Solving Strategy	I like problems to look familiar so that I can readily solve them
1☐ 2☐ 3☐		I use the same process for solving most kinds of problems
1☐ 2☐ 3☐	Narrowed Solution Space	I generate a few ideas I think will work and then move on
1☐ 2☐ 3☐		I act as if there is only one good way to solve a problem
Expression		
1☐ 2☐ 3☐	Idea Expression Languages	I stick to the one way of communicating that I'm good at
1☐ 2☐ 3☐		I never present my ideas with drawings, charts, or props
1☐ 2☐ 3☐	Limited Vocabulary	In my field of work, there is only one right way to say things
1☐ 2☐ 3☐		I use only language that everyone else can understand when discussing problems
1☐ 2☐ 3☐	Miscommunication	I get into conflicts where I am saying the same thing as the other person
1☐ 2☐ 3☐		People have trouble understanding my ideas

Using the Results

Note the total number of statements that you rated as "Highly Descriptive." If you have rated more than six of them this way, then working on your individual constraints will be a productive effort. Now that you have identified the specific constraints, you can take action. You may wish to turn back and reread the description of the problem and of the specific strategies for addressing that constraint. You may also find that strategies are obvious given the symptom you have identified. For detailed instructions on working with your assessment results, use the steps outlined in Appendix A,

Using the Assessment Results, to determine whether individual constraints are a significant impediment for you in your organization and to develop strategies for overcoming them.

Later, after completing assessments for the other chapters, you will be able to compare constraints and see if one of the other levels poses a greater challenge for you overall than do these individual constraints. Of the six levels of constraints discussed in this book, you will find that the individual-level constraints are the easiest to fix, assuming of course that you want to fix them.

Perception Constraints: Looking Without Seeing	
Selective perception and stereotyping	Broaden your sources of data
Limiting the universe of "relevant" data	Use practiced empathy
Not getting close to the data	Change your perspective
	Enrich the input
Intellection Constraints: Old Thought Patterns for New Problems	
Becoming captive to the way you frame the problem	Reformulate the problem
Being seduced by your problem-solving strategies	Use multiple problem-solving approaches
	Set an ideation goal
Prematurely narrowing the range of possible solutions	Explore, don't search
Expression Constraints: Difficulty Articulating Your Ideas	
Having only one language for exploring and expressing ideas	Stay mindful of your favored ways of talking (and thinking)
Insufficient vocabularies	Get out the crayons
Failures of communication	Sell your ideas
	Sweat the presentation

Summary

Creativity is not something magical, mystical, or built into our personalities. Spence Silver had nothing that every other chemist at 3M didn't have, except maybe curiosity, persistence, and an intense refusal to be hemmed in by everyone else's thinking. You too can enhance your ability to think in fresh ways by removing or mitigating the common constraints on individual creativity. The chart on page 55 offers a recap of the constraints discussed in this chapter, along with some strategies for overcoming or living with them.

Chapter Reflection: Individual Constraints

It can be helpful to reflect on your insights about individual-level constraints and the process of diagnosing them in yourself. You may wish to consider these questions:

- What evidence is there for the existence of the constraints you named?

- How important are these individual factors compared to the group, organizational, industry, societal, and technological constraints you identified?

- Are there any additional constraints you perceive that were not identified by the individual-level diagnostic?

- Would others agree that there is a need for you to fix these constraints?

CHAPTER

3

Why a Brainstorm Meeting Can Be Worse Than No Meeting at All

Innovation Constraints in Groups

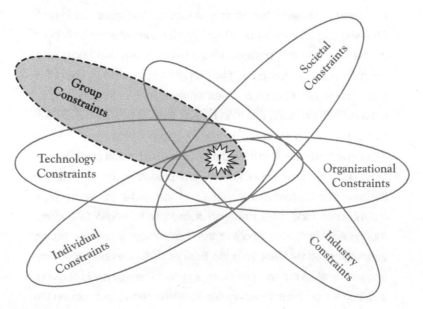

Societal Constraints

Group Constraints

Technology Constraints

Organizational Constraints

Individual Constraints

Industry Constraints

Figure 3.1

The board of ShowArts, a midsize performance arts organization, asked Josephine, the executive director, to come up with a plan to attract a larger and more diverse audience to their venue. They named the project Think Big because they wanted some fresh new thinking in anticipation of a planned capital campaign.

Josephine pulled together a team of nine people who represented a diverse mix of functions and departments from inside ShowArts. She consciously picked a couple of people she knew to be big thinkers and a few others she thought of as being very pragmatic and operations focused. Because she also realized that there might be some rocky points, she included only people she knew well and had worked closely with before.

For their first kickoff meeting, Josephine decided to have them brainstorm ideas to start the team off on a positive note. They gathered around the conference room table, and she told them the mandate: "to enlarge and diversify ShowArts' audience base." Without much further ado, they began to suggest ideas while she wrote them on a notepad. Heinz, the IT specialist and a generally soft-spoken person, wondered to himself what, exactly, the board had meant by *larger*? And what did they mean by *diversity*? Not sure whether to bring it up, he reasoned that because things were already well under way, it might embarrass Josephine if he brought it up now. Plus, she didn't seem concerned. After all, she was extremely competent and had far more experience doing this than he did; that's why she was chosen as the executive director of ShowArts just over a year ago.

Sonya from marketing offered a number of big radical ideas, among them doing a teaser show for the new production on "a stage on the back of a tractor-trailer that stops at various hip places throughout the city." Todd, who managed subscriptions, began to suggest "buying Ad-Words from Google if the data showed it to be—" but he was interrupted by Mark from the business office, who insisted that they first "analyze current audiences, segment them by levels of giving, and then survey them for willingness to attend shows and support the coming capital campaign." In an annoyed tone, Sonya reminded Mark that the problem was "increasing the audience, not bean-counting the capital campaign." Mark retorted that at least his ideas "were not delusional fantasies." The room became uncomfortably quiet, so Josephine called the meeting to an end, suggesting that they had "a couple of good ideas to work with." Sonya, however, disagreed, saying she didn't think they had a really exciting idea, to which Mark mumbled something in reply about "moving on and getting some real work done."

At the next meeting, Josephine had the Think Big team continue with their brainstorming, and said that she'd like by the end of the meeting to choose the idea they'd pursue. After some initial confusion about what the ideas were—Josephine had forgotten to bring the notepad from the last meeting, and none had been written down from this meeting—they resurrected most of the ideas from memory, writing them on the whiteboard. Then, just as the voting process was about to begin, Josephine's cell phone rang and she answered it. She put her hand over the mouthpiece and said to the team, "I've got to get this—go ahead and vote without me. I trust you and will go with whichever idea you choose," and stepped out of the room.

Calling out each idea, Jason tallied the votes. After a bit of horse-trading, they finally came to a choice that seemed to be acceptable to everyone. Or, as Heinz commented later, "one that was not unacceptable to everyone." When Josephine returned to the room, they told her the outcome of the vote. She was a little surprised and not fully convinced that it was the best option. But she decided to go along with their choice, reasoning that it had been hard enough to get them this far; any setback at this point would mean that all the time already spent would have been wasted.

The next meeting was intended for planning implementation. As Mark led the planning, Sonya lost interest; she couldn't get excited about the approach the team had decided on. She left halfway through the meeting, a pattern that persisted throughout the rest of the project. After six weeks of meetings, the team began closing in on their "opening day," as they referred to the project launch date. Their idea was to record a short video of the preparations for

ShowArts' new production along with a short teaser staged by the performers. This video was to be posted online and linked in a marketing email, and would begin playing when the recipient opened the email. The email was to be sent to several thousand people on a mailing list purchased exclusively for this purpose.

At the final coordination meeting, a week before the first round of recording was to begin, Anish, who was the ShowArts artists' representative on the board, told the team that he had gotten a concerned call from one of the artists. This prompted him to do a little research that quickly confirmed a fear he had been harboring all along. Recording and posting a digital video was a violation not only of the ShowArts labor contracts with artists and with stagehands but also of the licensing agreement with the creators of the production.

The story of ShowArts is a composite of tales I've been told scores of time by members of actual groups in businesses, nonprofits, and other organizations. The story brings to mind several questions about the difficulties of working in teams focused on innovation, even in a creativity-focused organization. For example, why does Heinz, who seems to know what's going on, just sit back and watch the team struggle? Why doesn't Anish do the critical research, or at least voice his suspicions, earlier? Why do Mark and Sonya not get along, and what effect do their behaviors have on the group? Why does the team fail at this relatively simple project despite succeeding at putting on hundreds of complex productions each year? And then there's the most important question of all: Why didn't Josephine see this coming?

Two Brains Are Better Than One— Except When They Aren't

Understanding the individual constraints discussed in Chapter Two can get you quite far in overcoming common innovation killers within individuals. But this story illustrates a different order of difficulty. Here the problem isn't that people aren't able to gather data, process the data, or express their ideas to others. In the ShowArts story, when the creative process stops, it's for reasons other than a lack of vocabulary or an inability to grasp the concept. It happens because the group members are afraid, in conflict, unsure of what they are doing, or just in a hurry to get things done, all of which can defeat the purpose of forming a group in the first place.

Before considering in detail the constraints that operate in groups, it may be worthwhile to remind ourselves of the advantages of group work, those that we want to maximize in the context of innovation. When a group is formed to address an innovation problem, the group members can be expected to perform the following activities: analyze the problem, generate a set of potential solutions to the problem, test those potential solutions against the constraints of the situation, and then execute the most optimal of the solutions. These tasks imply a "more is better" *information processing* function of the group.

Of course, one person can do all these things, including generating and testing a variety of ideas. But a group, by definition, can produce a larger number of perspectives on the problem, thus increasing the potential accuracy and scope of the diagnosis. And after the problem has been framed, the diversity of perspectives means that groups can produce a wider range of potential solutions than any one individual is likely to come up with. This divergent activity is what we call "brainstorming." Apart from increasing the number of ideas—and hence the likelihood of generating a really good one—using a group to tackle an innovation challenge provides access to a wider diversity of problem-solving strategies and a wider base of experiences to draw upon. This access increases the chance of devising a realistic and implementable solution to the challenge at hand.

Finally, a group provides access to a wider range of those skills and capabilities that might be needed during the implementation phase of the innovation project. All of these considerations, by the way, argue not only for the advantages of groups but for the particular advantages of *diverse* groups, such as cross-functional teams and groups that include people with different levels of experience and responsibility.

However, as we all know from experience, groups don't often work optimally. This is especially true when groups are working on problems of innovation, which by definition challenge the group members to do something new, often in an atmosphere that is fraught with pressure. Social psychologists have studied a number of factors that affect group interaction, but in this chapter I will focus on four factors that can most damage—or foster—creativity and innovation:

- *Emotion:* the kinds of feelings we have simply by being with others
- *Culture:* the group members' shared but often unconscious understanding of how they will work together
- *Environment:* features of the group's physical and social surroundings that help or hurt productive interaction
- *Group process:* the way the group goes about its work

Whether you are creating or overseeing groups and teams, leading a group, or simply participating in one, this chapter will help you identify the common ways groups kill innovation and what you can do to help overcome these constraints.

Emotion Constraints: Ego and Social Status

The fact that humans are social animals explains some of the constraints on creativity we experience in groups. As social animals, we seek a legitimate and honorable place, and this is represented by our status in the groups we are part of. Whether or not we are conscious of it, the human need to gain status—or to avoid losing it—is a prime driver of our behavior in groups.

In fact, one way to think of meetings is as *status contests* in which the participants' behavior serves to drive their relative social status up or down. It's easy to see this in conspicuous behaviors like running the critical finite element analysis for the project without being asked. More subtly, status can be affected by body language, by the ways we dress, and by what we say, how we say it, and to whom. Research has shown that people in groups watch behaviors like touching, interruption, and members' unconscious reactions to ideas as clues for assessing relative status (e.g., Knapp, 1978). Being the one who is touched, who is interrupted, or whose ideas are ignored (for example, by not being written on the board) are all signs of low or decreasing status. In contrast, status can increase if members contribute insightful thoughts, show how connected they are to powerful outsiders, or bring important resources to the group.

These dynamics often lead group members to adopt counterproductive attitudes and behaviors. Here are three of them.

Fearing Criticism

If being perceived as smart has a positive effect on our status, being perceived as *not smart* has the opposite effect. A common problem in group interactions is members' openly criticizing the ideas of others, particularly during brainstorm activities. Although such criticism can be motivated by an individual's desire to help the group—for example, by pointing out dead-end paths or showing why ideas won't work—it probably doesn't hurt that it also displays the person's critical analytic abilities and his or her knowledge of the problem to the group. In other words, delivering such criticism can make one seem smart and valued to a group, so why not do it?

Although it can be an advantage for a group to have members who are smart and analytical, criticism delivered at the wrong time or in the wrong way can have an inhibiting effect on the sharing of creative ideas. Teresa Amabile's research (1979) has shown that even the expectation that others will critically evaluate our ideas or evaluate them in a way that threatens our self-esteem will lead us to generate fewer and less creative ideas.

You probably know people who, deliberately or not, use criticism to try to look like the smartest person in the room. Naturally this behavior can cripple a group's efforts to be innovative, as it can cause members to stay quiet rather than risk losing status by having their ideas shot down.

Avoiding Mistakes

In his famous book *Conceptual Blockbusting: A Guide to Better Ideas*, James L. Adams (2001) points out how risk aversion sets in as people overestimate the negative consequences of making an error. This happens because we often lack information about the actual probability of each event in a causal chain of events. Instead of making realistic estimates, we have mental scripts that may predict the worst: "If I take a risk by proposing my idea for cleaning the parts using lemon juice instead of that awful chemical we use now, Joe will shoot down the idea, just like he always does, and I'll look like a fool. Or if the idea gets adopted and doesn't work, the boss will think I'm a dumb SOB for proposing it in the first place. Then I'll get passed over for the promotion I'm angling for, and Jeanne will never let me hear the end of it—if she doesn't divorce me. No way am I making that kind of mistake; I'm going to keep quiet and let somebody else take the fall." Of course I've dramatized this a little, but only a little. Often even an objectively small risk evokes a mental script that leads us to back out of trying or proposing new ideas.

Avoiding Good Conflict

People have a natural tendency to avoid conflict in groups. Conflict is uncomfortable, may put our status at risk, and can hinder our ability to work together with others in the future. We may avoid conflict out of a sense of propriety—for example, by choosing to remain silent even when we know that someone is making a false or wrongheaded claim. Maybe we feel that our silence is justified because having the *correct* answer in this particular case is just not that important—certainly not worth embarrassing the person over. One hopes that we can predict how important any given answer will need to be in the life of a project. We may also act to protect our status in the group. Going along with a proposal or decision being promoted by a high-status member of a group—even when we know it to be suboptimal or wrong—will feel less risky than supporting a proposal that may be wrong or that puts us on the losing side of an argument with a high-status person. Besides, we think, maybe they are high status because they are smarter than we are or know something we don't, which, of course, may or may not be true. Finally, we will also tend to avoid those behaviors that might lead others to brand us as being uncooperative, a "jerk," or worse.

In each of these cases, we tend to avoid those ideas or topics that we believe may cause others discomfort or that may get us into an argument we don't want to have. Unfortunately, in the service of innovation, those challenging ideas, topics, and perspectives are exactly the ones we are searching for.

Overcoming Emotion Constraints

You've probably known managers or group leaders who believe that the solution to the problems emotions can cause in groups is to try to keep emotions out of the group process altogether. "Come, let us reason together" is a useful approach up to a point, but emotions are not in themselves good or bad. In fact, they can be a big part of fueling our thinking and motivating our efforts to solve problems. The key is not to banish emotions but to channel their power so that they support our efforts to innovate in groups.

Support Psychological Safety

A *psychologically safe* group environment is one in which people feel supported and able to explore and learn (both activities that require trial and error) without risking painful emotional consequences. How do we create such an environment? One powerful tool is a formal set of rules for behaviors during meetings that the group is reminded of at the start of *each* meeting. For example, clear rules can help the group keep the powerful impulse to criticize in check. This is especially key in the early, idea-generating phases of the group's work. Of course there will be a need for significant critical analysis of the ideas, but that should happen during the *assessment* phase when that is the group's job, and not during data gathering or ideation early on.

At IDEO, the rules of brainstorming are written on the walls of every conference room and even on the back of business cards (see Figure 3.2). These rules are reviewed at the start of *every* brainstorm, even though most employees participate in multiple brainstorming sessions each week. They are reminded not because they are a forgetful bunch but because the social and emotional incentives to criticize are so strong. The penalty for repeatedly criticizing others' ideas is ejection from the session (and possibly not being invited to future ones). The model of brainstorming shown in the *Nightline* segment "The Deep Dive" provides excellent examples of ways that groups can avoid many of the negative emotional dynamics.

Brainstorming:

- *Defer Judgement*
- *Encourage Wild Ideas*
- *Build on the Ideas of Others*
- *Stay Focused on the Topic*
- *One Conversation at a Time*
  Extra Credit: Be Visual

Figure 3.2

Suppress Idea Egotism

Claiming ownership of our ideas is pleasant when the group approves of them. But what if the group rejects the idea, or we fear that it will? Then we may not be quite so enthusiastic about proposing it in the first place. Sometimes we feel the sting of rejection even when those around us actually like our idea—just not as much as we do. And even if we're perfectly comfortable having our ideas examined and criticized, encouraging individuals to own their ideas can lead to the kind of status competition described earlier.

The strategy for combating this dynamic is to discourage individual ownership of ideas in favor of group ownership. There are several ways to do this. First, have each person generate *lots* of ideas. Besides more thoroughly exploring the potential solution space, members are less likely to become overly enamored of any one favorite idea. Have members generate ideas before the actual meeting; the overlap of good ideas across their lists will spread ownership throughout the team.

Second, have members post their ideas on the walls instead of presenting them to the group one person at a time. When we vocalize our ideas in front of the group, we perceive the audience to be looking at and judging us. If approval isn't immediate and wholehearted, we're likely to feel rejected and become less motivated to help the group succeed. If instead interactions occur informally in front of the idea wall, the originator of an idea is less likely to feel put on the spot. And this simple tactic implicitly encourages shared ownership of all the ideas.

Leaders and managers have a significant role to play in modeling the collective ownership of ideas. I have worked with companies run by people who had founded their enterprises on a brilliant idea they had had. Ten years later, the success of the company had outgrown the founders' ability to generate sufficient ideas to keep the company in business. Yet the founders still acted as if *their* ideas were the vital key to success and paid little heed to input from others. When a good idea was finally extracted through a painful group interaction, the leader would attach the term "my idea" to that which the group knew perfectly well was "our idea."

If we want to foster the emotional gratification that comes from group ownership of ideas, we have to walk the talk. Especially for higher-status individuals, that means learning not to say "I" and "my" when the appropriate words are "we" and "our"—and making sure that our nonverbal behavior matches our words.

Have a Good Fight

Despite our natural tendency to avoid it, there are many good reasons to have constructive conflict in a group. If group members always shared the same perspective about everything, there would be no need to have a group in the first place.

There are three kinds of conflict, and the effect each has on the group depends on when it occurs in the group's process. The first kind is *process conflict*, or disagreement about how to arrange the required parts of the task at hand. Which should we do first, brainstorm or gather data? Conflicts like these are good to have early in the group's work because they may surface useful alternative paths to the group's goal. Once the order of tasks is agreed to, however, then it must be considered final. Everyone needs to be committed to the same process if things are going to get done in an effective manner.

The second kind of conflict is *task conflict*. This includes any kind of disagreement about the correct answer to a question connected with the task (as opposed to the process). We want this kind of conflict to the extent that having the right answer is important. For example, I think 15.8, but you say 24.7. If the two numbers refer to the minimum safe thickness of the stainless steel walls of a nuclear reactor, this is a very good argument to have. In contrast, if the right answer isn't critical to the group's work, try to minimize spending time and emotional energy on disagreements. Sometimes just pointing out that the right answer doesn't make that much difference is sufficient to defuse the argument.

The third kind of conflict is *relationship conflict*. This refers to conflict that doesn't have to do with either the task or the process. Sometimes people just bug us. "Why do you always eat garlic before the meeting and then sit right next to me?" "Why do you always interrupt when I'm talking?" "Why does it take forever for you to make a simple point?" Relationship conflict is generally unhelpful. It focuses attention on emotion processing instead of on the information processing that is the group's proper work, so should be avoided or minimized.

Relationship conflict is extremely uncomfortable, so groups may do everything in their power to avoid it—even if that means not risking engagement over important questions. What you can do is to establish formal roles in the team to be adopted by members during those stages in the process where asking the hard and conflict-engendering questions is desirable. For example, you can set a short time for doing the "devil's advocate" work of taking a contrarian and pessimistic view at the end of each meeting. Explain to group members that it is better to shoot holes in their own ideas than to have it done to them in front of an executive team.

Celebrate Failures

By reducing the emotional penalty for making mistakes, you can get people in a group to pay more attention to the information than to their fears. But how? In his book *Weird Ideas That Work*, Robert Sutton (2007, p. 103) offers a provocative dictum: "reward success and failure equally, but punish inaction."

What does it mean to reward failure? Consider framing the goal of the group's work not as finding the right answer but instead as *seeking and testing hypotheses for what might solve a given problem*. For example, if a particular idea—that is, hypothesis—isn't confirmed or is positively disproved, celebrate what was achieved by the "failure." Center the discussion on how much risk was reduced and costly investment avoided by determining that the particular approach was unlikely to work. In this view, success is not just coming up with the next great idea. It's also finding the showstopping constraint before more significant investments in time, money, and emotion have been made. The value of that kind of failure is well worth calculating—and celebrating. And when the group does come up with the next great idea, be sure that the celebration encompasses everyone's hard work, including the work of those whose criticisms helped refine the idea until it really worked. Remember, it's the group's idea.

Culture Constraints: Cohesion and Meaning

The culture of a group, which develops over the life of a project, is the set of understandings about what the group is for and how it works. The group's culture is made up of assumptions, often unconscious, about the group's goals, values, norms, and acceptable behavior.

What enables group culture to exist is a social force I'll call "cohesion." Cohesion is the glue that holds a group together, helping members stay aligned and cooperative according to the spoken and unspoken rules of their culture. However, although groups need a healthy degree of cohesion to perform optimally (or at all), every silver lining has its cloud. Groups often use a number of unconscious means of maintaining a high level of cohesion that can seriously impair their information processing capacity, particularly in the early, idea generation phase of an innovation process.

Forming Homogeneous Groups

The most direct way that groups establish and maintain cohesion is by deciding who gets to be part of the group. There is overwhelming evidence that groups engage in homophily—the tendency to choose and retain members on the basis of social similarity. Especially in work environments, we tend to like people who are similar to us in such characteristics as race, gender, level of education, social and economic status, and skills (e.g., Owens, Mannix, and Neale, 1998; Ancona and Caldwell, 1992; Newcomb, 1961). Because we can communicate more easily with "people like us" and are likely to share many values and habits with them, a group of socially similar individuals is likely to be more cohesive than a more diverse group. Managers know all this at some level, and they often encourage forming groups made up of people they think will "get along well."

Unfortunately, similar people are also more likely to share characteristics that inhibit innovation goals, such as generating a wide variety of ideas. They may have overlapping experience bases, social networks, and even problem-solving approaches. By limiting the kinds of input the group generates, the very similarity that helps the members "get along" can drastically reduce the group's information processing power—the very quality we seek in forming a group.

Enforcing a Shared Sense of Meaning

Organizational psychologist Karl Weick (1995) defines *sense* as the meaning that allows members to know *that* they are a group, *why* they are a group, and *what* it is that they intend to accomplish as a group. When answers to these fundamental questions are clear and obvious, groups can be extremely effective and efficient. When there are murky or competing goals, or when the situation changes precipitously and unexpectedly, or when members' behaviors no longer seem logical or reasonable, then members must engage in what Weick calls "sense making."

Sense making is natural and important to groups. If a group's mission or identity becomes indescribable or chaotic, or if members feel that the group is no longer in control, the loss of sense can threaten the group's cohesion and even its existence. You may have been part of a group that ended up dissolving or gradually fading away because it lost a clear sense of purpose or because the group members felt that its goals were no longer relevant.

Once again, however, the efforts we take to make groups function well may work at cross-purposes with our goal of fostering fresh, creative thinking. What can happen is that members work to increase buy-in and cohesion by adopting an easily shared, often standard definition of the problem they are trying to solve and by using generic, vague, and uncontroversial language to describe their goals and the process for reaching them. These behaviors will have the effect of bridging differences between members, but they can significantly reduce the group's ability to frame its challenge in multiple, paradoxical, and ambiguous ways, something needed to realize true innovation.

Adhering to Traditions and Taboos

As an organizational or group culture takes form, those ideas and activities that are considered sensible and valuable become a shared tradition. In one company, for example, every staff or team meeting begins with a "fun" icebreaking exercise that has nothing to do with the task at hand. Somewhere along the way this practice hardened into a tradition that no one questions, and it is now part of the organization's culture. By the same token, behaviors that are felt to be threatening to the culture become tacitly or openly forbidden. These prohibited practices are known as taboos.

Traditions and taboos help create a sense of group identity and establish familiar ways of working that don't have to be renegotiated with each new interaction. But they can also constrain innovation by reinforcing old ways of looking at problems or by making potential alternative approaches seem off-limits. More subtly, ways of thinking and talking that were valuable in the past may be unable to express today's problems, challenges, and potential solutions or facilitate fresh thinking about them. Although they probably did so for different reasons, the shift by some organizations to refer to their customers as "clients" or their employees as "associates" can force a break and opens new possibilities. In fact, innovation requires us to generate ideas that are as *different* as possible from the ones that have become second nature to us.

Overcoming Culture Constraints

A group culture will develop whether or not anyone consciously tries to influence it. Instead of letting nature take its course, group leaders and members can shape the culture of a team as it develops, in order to maximize the group's capacity to be innovative.

Mix Up Group Membership

In some research on early-stage R&D groups, I found that newly formed groups tended to seek homogeneity as a buffer against the uncertainty of the project's outcome. I find the same thing in teams of MBA students working on projects: by choosing people they know well as teammates, they are unlikely to get surprised by odd behaviors, especially around the time that assignments are due. Yet when projects are complex and don't fit a simple solution paradigm, what we need is a healthy variety of perspectives and skills. Unfortunately, by the time we recognize the need for greater diversity, often the cost of socially integrating new group members and bringing them up to speed seems too high.

Usually we don't like people *because* they are different from us. That is to say, they see the world in ways that aren't ours and know things we don't. That, of course, is why we should deliberately seek them out and invite them into groups working on innovation problems. As a marketing student put it to me recently while turning in a project assignment, "I don't like the attitude that the finance students have around here, but it sure would've been nice to have someone who actually knew how to use Excel."

You should also stay mindful of the group's composition as the group moves into different phases of its process. Different parts of projects require different skills, which means that some current group members may not have the knowledge or habits of thought they need in order to contribute to the work as productively as they did in earlier phases. Unless they show sufficient ability and willingness to learn and change, in such cases it's best to uninvite them from particular parts of the process. To make this kind of separation less painful for all, you can set the stage by being clear from the start that the makeup of the group may change as the work evolves and by warmly celebrating the contributions of a departing member.

Explore to Learn, Exploit to Produce

Most organizations are designed for efficiency. Whether it's assembling a car more quickly and cheaply or educating schoolkids in bulk, the goal is maximum output for the least amount of input. If routine production is the goal, this approach may work, as it preserves resources and minimizes waste. However, for groups pursuing innovation, valuing efficiency above all else will severely constrain them. In groups dominated by a culture of efficiency, members will want to get any needed learning over with and move toward implementation as quickly as possible.

Common strategies are to use a solution from a problem that we have already mastered or to find an expert who already knows how to do it. Maybe it's not innovative or even ideal, but at least it makes us feel as though things are moving. For one-time projects performed under time pressure or for problems that don't require a new approach—for example, organizing a mailing list or reporting financial performance—these strategies can work well. However, for a group seeking a new approach and desiring to build innovation skills, these tactics don't help. Not only do you lose the actual learning, but you lose out on improving your process of learning as well.

To overcome this tendency, reframe your group's view of learning and progress. Don't think of progress as being a move from ignorance to mastery, and of rapid progress as an even faster move. Rather, consistent with the ideas of James March (1991), consider that your group starts in an *exploration* mode, where you are focused on gathering information, testing relationships, and developing understanding. You are not "ignorant"; you are rigorously exploring the space. Next, you engage an *exploitation* mode, taking advantage of your insights to develop a highly efficient and effective system. You don't end in "mastery"; you develop an effective and efficient way to exploit the ideas and insights you have gained.

Rapid progress is not achieved by getting from the start of the project to the finish as quickly as possible. Rather, it comes from the group's ability to know how and when to move back and forth between these mutually reinforcing modes, as the project requires.

Prize New Problem-Solving Methods over Traditions and Taboos

In the course of a study on R&D teams, I observed as a group of hardware engineers (people who design circuit boards and microprocessors) grappled with a particularly hard problem in the design of a computer. At one point, one of them offered that maybe the problem could be better addressed by software. If the group passed the problem to the software engineers, she proposed, the problem would be solved more efficiently than it would be if the group insisted on solving it using chips and circuits.

The other members of the team just looked at her incredulously. Even though they could see that she was correct, passing problems to "those guys" was obviously not an acceptable solution in the culture of the hardware engineers. She got the message, and the group continued struggling to solve the problem in hardware.

Taboos like this can be good if they prevent bad or dangerous decisions, like the taboo I grew up with against eating the wild mushrooms that my uncle had picked. However, unless you are a fraternity or a gang, when the taboos in the group serve only to reinforce turf claims or become a test of loyalty for members, they do nothing but close down alternative sources of ideas and insights that might apply to your problem.

As any anthropologist will tell you, it is extremely difficult to determine your own group's cultural traditions and taboos, but there are ways you can flush them out. Enlist someone not trained in your field to sit in on a meeting of your group and ask him or her to report some observations afterwards. You can also learn by consciously observing your team at the next meeting with "those guys." See if you can determine whether any points of conflict that emerge are ones of substance or of tradition and culture.

Once you know the rules, it'll be easy to catch yourself and the team when you fail to think differently. Ask persistently and politely, "Why aren't we considering another way of doing this?"

Environment Constraints: Comfort Versus Collaboration

Many of us find that we are more productive in some environments than in others when tackling specific kinds of tasks. When generating ideas, some people prefer absolute quiet, whereas others do their most creative work in noisy, stimulus-filled places. For individuals, this constraint is usually straightforward to overcome: simply change places. But what about working environments for groups, in which preferences differ and interaction needs to be facilitated? The spaces that groups use are usually chosen by what is available and possibly comfortable to members of the group. Rarely are they chosen or designed so as to enhance the kind of interactions needed during an innovation project. But as we are about to see, a group's working environment can seriously constrain innovation by affecting the way the group processes information and emotion.

Using Spaces That Impede Interaction

Our physical environment shapes interactions in a number of ways. For example, when individuals sit face-to-face across the table, the seating arrangement sets up an implicit competition between them. Studies looking at communication patterns find that the most argumentative and oppositional statements made in a group sitting at a table tend to be directed at the individual seated exactly opposite (e.g., Sillars, Pike, Jones, and Murphy, 1984). Rectangular tables reinforce this dynamic, which is why many "creative design" tables have irregular shapes.

Other aspects of the physical space also affect a group's ability to fulfill its mission. Offices and conference rooms are usually designed for routine work. Recognizing this, many interior designers suggest fashioning a "creative workspace" by omitting walls, lowering cubicles, and encasing conference rooms in glass. Although the end result may look cool, it can become problematic for a group trying to do creative work.

The problem with glass-enclosed conference rooms, for example, is the distractions outside. The knowledge that the group is virtually under surveillance can create social pressure on the group members, encouraging them to restrict their behaviors to those that will seem normal and justifiable to anyone who happens to be passing by (such as the boss). Such behaviors as becoming playful or engaging in healthy conflict are necessary to spur imagination, but they will be suppressed to the extent that they might be perceived as not being real work.

Communicating Using Limited Media

In addition to spatial arrangements or geography, other aspects of the physical environment, such as the tools provided to a group, can powerfully shape its work.

Although it can be nice to have a large screen and a digital projector to illuminate it, these can only be driven from one person's computer at a time. We also default to using programs like PowerPoint or Keynote, which require the content to be developed in advance and make it all but impossible to change the presentation or even capture comments or insights as you go. IT staff and other expert users with access to digitizing tablets or touch screens might bristle at this assertion, suggesting that you can use the "digital ink" feature of these programs for annotating presentations. True, but the feature is limited to one person's input and is clunky at best.

This is not to say that these tools have no value; they are great for sharing information that one person has collected and organized into a "presentation" for the group. However, this is only a small part of an innovation group's work. Beyond perceiving the information, they need to interactively share, debate, and document the insights they develop *as* they develop them. When members lack access to the shared stream of thoughts and the progression of one another's ideas, much of the value of using a group can be lost.

These constraints are not just a function of our digital environments. An organization development consultant recently told me about trying to help a group of administrators at a college brainstorm ways of improving student achievement and faculty satisfaction. She reported that the conference room had one small whiteboard, about two by two feet in size, mounted in an awkward place on the long side of the room, and half the participants had to turn their chairs around to see it. There was one dried-out marker for the board, and it spent the entire morning in the hands of the school's dean. Clearly this was not a context for nurturing collaborative ideation.

Not Sharing or Documenting Insights

I often see innovation teams using spaces that, though pleasant, don't allow the capture of a variety of types of data and insights. Large windows are nice, but they don't let you display text, images, reports, or the resulting insights that they generate in the team. Even the physical position of documents can relay information— for example, by arranging them in sequence or priority order. Ideally the information being discussed can be displayed in a place that everyone can see, in a way that everyone can access it, and in a mode that best expresses that idea.

Understanding, comparison, collaboration, debate, and decision making in a group might be far better supported with a few pictures ripped from a magazine and taped to the wall, as opposed to a detailed thousand-word email that no one bothered to read before the meeting. And once you ask them to kindly pull out their BlackBerry to read the email, the meeting is doomed.

Overcoming Environment Constraints

Groups need a space where members can interact, and the places they choose will affect their interactions. Instead of letting facilities planners or geographic convenience dictate the nature of your interactions, choose and modify your space carefully to support innovation.

Reconfigure the Group's Working Space

The goal in claiming a space should be to create an environment that facilitates the behaviors dictated by the current stage of the innovation process. At times group members may be working primarily alone, and at other times together. At times the group's findings will be collected in the form of survey responses on a computer printout, and at other times they may take the form of hundreds of Post-its on whiteboards.

The most radical versions of effective high-end innovation spaces that I have used are those that are designed for creative interaction by MG Taylor Corporation. The tables come in a variety of nesting shapes and sizes and are deployed based on the group size, task, and need for interaction. When they are not being used, they break down and can be put into a closet. Rolling bookshelves are ubiquitous, as are power outlets and network connections. If a team needs them, large LCD screens can be rolled to the place where groups are working. Everything is on wheels—even the six-foot-tall whiteboard walls—and it all looks inspiring.

However, I have also seen less expensive approaches that were equally effective. Starting with nothing more than a large bare room, some simple tables and chairs on wheels, some movable screens and partitions, and a set of portable whiteboards or easel pads, a number of start-ups, arts organizations, and corporations have easily and inexpensively gained the flexibility they needed to accommodate different phases of work by their teams. For some of them, all it took was a trip to IKEA, the Swedish furniture store, and an Allen wrench to assemble it all.

One expense I would not spare, however, is for porcelain-on-metal magnetic whiteboards; they are expensive, but worth it. You can not only write on them but also use an ever-widening variety of magnetic pins, clips, and even shelves to display articles, charts, photos, and the like. Especially in the early data-gathering phases of a project, just the ability to stand together and look at all the materials the team has collected will be worth the price.

Facilitate Multiple Modes of Expression

Just as innovation demands multiple ideas and problem-solving strategies, it also demands a variety of means for expressing ideas and sharing information. Consider developing a group norm that requires using multiple modes of expression, and then provide the appropriate space and tools. If you get a chance to tour a truly effective "innovation space," you will note that it provides for multiple communication modes. You will see affordances for creating and sharing electronically created slides, photos, charts, and graphs. The space will also enable collaboration on whiteboards and easel pads, and will support the display and storage of physical models, all in the service of communicating ideas. Ready means for videotaping the proceedings are also likely to be built in and require little or no effort on the part of group members to operate.

Providing the means for visual expression is especially useful. I routinely bring a ream (one package of five hundred sheets) of white copy paper to meetings where ideation is going to happen. When people begin grasping for words to express their nascent ideas, I feed them paper and ask them to show me in drawings, diagrams, sketches, or any other way they can what it is they mean. Even if they simply start writing words on the paper, taking pen in hand can often help them get past the mental logjam.

Similarly, providing ample whiteboard space, flip charts, paper of different sizes, and other tools for visual expression can work wonders. Some brainstorming exercises, for example, benefit from forcing people to express an idea concisely on paper the size of a large Post-it. In other cases, a group might want huge sheets of butcher paper for listing or drawing ideas. Making sure everyone has a pen or marker in hand as the meeting starts and has ready access to a variety of writing surfaces will facilitate expression and communication of ideas.

Automate Documentation

Beyond having a place to interact, groups need a place to document their ongoing work. In this age of broadband, I find it astounding that so many groups do not take advantage of online collaboration tools, many of them free, to communicate about and document their work. Often I hear reasons like "the IT guys are worried about security" or "the company won't let us get access from home." Security is a real concern, but isn't solving this kind of problem what IT people get paid to do?

At a large R&D lab I studied in the early 1990s, even before the Web existed, teams used USENET groups (the equivalent of today's group mailing lists) for all their communications, even interpersonal ones, that had any potential relevance to the project. Agendas, minutes, questions, decisions, and timelines were all copied to the list. This allowed members to reference them as needed, and also provided a way to easily record the development of intellectual property, because the progression of ideas could be traced back in time by source. Today groups have access to many useful online tools for these purposes, such as dedicated Web sites, shared documents, and wikis (collections of documents any of the members can edit or comment on, similar to Wikipedia).

Another simple tool for documenting the group's work is to use digital cameras to collect visual materials, such as pictures of drawings, prototypes, and whiteboards. These days, with a digital camera that has built-in Wi-Fi, groups won't even have to remember to transfer the photo files. Instead, pictures can be transmitted to a server or Web site automatically and immediately.

Process Constraints: Directing Members' Behavior

The last group-level constraint I'll consider is that of the *process* through which a group does its work. Most groups do not use formal innovation processes at all, and when they do, they rarely consider the constraints inherent in the process. This forms the basis of a significant constraint: the lack of process in a group. Without an established and accepted process, members will tend to do what comes naturally. Unfortunately, what is natural for me may not be what's natural for you, and this sets up the group for unnecessary conflict. As discussed earlier in this chapter, this conflict will result in members' addressing the social and emotional issues in the group rather than focusing on the information processing that must occur if the innovation challenge is to be solved.

Although some organizations have formal processes in place, groups are often unaware of the constraints inherent in using these processes. For example, continuous improvement processes (e.g., the Six-Sigma approach) may be ideal for incremental improvements, but are generally unsuited for the pursuit of radical innovations. Or perhaps the formal, tried-and-true process worked for the last problem, but this problem may be completely different. And when the process doesn't work (or even make sense to the members), they lose trust in the process and revert back to the natural behaviors that characterize a lack of process.

When groups have a process and it is the right one for the task, they may still have difficulty managing the phase transitions as the project moves from one stage to the next. To the extent that different phases call for different behaviors by members, a lack of consensus about which phase the group is in leads to a loss of effectiveness as members work at cross-purposes. So although the innovation process may seem simple—just establish and follow the steps—there are a number of dynamics in play that can make the process anything but straightforward.

The Seven Phases of an Innovation Process

Figure 3.3 depicts the seven basic phases of a purposeful innovation process. Although the nomenclature may differ among the many books that discuss group creative processes, the basic steps they depict are the same. As we're about to see, a key point illustrated in the diagram is that an innovation process requires group members to enact completely different behaviors in different phases of their work.

Phase 0, Identify Problem, requires someone to identify and articulate the problem the team is to solve. It gets the number zero because it is of such fundamental importance, though it doesn't

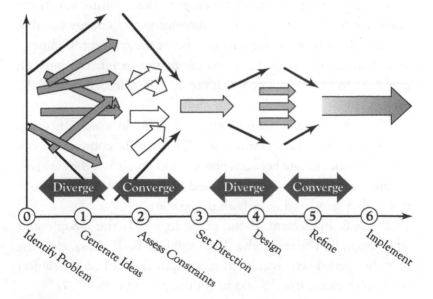

Figure 3.3

often get a lot of careful attention, as groups want to move quickly into the next phase. A group may develop its own mission, or the problem may be assigned from outside the group.

Phase 1, Generate Ideas, requires *divergent* behavior from the members, which simply means that they have to think as differently as possible from each other, with the goal of coming up with the widest variety of possible solution ideas. This generates the primary space of potential solutions for the team.

Phase 2, Assess Constraints, requires *convergent* behavior from the group as it critically examines the ideas alone and in combinations to determine those that might have a chance of actually working in the intended context. The goal for this phase is to develop a set of solution concepts that have a chance of solving the problem, along with an understanding of the different constraints that each of the particular approaches would face.

Phase 3, Set Direction, is the peak of convergence, where the team makes a commitment to the direction it has chosen. This is also a time when teams seek external opinion about the wisdom of their choice.

Phase 4, Design, is another *divergent* phase, during which the team has to generate ideas for overcoming the constraints that stand in the way of the implementation of the concept. If immovable constraints cannot be overcome at this point, the problem may need to be reformulated, or it is considered unsolvable and the project stopped.

Phase 5, Refine, is again a *convergent* phase in which the group molds its solution into a form that will work in its context. Groups can sometimes iterate between phase 4 and phase 5. If they are successful, they will become aligned and ready to move into phase 6; if not, they may need to go back to the start.

Phase 6, Implement, is the phase in which the group enters what might best be called the "Pizza and Red Bull" phase. Here the team hunkers down, avoids any new input (lest it become subject to "feature creep"), and works to get the project done.

Overcoming Process Constraints

As we have just seen, the innovation process involves significant transitions in the way the group goes about its work. Even if the group understands that different phases of the process demand quite different kinds of behavior—and many groups do not—the social forces operating on groups tend to be much more powerful than reason. I'll point out some adverse dynamics that can occur as I've observed them in teams in a variety of industries, as well as ways to overcome them. As an example, I'll use the story from the start of this chapter about Josephine, the executive director of ShowArts who was asked by her board to undertake project Think Big aimed at attracting a larger and more diverse audience. The lettered paragraphs here correspond to the labels in Figure 3.4.

A. Before generating divergent ideas, a group needs to share an understanding of the project (a convergent step). Unfortunately, Josephine's board wasn't clear about what it considered as "large"

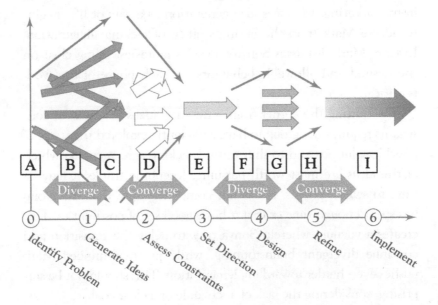

Figure 3.4

or what it defined as "diverse." Often organizations don't provide a well-developed brief to help them start, so team project leaders will have to insist on creating and vetting one. Make sure everyone understands the goal. Then take the time to create a process map that shows the required phases, the timeline for those phases, and the expected outcomes for each phase.

B. In the idea generation phase, participants may not be sure of how narrow or wide to set the scope. Each person must decide if his or her ideas should diverge wildly from those of others as a way to enlarge the search space, or if he or she should explore nearby with more closely related ideas in an effort to be more thorough in the search. Without explicit guidance, group members can only do what comes naturally. Some will go wild and radical with revolutionary ideas; others will stay in an adaptation mode, seeking evolutionary ideas with implementation in mind. Of course you need both kinds of exploration to be truly effective; but when we are not aware that both are happening at once, the result is debilitating frustration. Recall how Sonya from marketing, who sees idea generation as a way of life, begins to accuse Mark from the business office of lacking imagination. In turn, Mark dismisses Sonya's ideas as fantasies. Being clear on the desired and allowable behaviors for each phase of the work is critical.

C. Turning the corner from generating ideas to assessing constraints requires the group to have sufficiently explored the space of possible solutions and to shift toward seeking agreement on which of the ideas are most worth pursuing. Josephine thinks it may be time to switch phases, but is not completely sure that the group has spent enough time or that it has a good set of possibilities. This creates a vacuum wherein Sonya tries to delay the transition and continue divergent brainstorming, while practical-minded Mark pushes even harder toward implementation. This should not be surprising, considering the lack of a schedule or a clear goal.

If you have created a process map, revisit it at every meeting, plotting the team's progress and reminding everyone of the kind of thinking and action needed in the current phase. This may generate process conflict in the short term, but agreement about the process is paramount.

D. Assessing ideas is a very different behavior from generating them. Once again, the group needs an explicit understanding of the behaviors required in a new phase of the process. It is sure to lead to relationship conflict if you keep generating ideas and I keep critiquing them, both of us sure the other is being stubborn or mean. At ShowArts, with Josephine out on a phone call amid general confusion about the process, Barry's proposal for them to vote does restore some small amount of meaning and order: voting means making decisions, and making decisions means we're making progress. Unfortunately, what was needed at that moment was not a solution for "moving on" but a reminder of what phase the group was in and what its purpose was.

E. Committing to a direction is always hard, but it is even harder when you believe a different direction to be better or when you are not even sure, anymore, of the direction. Not fully convinced that the group has found a good solution, Josephine nonetheless goes along with its vote, possibly believing that reversing its decision will undermine harmony and commitment in the team. Even so, Sonya, disagreeing with the choice, checks out and never fully rejoins the team. The commitment being asked for at this stage is substantial; people are being asked to step forward into an uncertain future they may not understand or believe, possibly putting their social status and careers at risk. This must be acknowledged. Beyond a trustworthy process and a meaningful schedule, people like Sonya need to understand why the group is going the direction it is and why that's the best way for it to go.

F. The design phase requires that we have a good understanding of the goal so that we can make informed choices about the inevitable trade-offs that will have to be made in this stage. It also requires that we test and iterate possible solutions. Team Think Big seems to have bypassed this phase altogether, instead rushing into implementation by purchasing a mailing list.

Groups have a natural desire to get past the confusing early stages and move into the more stable production phase. This is where a well-planned schedule, with appropriate amounts of time allotted to each phase, can help a group resist the urge to converge prematurely (or, for that matter, languish too long in a particular phase). A better approach is to feed the desire for concrete action by starting small experiments to test your ideas to see what will work. Doing a small pilot project of recording and emailing, for example, might have shown the team that the real constraints for ShowArts were going to be legal.

G. This is a critical point for inviting supportive but straight-talking outsiders to give hard feedback about the problem, the proposed solution, and other contextual issues that may affect them. Of course, a team should be doing this all along, but at this juncture getting feedback is essential. Often we don't seek outside scrutiny for fear of criticism or because of a fear that others might uncover a showstopper flaw or a deadly mistake in our approach. But of course this only sets us up for a bigger setback or failure later on during implementation, after we've begun to sink not just time but also money into our approach.

H. As they refine their ideas into a final approach, team members must again be convergent. As before, it is critical that they understand (and agree) about the phase they are in and their current goals. Groups will tend to be short on time at this point due to poor scheduling or lack of time resources and will try to rush into the implementation stage to get it done. However, they must accept that they may need to iterate between designing and refining to overcome obstacles that may appear—or, god forbid, that they may even have to abandon their approach.

I. The implementation phase is when you transition from exploring, critiquing, and refining to going head-first down the luge toward your ultimate goal. Some naturally divergent thinkers like Sonya will want to abandon the project at this point if they feel that it lacks excitement or impact, and some naturally convergent thinkers like Mark may bail because they sense too many unresolved issues and are afraid the solution is not going to work. Two ways to keep the momentum going are (1) to pull in fresh people who can add energy and expertise and (2) to ensure that the project has sufficient resources.

Putting the Framework to Work: Group Constraints

To aid you in assessing the constraints at this level, use the following diagnostic survey. It is intended to help you assess the extent to which the constraints described in this chapter may be unintentional hindrances to innovation in your organization.

Group Constraints Diagnostic Survey

The survey lists twenty-four statements describing symptoms that can be caused by the constraints discussed in this chapter. As you read each statement, consider how closely it describes the situation in your current working group or project team. Think of your group as consisting of the people you interact with on a weekly basis and who have an impact on the group's work. Record your assessment by putting a checkmark in the box that indicates how accurately the statement describes your situation.

1 = Highly Descriptive; this occurs often or on a routine basis in the group

2 = Moderately Descriptive; this occurs sometimes or occasionally

3 = Not Descriptive; this occurs rarely or not at all

Constraint Level	Constraint Type	Diagnostic Statement
Emotion		
1☐ 2☐ 3☐	Fearing Criticism	Members don't share weird or half-baked ideas with the group
1☐ 2☐ 3☐		Members criticize and point out the weakness of ideas during brainstorms
1☐ 2☐ 3☐	Fearing Mistakes	Members are afraid to admit when they've made a mistake
1☐ 2☐ 3☐		Members blame each other and do not share responsibility for problems
1☐ 2☐ 3☐	Avoiding Conflict	Members do not challenge one another or ask difficult questions
1☐ 2☐ 3☐		Manager's ideas are considered "better" than those of everyone else
Culture		
1☐ 2☐ 3☐	Homogeneous Groups	Members are more similar to each other than they are different
1☐ 2☐ 3☐		Members are assigned for relationship reasons and not because of training or knowledge
1☐ 2☐ 3☐	Fearing Loss of Meaning	Members avoid considering ideas that may disrupt operations in the short term

Constraint Level	Constraint Type	Diagnostic Statement
Culture		
1☐ 2☐ 3☐		Members avoid "wasting time" on learning activities
1☐ 2☐ 3☐	Enforcing Taboos	Members consider only "hard data" or only "intuition" (not both) when deliberating
1☐ 2☐ 3☐		Members are openly critical or disdainful of new ideas or alternative approaches
Environment		
1☐ 2☐ 3☐	Impeding Interaction	Meeting space configuration is difficult or impossible to change by the group
1☐ 2☐ 3☐		Meeting and working spaces are chosen based on convenience or availability
1☐ 2☐ 3☐	Limiting Media	Our group space does not facilitate collaboration or information sharing
1☐ 2☐ 3☐		Members are distracted by outside activities during meetings
1☐ 2☐ 3☐	Lack of Documentation and Sharing	Our meeting or working space must be cleared after each meeting
1☐ 2☐ 3☐		Members don't capture and review the team's discussions and insights
Process		
1☐ 2☐ 3☐	Lack of Process	Members are confused about the current state or phase of a project
1☐ 2☐ 3☐		Members cannot articulate the innovation process we use
1☐ 2☐ 3☐	Poor Phase Transitions	Members are unclear when projects need to move from phase to phase
1☐ 2☐ 3☐		Schedules slip early in projects, causing missed deadlines
1☐ 2☐ 3☐	Not Trusting Process	Members are suspicious of attempts to use "exercises" or "process" during meetings
1☐ 2☐ 3☐		Members do not consult the process guidelines once a project is under way

Using the Results

Note the total number of statements that you rated as "Highly Descriptive." If you have rated more than six of them this way, then working on group constraints will be a productive effort. Now that you have identified the specific constraints, you can take action. You may wish to turn back and reread the description of the problem and of the specific strategies for addressing that constraint. You may also find that strategies are obvious given the symptom you have identified. For detailed instructions on working with your assessment results, use the steps outlined in Appendix A, Using the Assessment Results, to determine whether group constraints are a significant impediment for you in your organization and to develop strategies for overcoming them.

Later, after completing assessments for the other chapters, you will be able to compare constraints and see if one of the other levels poses a greater challenge for you overall than do these group constraints. Of course you need to recognize that fixing these issues in a group is going to be far more difficult than fixing them in yourself, especially if you haven't yet convinced others in the group of the value of the change.

Summary

Groups can be powerful agents of innovation. When members provide multiple perspectives, alternative problem-solving approaches, and production capability together, they can achieve things no individual can achieve on his or her own. To use groups to their highest potential for innovation doesn't require much, except a safe environment, a desire to innovate, an environment for collaboration, and a simple process. The following chart offers a recap of the constraints discussed in this chapter, along with some strategies for overcoming or living with them.

Emotion Constraints: Ego and Social Status	
Fearing criticism	Support psychological safety
Avoiding mistakes	Suppress idea egotism
Avoiding conflict	Have a good fight
	Celebrate failures
Culture Constraints: Cohesion and Meaning	
Forming homogeneous groups	Mix up group membership
Enforcing shared sense of meaning	Explore to learn, exploit to produce
Adhering to traditions and taboos	Prize new problem-solving methods
Environment Constraints: Comfort Versus Collaboration	
Using spaces that impede interaction	Reconfigure the group's working space
Communicating using limited media	
Not sharing or documenting insights	Facilitate multiple modes of expression
	Automate documentation
Process Constraints: Directing Members' Behaviors	
Lacking a formal process	Adopt an explicit process
Not using or trusting the process	Communicate the current phase and status
Failing to make phase transitions	
	Enforce needed behaviors for each phase

Chapter Reflection: Group Constraints

It can be helpful to reflect on your insights about group-level constraints and the process of diagnosing them in your group. You may wish to consider these questions:

- What evidence is there for the existence of the constraints you named?

- How important are these group factors compared to the individual, organizational, industry, societal, and technological constraints you identified?

- What constraints may have been overlooked because of your group process?

- Would other members of the group agree that there is a need to fix these constraints?

Why You'll Never Be a Prophet in Your Hometown

Organizational Innovation Constraints

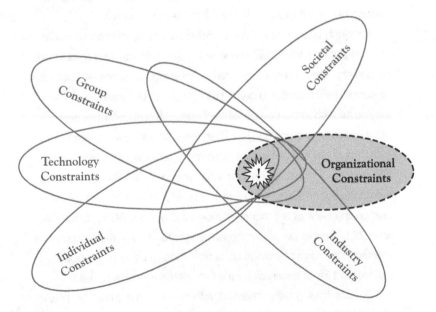

Figure 4.1

Xerox PARC, the Palo Alto Research Center, was founded in 1971 as an R&D center for the Stamford, Connecticut–based firm. Worried that new competitors from Japan would soon be entering the copier market as early photocopy patents expired, and concerned at what the "paperless office" of the future might entail for Xerox, the company created PARC with a mission of innovating for the future. As Larry Tesler, a researcher there recalls it, "The management said go create the new world" (Cringely, 1996, part 3).

From all reports, it was a very innovative place. John Warnock, a researcher at PARC and, after a stint at Apple Computer, a cofounder of Adobe Systems, said, "The atmosphere was electric—there was total intellectual freedom. There was no conventional wisdom; almost every idea was up for challenge and got challenged regularly" (Cringely, 1996, part 3). According to Adele Goldberg, manager of the System Concepts Laboratory, this was a kind of nirvana for researchers. They "came there to work on 5-year programs that were their dreams" (Cringely). They also had immense funding; Charles Thacker, one of the scientists there, said, "We felt comfortable in profligately wasting hardware to simulate the future" (Abate, 2004).

Although having lots of smart individuals is no guarantee of creative output, this innovative group really did produce. At a time when computers were gargantuan things, housed in controlled-access air-conditioned rooms and owned by IBM or the Defense Department, they developed all the components of personal computers as we think of them today: a graphical user interface with windows, a point-and-click mouse, a cut-and-paste command for use while working on documents, a "what you see is what you get" (WYSIWYG) display, the computer network, and even the laser printer. Much of this was built on the back of another revolutionary idea from PARC, SmallTalk, an object-oriented programming language. Taken together and implemented in the form of the Alto computer, these inventions represented a significant list of treasures for the late 1970s (Dernbach, n.d.).

Despite having been charged with creating the future by headquarters (and having done so), the researchers at PARC could not seem to get sufficient traction for their ideas. James Turner (2008), in an interview for *O'Reilly*, said, "I actually worked for Xerox AI Systems in 1986 and it was kind of frustrating because they really had the mentality there that if you couldn't sell paper and toner for [them] they weren't interested." Andy Herzberg, one of the original designers of the Macintosh, offered that "most of the best PARC people were really frustrated by the Xerox management" (Turner). Steve Jobs characterized management as "copier heads that just had no clue about a computer or what it could do" (Cringely, 1996, part 3). Apparently headquarters did not care for anything that did not work with a copier or that they could not conceive of working with one. Ignoring all the rest of the PARC treasures, they did seize on the value of the laser printer in moving paper and toner ("Adopting Orphans," 1999).

This situation might well have turned out to be one of lamentable frustration on the part of the researchers, and not much else. Just as the Post-it almost did, the inventions might have died in the lab; everyone would have moved on to new pursuits. This would likely have been the case had it not been for a visit by Steve Jobs. PARC was an intellectually open place and had a continuous flow of visitors, but this visitor in particular was smitten by the Alto. Jobs reported that "within, you know, ten minutes it was obvious to me that all computers would work like this some day" (Cringely, 1996, part 3). Jobs then resolved to align Apple's strategy with the graphical user interface he saw at PARC (Dernbach, n.d.). Days later, he arranged an intimate technical demo of the Alto with senior members of his Macintosh development team, over the loud objections of the Alto project manager. HQ executives overruled her, however. In exchange for the right to purchase $1,000,000 of pre-IPO Apple stock, they had agreed to allow the demo along with three days of access to the PARC facilities (Landley, 2000; Pang and Marinaccio, 2000).

There is a great deal of speculation about what the Apple team actually learned and whether it appropriated Xerox's intellectual property, especially considering that Apple's Lisa computer, the predecessor to the Macintosh, had already incorporated a number of the ideas. Bill Gates had his own thoughts on the matter. After being accused by Jobs of "ripping off" Apple in the development of Windows, Bill Gates is said to have replied, "Well, Steve, I think there's more than one way of looking at it. I think it's more like we both had this rich neighbor named Xerox and I broke into his house to steal the TV set and found out that you had already stolen it" (Hertzfeld, 1983).

The story of PARC's development of the Alto may seem to suggest that Jobs's visit made the difference between Xerox's failure to capitalize on its own innovations and Apple's success. Yet there is obviously much more to the story than that. Given that numerous "Leonardo da Vincis" were hard at work and that groups in Xerox were sharing and collaborating (they built more than two hundred Altos), it's clear that individual and group constraints were not the issue. And although we might like to find fault with the executives at HQ, they were focused exactly where they should have been: on protecting the business at hand. One technology they did pay careful attention to, the laser printer, turned into a $1 billion business for them, so clearly they were not asleep at the wheel. They knew there were problematic issues on the horizon, which is why they had founded this research organization in Silicon Valley.

So how do we explain this story of innovation? Although Apple may have come away with some ideas, we also know that the *idea* is the easy part; it's *implementation* that's the hard part. Why was Apple able to enjoy the fruits of PARC's efforts in a way that Xerox never was?

Do "Innovation" and "Organization" Belong in the Same Sentence?

The purpose of *organizing* is to get people into a configuration that allows them to achieve a predefined output, and to do so in an effective and repeatable way. Successful organizations are quite good at doing this. For example, Maxim (www.maxim-ic.com/), a manufacturer of integrated circuits, or chips, reports a failure rate for its products as 0.49 FITs. This means that the company expects a chip to fail only once in *two billion* hours of operation (once in 5.5 million years)! Xerox's copier business was so successful and its machines so ubiquitous that its name became a verb. Instead of photocopying something, you Xeroxed it.

Although organizations have many advantages over individuals and groups in achieving complex goals, this increased power comes with its own set of constraints. These constraints are not the result of malice or conscious efforts at sabotage on the part of change haters (though at times it may feel that way). Rather, they are inherent in the very act of organizing. For example, the organizational goal of reducing variance can be in direct conflict with the goal of innovation, which requires constantly questioning and changing the things we do.

This chapter focuses on three aspects of formal organizations that can seriously impede innovation:

- *Strategy:* the organization's mission and the employees' understanding of how they will achieve it

- *Structure:* the mechanism for coordination and control in the organization

- *Resources:* the assets an organization has control over that can be used to achieve the mission

Whether your role in an organization is one of managing others or of being a sole contributor, these constraints limit your ability to innovate. This chapter will help you understand how this happens and suggest ways of overcoming these constraints.

Strategy Constraints: Knowing the Intent

An organization's strategy is an articulation of its intentions and embodies a judgment about appropriate ways to achieve that intention. It is designed to tell you what to do and, at least in broad terms, how and when to do it. Business thinkers and executives alike will readily agree that a solid, well-articulated strategy makes decisions easier—you need simply align to it. Use it to make new product or service decisions, resource allocation decisions, operations decisions, and even decisions about which customers to serve or to ignore in the face of the actions of your competitors and of other agents in the environment. If you have a good strategy and if all your decisions are aligned with it, you should be on your way to achieving your goals. But several factors can complicate this simple picture.

Innovative Ideas Don't Fit the Organization's Strategy

One of the basic pitfalls for would-be innovators in an organization is a lack of "strategic fit" between their ideas and the organization's goals or plan for achieving them. This gap can lead to a failure of innovation—and significant frustration for the innovator—and for all the right reasons. If a proposal for change violates the what, how, and when of the organization's strategy, then it *should* be stopped because it is a waste of organizational resources.

It follows that employees' ability to respond to a call to innovate will suffer if they don't know or understand the organization's strategy. Why would they not know the strategy? Sometimes executives keep the strategy secret out of fear that it will be revealed to competitors. Sometimes the strategy is too complex to be easily shared. Sometimes employees do understand the basic strategy but not underlying risk factors, such as the organization's financial condition, or legal considerations, such as patents or liability. And sometimes, as in the PARC story, the strategy "go create the new world" is so ill defined that even the senior leadership may not recognize when employees are fulfilling it.

The Organization's Strategy Doesn't Reflect an Ever-Changing Reality

It can easily happen that even a well-thought-out strategy no longer makes sense because of changes in the environment—for instance, a new competitor moves into your market, your core product loses its patent protection, or changing technology threatens to take away your ecological niche (think of newspapers). In fact, this kind of gap between reality and even our best-laid plans is bound to exist because of the way we make strategy in organizations. We do the analysis to develop the strategy and communicate it at Time 1, but we don't finish enacting the strategy until Time 2. If there is a substantial interval between T1 and T2—many organizations use a five-year strategic plan—you will likely be facing a completely different world than the strategy was intended for. What is more, this change is accelerated as competitors in a market respond to one another's moves in a process called *coevolution*. You lower your product's prices, then your competitors do the same, then you respond again. Or you improve your valet parking, and they install luxury seating; the next move is yours.

Faced with these situations, people generally do the rational thing, which is to change their perspective to match the new reality. If everyone in an organization saw exactly the same changes in the environment, they could all change their behavior uniformly (and presumably update the strategic plan accordingly). But organizations typically group people by the kind of work they do, so employees necessarily see different parts of the environment that might call for different kinds of responses. The gaps between strategy and perceived reality—and therefore appropriate action—are likely to be many. This situation creates confusion and uncertainty that are exacerbated when there is significant divergence between the views. The employees at PARC, for example, could not understand why HQ would be so dense as not to see what they saw in Silicon Valley: the clearly emerging future of the personal computer.

The Strategy Is Risk Aversion First, Innovation Second

Some organizations adopt a strategy of pursuing new products only *after* the market is proven and the technology has been mastered. Most car companies are taking this wait-and-see approach toward the electric car, preferring to sit on the sidelines as Nissan launches the LEAF. Seeing the battery technology to be immature and the market risk as high and unknown, they won't pursue this innovation until they see whether it actually works. The problem for firms that might like to be "fast followers" is that they may not be fast enough to ever catch up. Surprisingly, many of these same car companies had just recently learned this hard lesson with their wait-and-see approach to Toyota's launch of the Prius hybrid car. When it did take off quickly, other firms struggled to respond by developing their own hybrid technology, which they learned was harder than it looked, and they never caught up. In 2011, Toyota remained the hybrid market leader, having sold more than three million hybrid cars.

When a genuine willingness to assume the risks that come with innovation isn't part of the organization's DNA, then innovation-as-strategy will not be valued, no matter what the strategic plan says. The risk-averse types (and there are always plenty of them in an organization) will act to stifle efforts to innovate on the grounds that they are a waste of organizational resources.

Overcoming Strategy Constraints

Innovative organizations make innovation a guiding principle and core part of their strategy. They also demand the participation of all employees in pursuing it. When the organization is aligned toward innovation, employees are less frustrated because their innovation efforts will be directed toward ends that are truly valued by the organization. Employees also know that everyone has an obligation to support their innovative ideas, reducing the likelihood that those ideas will be arbitrarily maimed or killed.

Know the Strategy

Do you know your organization's strategy? If you think you do, go ahead and write it down. Then ask other people in your organization to do the same. Do an honest "compare and contrast." If you have clear articulation, fair agreement, and coherent alignment, then this is not your constraint. However, if the strategy statements are so vague that they cannot give direction, if they disagree, or if they are likely to drive different parts of the organization in different directions, then you have work to do.

Without clarity about the strategy, people may aim their innovation efforts in completely different directions, resulting in unnecessary conflict that can kill innovation. At Xerox, the strategy that the people in PARC assumed to be operational and valued was completely different from that on the East Coast. With HQ insisting on a strategy of protecting the copier business at all costs, PARC scientists and engineers couldn't support or understand it, and as a result they left to join Apple after realizing that the strategy there was one they could value and that could value them. Had Xerox executives been able to articulate earlier what they later realized, that they were in the document management business, they might have seen the immense value of what PARC was doing, and the PARC scientists might have been able to show how their ideas were relevant to the strategy of the company.

Tell the Story

Senior managers should work to ensure that everyone understands the goals of the organization and, ideally, that they are willing to help achieve them in valued and meaningful ways. To achieve this understanding, no one needs (or wants) a four-inch-thick binder full of the strategic plan documents. Those documents were already out-of-date by the time they came out of the printer, given the months-long time lag between the analysis that drove the insights and the bureaucratic approval process used to authorize them. Rather, most employees would do better with a simple understanding of how the company competes and why.

There's a story I've been told by executives and senior leaders at Nissan that they share in response to fear among managers over the riskiness of the LEAF electric car initiative. In the mid-1970s, the Datsun "Z car" was introduced to the U.S. market and took it by storm. It was a high-performing, inexpensive Japanese sports car that proved that Nissan could do something bold and amazing, much more than simply make cheap economy cars. Resting on its laurels, Nissan didn't do anything so meaningful for a long time afterwards. As a result, the late 1990s found Nissan on the verge of bankruptcy. An alliance with Renault and severe austerity under the "Nissan revival plan" brought an unbelievable turnaround in its financial health. But what would Nissan do about its psychic health? Executives tell the managers that it's been a long time since the company did something so innovative, radical, and amazing that it changed their world. "The LEAF is our chance, now, to change the world again. Are you ready to help?"

The story is compelling. The timeline is simple and easy to follow. It is a clear demonstration of the villainy of resting on your laurels and the high price of the climb out of difficulties of your own doing. It gives us perspective by showing that Nissan is now financially healthy and stable, but still longing for something. Finally, it insists we make a choice: rest on laurels once again or satisfy the longing by changing the world.

Take the time to tell your story and make it compelling, too.

Trust the Doers

The people who are going to be sources of innovation in the organization (and there may be many more of them than managers imagine) *want* to do things that are valuable in their organizations. They want to innovate in ways that help the company and that advance their own careers. And often those who are in the trenches have a better understanding of where the opportunities are, given that they are closer to the problems and more versed in the details of those problems. Yet too often their leaders don't trust them to be the loyal, smart, and determined employees they were hired to be.

At some point we have to trust the doers. If you're a manager, your role is to get people to a point where they are competent and empowered and where they are willing to give their best ideas to the cause. If you are able to communicate the strategy (and show how it leads to the achievement of the organization's goals) and if you can articulate what considerations to account for in a meaningful and acceptable solution, you have the problem mostly solved. Then get out of the way. With a clear sense of direction and the feeling of being trusted to figure out what to do, most people will take to the problem with great gusto and work hard to solve it. Instead of micromanaging, focus your efforts on helping remove the individual and group constraints on innovation you have already read about. And think about this: you can't get a promotion until someone can do your job.

Understand (and Communicate) the Risks

Even when the strategy is clear, the risks associated with specific ways of achieving it may not be. Initiatives that look like good ideas to people in one place in the organization may create problems for those in another.

In a consumer electronics company whose strategy was to be first to market with the most innovative products in a fast-moving competitive environment, Noah, the head of the R&D group, approached Connie, the CEO, seeking permission to purchase a rapid prototyping machine that would allow them to cut *weeks* off a tight development cycle, but that was also very expensive. Connie immediately said no once she heard the price. Questioned, she could give no satisfying reason for saying no, but that was the answer. Noah went away frustrated, confused, and slightly demoralized. After all, this purchase clearly supported the strategy, and for all he knew, the company could afford it. Was she not in support of her own strategy?

Only a year later did Noah learn the real reason for the refusal. At the time he asked, the firm was experiencing a shortage of working capital (cash). The CEO had worried that sharing this information about the company's precarious financial situation might drive Noah right back to the lab, where he would polish his resume in anticipation of the company's impending demise. But Noah suggests otherwise. He says that had he been told the true reason for the denial, he would have gotten creative about cutting costs in less value-adding areas and then working on a financing arrangement with the machine vendor.

Ironically, not communicating the real level and nature of risks can *create* a culture of paralyzing fear instead of preventing it. Once this culture starts to take hold, it can require an immense amount of work to undo.

Structural Constraints: Efficiency and Control

In early 2011, Steve Jobs, cofounder, chairman, and CEO of Apple Computer, announced that he would take a medical leave of absence from the company. Immediately, the debate started about whether the company could continue to be successful without his leadership. Much of the debate was about where the amazing ideas would come from without Jobs. But this may be a misreading of the situation. Although Jobs's creativity may have contributed to Apple's resurgence, perhaps his greatest value was as a hard-charging, bulldozing roadblock remover. There must have been countless conversations inside Apple that went something like this:

Innovator: I'm going to need help from a bunch of people to move this new idea forward, including a few from other departments.

Manager: Sorry—the idea is interesting, but everybody in our group is maxed out, and getting help from other departments is out of the question.

Innovator: But Steve wants this done yesterday!

Manager: How many people do you need?

In many organizations, conversations like this would only turn up a litany of reasons why the innovator's request was impossible. What are the sources of this inertia that so often stifles good ideas?

The Price of Efficiency

The magic of an organization is its ability to coordinate the behaviors of large numbers of individuals. Efficiency is served by breaking down the work into distinct pieces that individuals perform routinely and reliably. The hierarchy fixes inputs to and outputs from any particular individual's role. With fixed inputs, a defined role, and predetermined outputs, reliability is the desirable result. If you work in the sales department in a large company, for example, your input might be a list of who wants how many of what. Gathering orders from across all the sales force, you enter these into a spreadsheet to determine how many of X to make and how many of Y. You send part of your output to the production group to start making the stuff and the other part to the distribution group to prepare to ship it. This can be very efficient and reduces the possibility of all kinds of errors.

But when all the vital communications among the parts of an organization begin to take the form of standard reports and electronic data interchange, they can constrain the possibilities for innovation that might be generated by chance encounters between information and people. Standard reports are designed to remove all ambiguity about the information contained within. Although it may be important to fix communications in this way to achieve routine outputs, innovation can suffer. Imagine if Art Fry of 3M, instead of having seen firsthand what Spence Silver's idea was, had been given a standardized report that said something like "Item 43; Formula X developed; mediocre adhesive that only sticks to itself; no known use."

The Downside of Size

Hierarchical structures allow organizations to grow extremely large and to become distributed across a wide geography. To grow large, organizations divide and coordinate the thinking and the labor that is to be performed, among various functions and specializations inside. But increased size and spread can be a mixed blessing. On the one hand, the organization potentially gains access to more kinds of information and multiple perspectives that could inform innovation. On the other hand, larger size means more coordination and communication difficulties, and having multiple perspectives means a greater likelihood of significant divergences of opinion about the desirability of one decision or another.

To solve the problem of supervising a far-flung operation, Xerox did what many organizations do: require that headquarters approve any large expenditures or new programs. Although solving the supervision problem, this approach did not solve the information-sharing problem. To make good judgments, especially the kind of tacit and nuanced judgments that would be required to decide the fate of early-stage and revolutionary programs like the Alto, HQ executives would need to see the full spectrum of information that the PARC researchers themselves had seen that led them to believe that this was the way of the future. Unfortunately, accounting statements or even progress reports are not sufficient to communicate the information. This exemplifies the problem of generating ideas in one context but requiring they be approved in a completely different one.

Rewarding Survival Instead of Experimentation

Other things being equal, we get the behaviors we reward. Handing someone a bonus for coming up with a great new idea is one way of rewarding innovation, but it won't go that far if the more powerful incentives in an organization fail to reward innovative behavior. Over the long term, who tends to get raises and promotions: the individuals who are rich sources of ideas, only some of which succeed, or the ones who survive as long as possible without a single failure?

Regardless of what an organization espouses, you can get a good read on how much the organization values creativity by asking individuals which workplace behavior is more likely to result in advancement: putting yourself on the line on behalf of potentially risky ideas, or keeping your head down and doing exactly what you're told.

Overcoming Structural Constraints

In 2011, Steven M. Anderson, a retired brigadier general in the U.S. Army, wrote about how the military could reduce battlefield casualties by conserving energy. A great many lives are lost feeding the military's ravenous energy appetite: at last count, more than a thousand American deaths in Iraq and Afghanistan could be attributed to fuel-related missions. Not only that, but the fuel itself is very expensive. Answering his own question about why the Defense Department does not address this important issue, Anderson suggested that the reasons for aversion to change were the same as those in any big organization: "Passive leadership, lack of accountability, competing priorities, skepticism about environmental concerns" (p. A29). His solution? Strong leadership. Although cultivating strong leadership is clearly vital, a structural analysis suggests that other approaches will also be needed to overcome organizational inertia.

Use Fluid Structures

To reduce the constraints introduced by rigid hierarchical forms, you may need to restructure parts of your organization to optimize information gathering and processing rather than operational efficiency. Innovation requires multiple paths of information flow and the ability to stop the process to absorb and evaluate data that don't seem to make sense. It also requires that insights and initiatives be able to come from anywhere in the hierarchy. These are all inefficiencies from a process-flow, variance reduction perspective.

If bureaucratic structures help promote routine, ad hoc structures that arise in the moment and that have fluid and changing memberships can be great at supporting innovation. Take consulting teams as an example. Consulting firms are not organized in neat multilevel hierarchies. Rather, they form teams on an as-needed basis, pulling people in as more are needed and sending them out when their role is fulfilled. The team is built around a project and organized around the process the team uses to complete the project. Movie production works the same way. With a core group running the show, people with unique information and special skills are pulled in and sent out as needed. While engaged in the project, they direct their behavior according to their place in the process and not where they might fit in the hierarchy.

Mix It Up

You can improve information flow in your organization by allowing (or even forcing) people to meet and work across functional boundaries. Considering that at the beginning of a project, you are not usually aware of which piece of information might need to come from or go to which part of the organization, err on the side of allowing as much access to information as possible. Many R&D and consulting organizations have company-wide weekly gatherings during which teams share information about their projects, their progress, and their process, in case someone in another part of the organization knows something the team needs to know. Although these weekly gatherings are usually informal (on Monday mornings over bagels at IDEO), some companies hold more formal seminars where teams are able to share more specific information and get input into their projects. It was at this kind of seminar at 3M that Spence Silver presented his progress in a way that stimulated Art Fry's thinking about a solution. Rather than merely giving permission to attend these meetings, overcome organizational constraints by requiring some consistent level of participation or attendance.

Stay Aligned

Innovation efforts, especially radical innovation efforts, are likely to create confusion and misalignment. For this reason, keeping everyone aligned requires conscious effort. If multiple parts of your organization are working on complex problems related to a particular initiative, take the time to get them into the same room to discuss how the pieces fit together. You can use the chart of innovation process phases discussed in Chapter Three (Figure 3.3) to help groups locate where they think they are in their own project and at what points of convergence it makes sense to bring the teams together.

Innovate Outside the Lab

Structure in large organizations is based on the division of labor, separating people into functions. Unfortunately, that means innovation is separated off as well. In structure and in mind-set, many organizations enforce the idea that innovation is done in the lab by the scientists or engineers, and everyone should stick to his or her work. But as a manager, you know this is not the way it should be. Shouldn't the payroll clerk also be encouraged or required to innovate? There are as many ways to add value in the administration of a business as there are in the products it creates. Dell Computer's business model innovation that built the company had little to do with changing the performance of the computers themselves. Rather, the innovation was to hold no inventory of computers and to get paid by the consumer for the computer long before paying the contract manufacturer who builds and ships it.

By outsourcing innovation only to certain parts of the organization, you create frustration among the innovators in other parts of the organization who have useful ideas to share, but who can be ignored and derailed by those around them who prefer things as they are by simply saying, *Stop innovating; that's R&D's job*. But in today's competitive world, improved product performance is necessary but not nearly sufficient to keep an organization at the top of its industry.

Cultivate Dissent

In normal bureaucratic functioning, "skipping levels of authority" is considered improper, and there are often informal norms against this. In 1986, NASA learned a difficult lesson about how this norm impeded information processing. After the space shuttle *Challenger* exploded seventy-three seconds into flight, killing all seven crew members on board, the Rogers Commission was formed to investigate the circumstances surrounding the accident. After a lengthy investigation, the commission found that NASA's culture and decision-making processes had contributed to the accident. There was a previously known flaw in the booster O-ring, and when engineers warned of the danger it represented on the eve of the launch, their arguments and supporting data never made it past their supervisors for consideration. Had the dissenting opinions been allowed, the report suggested, the accident might have been averted. By 2008, it seems, things hadn't changed very much at all. A group of summer interns made a video parody, titled "Barriers to Innovation and Inclusion," about their internship experiences at the Johnson Space Flight Center. The plot centers on a young woman engineer trying to get her ideas for an innovative design listened to within the NASA bureaucracy; it shows all too clearly the barriers she faced as middle managers tried to stay in their comfort zones, continually reminded her that it was not in her job description to do design, and worked hard to prevent the young engineer from annoying their superiors.

When I was first shown the video, I was a bit shocked that the interns had actually made it and then aired it publically; it seemed they were very definitely burning bridges to future employment at NASA. But the last scene in the video suggests why they had acted as they did. The same young engineer, now a Google employee, is shown having a discussion with her new manager and finding exactly the opposite treatment: open discussion, respect for her ideas, and true excitement about them. The last line is a zinger: the engineer's manager says, "Maybe we can sell this idea to NASA!" I guess that with the option of working at a place like Google, these bright young engineers find the bureaucracy of NASA makes it a place where they don't care to work.

Cultivating dissent, however, is not easy. People tend to want to be cooperative and to fit in. One organization, the American Foreign Service (AFS), cultivates it through a mechanism it calls the "dissent channel," which is a communication channel for "expressing constructive dissent." By giving it a formal name and advertising its purpose, the AFS gives employees a place to express their dissent with current approaches and to voice those alternative perspectives that they feel are being blocked and not heard. The message is clear that dissent is appropriate and will be heard. Create your own dissent channel like the AFS by setting up an email address where people send their reports of blockage; or even simpler, make a few minutes' time at the end of each meeting and call for an expression of dissent. A few anonymous remarks on Post-its can work wonders for getting people to say what you need to hear: what they *really* think. After all, it's better for higher-ups in your organization to hear ideas from frustrated innovators than to have those innovators find that the only person willing to listen is your competitor.

Resource Constraints: Capital and Capabilities

The third category of constraint that is inherent in organizations has to do with the resources that the organization uses to achieve its goals, what we might think of as the fuel that powers the actions. Many managers I talk to believe that the tightest constraint on innovation is insufficient time or money. However, there are a number of other resources worth considering in this light. In addition to the many forms of capital—economic, political, social, and so on—organizational resources include the employees, their skills, the value chains, and the processes and systems that enable the work.

Getting Capital Where It's Needed, When It's Needed

A common idea about innovation is that it is expensive and that the expense is paid in money. We think of start-ups, for example, as becoming viable only after the infusion of (lots of) venture capital. However, even a cursory conversation with a venture capitalist or private equity fund manager will indicate that there are lots of things that innovative early-stage companies need, but that cash is usually not the most difficult to get nor the most important. Rather, experienced leadership, technical know-how, market power, and political and social capital in the form of powerful networks are often what will make or break a start-up. These resources are just as important in established organizations that are embarking on new ventures. Unfortunately, they can be difficult to acquire, store, and distribute throughout an organization in the service of innovation. In large measure, the focus that organizations place on money causes managers to lose focus on the value and power of these other types of essential resources.

At the same time, money (assuming money is to be had) can be accessed and distributed quite easily—so easily that organizations erect any number of controls and barriers to prevent it from being distributed and used in uncontrolled or illegitimate ways. Budgets, of course, are a primary way of controlling the flow. They enable the management team to allocate financial resources in ways they believe will best allow the organization to achieve its short- and long-term goals. A key word here is "will": budgets are always about the future. That budgets are created in advance does not pose a serious problem for supporting the routine functioning of an organization. However, when it comes to innovation, the world stubbornly refuses to behave the way we plan for it to behave. Budgets that require *all* allocations to be specified and approved in advance do not allow for the eventualities of an innovation process. Of course, R&D budgets are intended to account for and control "unplanned" expenditures. But what if your group isn't on the R&D gravy train? Then you'll probably have to account for every penny up front, which will likely entail being starved of the resources you need to support a meaningful innovation effort.

Having the Right People for the Job

It's hard to overstate the importance of marshaling "people" resources in support of innovation. People bring the knowledge, imagination, and skills that are the essential fuel of the innovation engine. But that doesn't mean that it's always easy to get the kinds of people we need or to motivate them to apply their talents to the problems the organization deems important.

In the spirit of efficiency (and in deference to inertia), organizations tend to recruit in conventional ways and in the same places that they have always looked for labor (and brains) in the past. Yet the people an organization needs to innovate may be very different from the ones it knows how to recruit and screen. Consider General Motors, for example. As long as GM was making conventional combustion-engine cars, it was fairly straightforward to find combustion engineers and even to help create new ones through such means as donations to university programs. But what happens when the company decides it's time to build an electric car? Suddenly it needs to find electrical engineers and battery experts to work in a field that is just emerging. To some degree, the company's routines for finding engineers are going to have to be reinvented. Similar issues arise any time an organization is branching out in a distinctly new direction. If we're lucky, we may choose well and end up with individuals who have just the skills and knowledge we need, but even then we may not be happy with them (or they with us) because of the different value systems they are likely to bring into the organization.

Complex and Well-Defended Value Chains

Another, oft-overlooked constraint on innovation is the existing value chain. The value chain is simply the set of linked steps involved in taking raw inputs and converting them into a more highly valued product. The value creation may occur with a product, as in manufacturing, or as a service. A proposed innovation will ideally take into account the organization's value chain and, in fact, strategically improve some part of that chain to create even more value. For example, Porter Walker, a company that distributes tools and safety equipment to manufacturing firms and utilities, creates value by getting its client organizations the equipment and supplies they need, when they need it. When the heads of the Tennessee Valley Authority, for example, take a nuclear power plant off-line for planned maintenance, the last thing they want to do is sit around waiting for needed tools and supplies. Porter Walker realizes this and focuses relentlessly on improving its ability to get the right stuff to the right place, which includes loading trucks more quickly and accurately, planning more optimal routes, and understanding and acquiring those supplies most likely to be needed. Innovations focused on the critical parts of the value chain are much more valuable than, for example, optimizing the spaces in the lot for employee parking.

To change a process may require changing what several people in the chain do, and how they do it. A simple change in the way you load a truck to make it quicker to unload, for instance, requires the involvement of not only the driver but also the warehouse workers, the stock picker, and the salesperson who is checking the order. And if your new way of loading requires additional space, you may have to involve the forklift drivers too, as the space you need is the same space they currently use for turning around in the tight warehouse. Changing processes may also require new equipment, rearranging old equipment, and entirely new sets of understanding about how to fix the inevitable problems that arise when implementing a new system.

Another hindrance to change is the belief that the current system works "well enough," a stance captured by the expression

"If it ain't broke, don't fix it." An inefficiently functioning but predictable process may be considered a small price to pay as compared to undertaking the risk that will be introduced by changing it. Someone might ask, "What if taking away the turnaround space causes more accidents in the warehouse?" After all, the process under discussion is what led to the current success of the organization and the individuals within it. No wonder they ask, "How can you guarantee me that the changes required by your innovation will make the process work better for us and for me?" They are right to ask the question, but it sets a high hurdle for seriously considering, let alone adopting, a new way of doing things.

Overcoming Resource Constraints

Resources need not be a constraint to innovation in an organization. Key to improving your organization's ability to innovate is paying attention to the amount and types of resources in the organization and allocating them in ways that support innovation.

Feed and Starve Innovation

Some innovations require a massive investment of resources to make them happen. The Manhattan Project, which created the first atomic bomb, was awash in resources. The project was started in 1940 with wartime funding and a life-or-death mandate, and scientists working on the project could get virtually anything they asked for. By 1945, the project had employed thousands of scientists and spent over $2 billion, which would be over $30 billion in 2010 dollars (Schwartz, 1998). And in truth, nothing short of this massive commitment of resources could have gotten the job done in only a few years' time.

But not all cases of innovation are like the Manhattan Project. There are many familiar stories of individuals who were able to achieve amazing innovations with very few resources. For example, Steve Wozniak, the cofounder and technical brains behind Apple

Computer, designed the company's first computer as a teenager, on the floor in his bedroom. His design was revolutionary in the way that he used integrated circuit chips in combinations that had never been considered before. Although he has been called the "Mozart of Digital Design," as he tells it, his motivations were fairly mundane. He had wanted a computer that he could use to play games, but could not afford one. So he started out using only the chips that his allowance could buy. Precisely because he didn't have more capital to work with, he had to make a number of radical technical choices, such as using the same physical memory for data and for video. This was clearly a case where starving innovation actually helped make it happen.

What these stories suggest is that managers need to exercise judgment about the nature of the innovation and what will truly be required to achieve it. The leaders of the Manhattan Project harbored no illusions that what they did was going to be cheap or easy. Consider that plutonium, the critical ingredient, didn't even exist before 1940. In contrast, Woz, as he is affectionately known, didn't have a timeline and didn't have any more money. He would have used any amount of money he was given. What this suggests is that whereas budgets allow managers to "turn off their brains" while organizations are in a routine functioning mode, during innovation, an awareness of the goals and the current situation is paramount to avoid cases of overfunding or underfunding innovation initiatives because of ignorance about how the funds are actually being used.

Ignore the ROI

As discussed earlier, the larger an organization becomes, the more likely there is to be divergence of opinion about the desirability of a decision. Often organizations resolve these conflicts on the basis of political power. If powerful groups or individuals in the organization view a proposed innovation as too risky or as too inconsequential, they'll use their influence to stop the initiative.

One favored mechanism for doing this is to insist on a calculation of projected ROI for an early-stage project. Certainly this tool, used properly, can assist organizations in deciding whether a particular investment will help move it toward its goals, but insisting that early-stage innovations, particularly radical ones, show ROI is an easy way to kill them.

ROI is notoriously difficult if not impossible to prove in early-stage projects, especially when a market does not currently exist for the innovation. The late Ken Olson, the CEO of Digital Equipment Corporation, said that trying to calculate the potential market for a radically new product is "like deciding where to build a bridge by rowing to the middle of a river in a boat and counting the number of cars that drive by" (Victor, 2009). Although organizations must necessarily consider issues of strategy and ROI in the assessment of innovations, it matters a great deal when in the process such an assessment is made.

If It Ain't Broke, Give Them Something to Break

A good friend related the story of his early days at a well-known company in the diaper manufacturing industry. When he arrived at the manufacturing facility as a newly minted industrial engineer straight out of college, he was thinking of the amazing improvements he would be able to make with his newfound knowledge. As he entered the room where the giant machine was, an old-timer said, "Take a good look at that machine, 'cause it is the last time you are gonna see it. You are not to touch that machine or even to think about it! You mess that thing up, and not only will we miss production but we'll be cleaning up the mess for weeks. Go back to the engineering building and leave us alone!"

The old-timer was correct in thinking that tampering with a crucial piece of technology (or a crucial process or any other part of the value chain) can carry significant risk. Granted, but why bother hiring bright young engineers if you don't intend to take advantage of their knowledge and fresh perspectives?

One answer to this dilemma is to provide your innovators with a test rig or simulator to use in their "fail forward" work. Apple, for example, built a complete mock-up of an Apple Store inside a warehouse to try it out and tinker with it. Although it may seem hard to justify the expense of a rig that won't be used for production, it can be a small price to pay if you truly seek significant improvements in the way you do business.

Know the Value Chain

Knowing the value chain is key to meaningful innovation. Without an understanding of exactly how and where value is added in the process, individuals can waste time and resources in an effort to improve things that in the end create very little value. By the same token, they may miss significant opportunities by ignoring areas where the organization creates a great deal of value.

In an interview with *McKinsey Quarterly*, Bill Campbell, founder of Intuit Software Company, relates a relevant anecdote about working with software engineers to build Quicken.com (Mendonca and Sneader, 2007). During one meeting with the engineers, a product manager said, in the fashion of product managers everywhere, "I want these features." To which Bill replied, "If you ever tell an engineer what features you want, I am going to throw you out on the street. You're going to tell them what problem the consumer has, and then the engineers figure out how to solve it." Drawing this kind of distinction is possible only with a thorough knowledge of where—and how—value is created in the value chain.

Putting the Framework to Work: Organizational Constraints

To aid you in assessing the constraints at this level, use the following diagnostic survey. It is intended to help you assess the extent to which the constraints described in the chapter may be unintentional hindrances to innovation in your organization.

Organizational Constraints Diagnostic Survey

The survey lists eighteen statements that describe symptoms that can be caused by the constraints discussed in this chapter. As you read each statement, consider how closely it describes the situation in your organization as it affects those in your workgroup or project team. Record your assessment by putting a checkmark in the box that best indicates how accurately the statement describes your situation.

1 = Highly Descriptive; this occurs often or on a routine basis

2 = Moderately Descriptive; this occurs sometimes or occasionally

3 = Not Descriptive; this occurs rarely or not at all

Constraint Level	Constraint Type	Diagnostic Statement
	Strategy	
1☐ 2☐ 3☐	Not Knowing the Strategy	Our people don't know the strategy
1☐ 2☐ 3☐		Different parts of our organization see our strategy differently
1☐ 2☐ 3☐	Outdated Strategy	Our strategy does not match our situation or capabilities
1☐ 2☐ 3☐		Our stakeholders don't understand or value our innovation efforts
1☐ 2☐ 3☐	Innovation Not Strategic	We don't require everyone to participate in innovation
1☐ 2☐ 3☐		Our leaders prefer that we keep risk to an absolute minimum
	Structure	
1☐ 2☐ 3☐	Organized for Efficiency	We avoid positive changes if they risk short-term inefficiencies
1☐ 2☐ 3☐		We prize efficiency over all other values
1☐ 2☐ 3☐	Ineffective Size and Structure	We are the wrong size to effectively try meaningful new ideas
1☐ 2☐ 3☐		We do not reorganize around new ideas, even in service of our mission

(Survey continued on next page)

(Survey continued from previous page)

Constraint Level	Constraint Type	Diagnostic Statement
Structure		
1 ☐ 2 ☐ 3 ☐	Rewarding Survival	We do not have a mechanism for authorizing important experiments
1 ☐ 2 ☐ 3 ☐		Keeping your head down is a way to get ahead here
Resources		
1 ☐ 2 ☐ 3 ☐	Overplanning	Our budgeting process requires us to make all allocations in advance, even for innovation projects
1 ☐ 2 ☐ 3 ☐		We do not try ideas because we lack the financial capital or are unwilling to risk it
1 ☐ 2 ☐ 3 ☐	Gaining and Valuing New Resources	We have trouble finding experts with the new skills we need
1 ☐ 2 ☐ 3 ☐		We marginalize those groups working on our new products and services
1 ☐ 2 ☐ 3 ☐	Complexity of Value Chain	Our operations and processes are finely tuned; improvements to it are discouraged
1 ☐ 2 ☐ 3 ☐		Our primary value-adding processes are complex and difficult to manage

Using the Results

Note the total number of statements that you rated as "Highly Descriptive." If you have rated more than six of them this way, then working on organizational constraints will be a productive effort. Now that you have identified the specific constraints, you can take action. You may wish to turn back and reread the description of the problem and of the specific strategies for addressing that constraint. You may also find that strategies are obvious given the symptom you have identified. For detailed instructions on working with your assessment results, use the steps outlined in Appendix A, Using the Assessment Results, to determine if these constraints are a significant impediment for you in your organization and to develop strategies for overcoming them.

Later, after completing assessment for the other chapters, you will be able to compare constraints and see if one of the other levels poses a greater challenge for you overall than do these organizational constraints. Of course you need to recognize that fixing these issues for an organization is going be difficult, especially because you will need to convince others of the potential value of the change.

Strategy Constraints: Knowing the Intent	
Innovative ideas don't fit the organization's strategy	Know the strategy
	Tell the story
The organization's strategy doesn't reflect an ever-changing reality	Trust the doers
The strategy is risk aversion first, innovation second	Understand (and Communicate) the Risks

Structural Constraints: Efficiency and Control	
The price of efficiency	Use fluid structures
The downside of size	Mix it up
Rewarding survival instead of experimentation	Stay aligned
	Innovate outside the lab
	Cultivate dissent

Resource Constraints: Capital and Capabilities	
Getting capital where it's needed, when it's needed	Feed and starve innovation
	Ignore the ROI
Having the right people for the job	If it ain't broke, give them something to break
Complex and well-defended value chains	Know the value chain

Summary

Organizations are powerful primarily because of their ability to use large numbers of people to produce routine outcomes in an efficient way. In their normal functioning, these are the exact outputs we get. However, organizations can deliver innovative outputs if we remain aware of the basic constraints that organizing brings. It's not enough to have smart people working in creative groups, as Xerox did. Innovation also requires keeping people pointed in the right direction through awareness of a meaningful strategy, structuring and coordinating them on the basis of information processing and not simply a division of labor, and allocating resources in a way and in a form that enables people to apply them to the problems they face. The chart on page 123 offers a recap of the constraints discussed in this chapter, along with some strategies for overcoming or living with them.

Chapter Reflection: Organizational Constraints

It can be helpful to reflect on your insights about organization-level constraints and the process of diagnosing them in your organization. You may wish to consider these questions:

- What evidence is there for the existence of the constraints you named?

- How important are these organizational factors compared to the individual, group, industry, societal, and technological constraints you have identified?

- What constraints were overlooked because of your limited view into the organization?

- Would others agree that there is the need to fix these constraints in the organization?

If It's Such a Great Idea, Why Isn't Our Competitor Doing It?

Industry Innovation Constraints

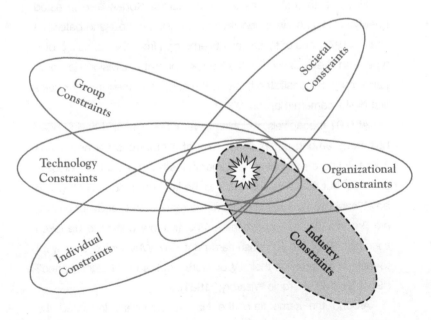

Figure 5.1

"You press the button, we do the rest" was the marketing phrase coined by George Eastman in the 1880s to pitch his idea to the American photographic market. Prior to that time, photography was an expensive and difficult process limited primarily to professionals because cameras were big and the negatives were made on glass plates that needed to be chemically processed soon after exposure. However, after Eastman's invention of a plastic-based negative film that could be formed into a roll and preloaded in a camera, photography was ready for the masses. Kodak's Brownie camera, which cost $1.00 at the time, came preloaded with film. Once you exposed the entire roll as a set of "snapshots," you sent it in to Kodak so that it could "do the rest."

Eastman's strategy of making photography for the masses continued successfully through the Brownie line and through the 1960s Instamatics, whose use of a film cartridge made loading and unloading foolproof. The cameras drove Kodak's strategy of selling the cameras cheaply but making serious money on the film ("Has Kodak Missed the Moment?" 2003).

Not one to rest on its technical laurels, Kodak also invested heavily in R&D and was generating more than a thousand patents a year. In 1975, one of these patents emerged from the lab as a prototype, and Steve Sasson of the Kodak Apparatus Division Research Laboratory demonstrated it. It was the camera of the future: Kodak's first digital camera (Sasson, 2007).

At 0.01 megapixels, weighing several pounds, and having been built from, among others things, bits of a tape recorder and a lens from the spare-parts bin, the camera was hailed as a technological success, but then was sent back to the lab. The feedback? It would be at least twenty-five years before the market was ready for a camera like this. It was too expensive and too low quality to be taken seriously. What would consumers print on? Why would they want to look at pictures on their TV or store photos on audiocassettes? ("Sony's New Electronic Wizardry," 1981).

Around the same time, the Noritsu Company launched the QSS-II one-hour photo-processing machine. Kodak's power in the market was now reinforced as the supplier both of the film the consumers used and of the chemicals and papers consumed by the photo-processing stations. Things could not have been better.

At a conference in Tokyo in 1981, the same year that Sony announced the 3.5-inch floppy drive, Sony's chairman, Akio Morita, presented the company's prototype of the Mavica Electronic Still Video Camera, which recorded images on a two-inch disk. The Sony announcement hailed its Mavica (*magnetic video camera*) as an "epoch-making innovation in the history of still photography" and, because it used no film or chemicals, as one of the most fundamental changes in the concept of photography "in the 140 years since the invention by Daguerre of France" (Sony Corporation, 1981).

Kodak vice president John Robertson begged to differ: "Why would anyone want a still camera that takes pictures only as sharp as those on your TV? It's an idea we've discussed for years and clearly decided that there's no market for the product." He continued, "We expect traditional photography to grow and continue to be the predominant form of amateur picture-taking into the next decade." The article reports Polaroid as commenting that it "has no plans at present to follow Sony down the route to electronic pictures" ("Sony's New Electronic Wizardry," 1981).

Kodak's failure of vision cost the company dearly. Despite being first to invent a digital camera, Kodak was late to its commercialization and was never able to catch up. This leaves the question of what Sony's executives saw on the horizon that Kodak didn't. Why were they willing to take the chance on the new technology, despite its shortcomings and flaws?

It's conceivable that they saw the rapid development of faster and more powerful personal computers powered by Intel's chips in the IBM PC and Motorola's in the Macintosh. It's possible that they saw Conner's revolutionary hard disk design that would enable 20 MB and larger-capacity hard drives on users' desktops. And maybe they saw HP's development of the DeskJet inkjet printer and the emergence of photo editing programs like Adobe Photoshop 1.0. It wasn't enough to see just one of these, but putting it all together would show characteristic features of a perfect storm: other companies in other industries driving the development of the entire infrastructure that would enable the adoption of the electronic camera.

Driving Competition with Innovation or Innovation with Competition?

Competition among rival organizations is considered a natural and healthy activity within sectors, markets, and industries. Competition is considered to be so important to innovation that the Federal Trade Commission (FTC) disallows mergers within markets if it believes the merger to be "anticompetitive"—that is, if it removes a significant competitor and therefore reduces a firm's incentive to deliver lower prices and better performance through innovation. For example, in late 2010, Comcast, in its attempt to acquire NBC, the nation's fourth-largest broadcaster at the time, was forced to agree to a number of conditions which ensured that satellite providers and other rival services, such as innovative Internet video distributors like Hulu, Netflix, Amazon, and Apple, would still have access to the popular NBC programming they would need to grow and compete.

Viewed in this way, innovation is rarely thought of as being constrained by competition. Yet sometimes competition positively discourages innovation. Especially when competition in a market or industry is intense, organizations can have difficulty mobilizing the knowledge, equipment, capital resources, and, not least, the focus they need to innovate.

This chapter looks closely at how the behaviors of the key actors in an industry can impede innovation. We'll focus on

- *Competition:* the tactical and strategic actions and reactions that organizations enact in order to remain viable in a field of rival organizations

- *Suppliers:* holders of the specialized capabilities and resources that organizations use to compete, including labor and capital
- *Markets:* the larger group of interacting agents that includes the producers, the consumers being served, and all other stakeholders, including, for instance, the regulators of that market

For many people in business, the economics-based perspective of this chapter is deeply ingrained in their vocabulary and thinking. Such terms as *profit, competition,* and *value chain* are part of everyday conversation. The same may not be true of many people who work for nonprofits, government agencies, and the like. But whatever kind of organization you work in, the material in this chapter applies to you. For example, I will use the word *profit* in this chapter in the technical sense of generating value in excess of the cost required to produce it. If you work in a tax-exempt (that is, nonprofit) organization, don't be intimidated by the word or alienated by its connotations. Instead, think about it this way: society expects your organization, like all others, to generate "excess value"—that is, to produce or output something of greater value than what was consumed in producing it. Profit is simply what's left when you subtract the value of the input you received from the value of the output you generated. Tax-exempt organizations are also subject to competition. They are competing not only with organizations with similar missions but also with all the other investments of time, money, and energy a potential donor, volunteer, audience member, or government agency might make in the sector or industry in which they operate.

Whatever kind of organization you work in, and regardless of your role in it, understanding the external constraints that limit your organization's ability to innovate is critical to guiding your own innovation behaviors. This chapter provides insights into why these constraints operate and suggests ways of helping you overcome them.

Competition Constraints: Innovation as a Last Resort

Competition arises from the efforts of organizations to extend their own survival and increase profits by better serving the needs of a market among a field of rivals. Although competition is best served when firms innovate new products and processes, thus improving the performance of the products or reducing the prices of those products or services, innovation does not come without its own cost to the organization. Depending on the source of competition—existing rivals, new entrants, or substitutes—the innovation constraints may take different forms.

Competition Among Strong Rivals

Competition is good for the consumers in a market, as it results in increased performance and decreased prices. However, competition can be problematic for the producers in that market. A basic theory of economics holds that successful competition—that is, purely efficient competition—will have the effect of driving profit to zero in a market. You may have observed this in your own market; each time you increased the quality or performance of your product or provided it at a reduced price, your competitors did the same. This reduced your profit by forcing you either to spend more to deliver the increased performance or to receive lower profit margins due to the reduced price.

If this tit-for-tat continues unabated, there will eventually be no profits to be had for any producers in that industry. This dynamic is the source of firms' desire to reduce the competition in their markets; they'd like to maintain profits at least long enough to pay off the investments they made in innovation to gain those profits.

This is the source of a paradox: organizations have a good reason to innovate, to create new products that generate profits; but they also have an equally good reason to kill innovation, to reduce competition and prevent the erosion of profits. One possible outcome is that an organization will abandon a market instead of rising to the challenge of an innovator's strong product. A senior executive at a large medical center told me how they had recently built a world-class children's hospital, but were perplexed when it reached full capacity *years* ahead of schedule, requiring them to start expansion far earlier than they had intended. Some diligent market research showed that they had not made an error in forecasting the market size; rather, competitors had begun to pull out of that market, rather than paying the costs of upgrading their own facilities or innovating in some other way to stay competitive. We can assume that these other firms focused their innovation investments in some other market that was less competitive.

Radical Innovations by New Entrants

In addition to competing with existing rivals in an industry, where innovation commonly takes the form of product performance improvements, organizations may require a different kind of innovation to compete with *new entrants* in a market. New entrants aren't necessarily new companies; they are often established organizations entering a new market or sector. The firm Tata, for example, was a new entrant into the automobile market in India in 1998; Apple Computer was a new entrant into the mobile phone market in 2007; and Sony, in 1981, was a new entrant into the photography market.

New entrants believe that they can meet the needs of the customers in a market at a significantly more attractive price or at a much higher performance level, which should result in more profit for them. They do this by introducing more radical innovations that can significantly change the basis of price and performance. Either of these approaches can increase profits and value compared to the existing firms in the market. Otherwise, why take the risk of competing?

The firm Tata bet that by introducing a "people's car," the Tata Nano, at a price point of $2,500, it would be able to compete in a way that existing companies could not. Although the jury is still out on the success of Tata's strategy, the company clearly bet on lower cost. The runaway success of the iPhone was a clear bet on performance: an enormous screen, a focus on media applications, and integration with the computer. Since its introduction, other smartphone companies have been struggling to keep up with Apple's trifecta of customer value.

Substitutes for Your Product

The third source of competition that can affect innovation takes the form of substitutes that completely displace the market need that the current industry of existing rivals is focused on meeting. As an example, consider the free music sharing service Napster, created by Shawn Fanning and Sean Parker. Launched in 1999, Napster (named after Fanning's hairdo) allowed music copied from CDs onto a computer to be easily, freely, and anonymously shared with others over the Internet. This served as a ready substitute source of music for large numbers of music fans. Rather than going down to the local record store and paying up to $20 for a new CD to buy eleven songs you hate to get one song you like, simply install Napster and belly up to the free all-you-can-eat music buffet. Not surprisingly, this was a pretty difficult substitute for existing record companies to compete with.

Substitutes often come from industries totally unconnected to the ones they disrupt. It shouldn't be hard to see why; surely the record industry had better means of innovating than two under-graduates at a small university. Why weren't record companies the ones doing the innovation that would revolutionize the industry? Probably because they didn't have to; they had music fans right where they wanted them—buying eleven songs they hated to get the one song they liked.

Overcoming Competition Constraints

Of course, organizations can't always single-handedly change the constraints that affect an entire industry. Still, you can gain strategic insights by understanding how your industry dynamics will shape your competitors' innovations and how you can drive innovation in your own organization in response.

Find New Ways to Compete

In normal competition against existing rivals, firms tend to try to increase profits and market share by improving product performance. Think of how much more performance you get from a personal computer at a much lower price than you did five years ago, thanks to the cutthroat competition in the PC industry. To fuel this competition, organizations invest significantly in R&D activities aimed at improving technical performance and reducing production costs.

Yet this is not the only or necessarily the best way to compete. The Doblin Group (2010) notes a number of ways that firms can innovate—for example, through *business model* innovation, which Dell Computer employed by preselling computers and then building them to order instead of building a large inventory of products that would go quickly obsolete as the computer industry evolved. Or a firm might use *process* innovation, as Walmart did, to build a core strength around its inventory management systems. Apple's iTunes music service was an innovation in the *delivery* of the product.

You might even consider combinations of alternative forms of innovation. Avis, Hertz, and Budget rental car companies competed mercilessly on product performance, waging a battle of increasing car availability, model variety, add-on services (for example, cell phones, onboard GPS, rapid pickup and return), and more. This had the effect of driving down prices and driving up costs, especially as the competition also encompassed jockeying for the space closest to the popular terminals in airports. As you can imagine, it would be quite expensive to enter that raging battle expecting to prosper if you approached innovation the way the current competitors did. Instead of joining the fray, Enterprise Rent-A-Car found an alternative path for innovation by creating a new *service offering* with a focus on insurers, fleet renters, and occasional renters; by focusing its *business model* on being efficient at charging insurers and fleet renters directly; and by using a mode of *delivery* that was innovative in that it would bring the car to the customer. By focusing on alternative forms of innovation in a cutthroat competition, Enterprise found a lucrative new customer base, which quickly became the largest in the industry.

Become Partners to Learn, Not to Kill Innovation

Mergers and alliances are usually justified with an argument that complementary strengths of the two firms, when combined, will make a stronger, more capable firm. But the end goal is always going to be an increase in profits and long-term viability through growth in size, revenue, and market share. From an economic perspective, an added benefit is that partner firms can reduce the need to innovate their products if the partnership co-opts or removes a significant source of outside competition. This is the reason that utility companies (that is, regulated monopolies) are often maligned as having such poor service quality; they don't have to improve the product or provide higher levels of service to stay in business. By merging or forming partnerships, firms take a step in that direction.

However, it is only a step. In most industries or sectors, firms still have to innovate to survive. And even though a partnership may reduce competition, it can increase the cost of innovation in the new entity, especially when an innovation requires both partners to participate. Pitched primarily as a way to cut costs during a downturn in the computer industry, the acrimonious 2002 merger of HP and Compaq caused palpable tension. Long after their merger, one predicated on complementary strengths and expected operational efficiencies, the new firm still seemed to lack the promised unity and effectiveness. One subtle symbol of the disunity was on the combined Web site landing page. The search box (see Figure 5.2) begged the question: Where do you *really* want to go? To HP or Compaq or both?

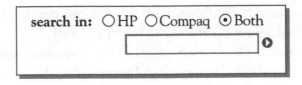

search in: ○ HP ○ Compaq ⊙ Both

Figure 5.2

Source: www.compaq.com.

If you are considering an alliance, think about it in terms of how it improves your competitive position through learning and innovation, and not simply through removing competitors. Once integration begins, stay focused on creating systems that decrease the cost of innovation in the partnership—for instance, by creating an entirely new R&D entity to service the new organization. This may seem costly in the beginning, but given the constraints that occur even in functional organizations, putting the innovators from both firms on equal footing and giving them a clear strategy can work wonders for innovation in the long term.

Don't Overinvest in Efficiency

Increasing an organization's production to drive economies of scale has the effect of increasing profits, because more products are produced at a lower cost. Achieving these economies also reduces competition by discouraging new entrants from entering a market. The ability to produce cheaply creates a significant hurdle for potential new entrants; they will have to compete with your significant cost advantage to enter the market.

Although it may act to reduce competition, this behavior may also have an unintended effect. If a new entrant is committed to entering your industry or market for strategic reasons or even ideological ones (for example, charter schools), it cannot compete according to the accepted rules of that market. There is too much risk; you will be too efficient to compete with head-on. Instead it will seek radical new ways to serve your market—and it will choose ways that give it significant cost benefits and possibly give the customers significant performance benefits as well.

Clayton M. Christensen discusses the disruptive innovation dynamic in his book *The Innovator's Dilemma* (2003). Using the disk drive industry as a case study, he describes how new entrants gained a footing by using altogether different technological approaches to disk drives than were current among the market leaders. For example, disk drives moved from ferrite heads to thin-film technology to magneto-resistive technology, with each change in technology offering an immense performance jump. He also shows how incumbent firms were unable to keep up; they had too much invested in the efficient old technologies to be willing to abandon them.

This is not to say that efficiency is not a good thing; it is. However, as your organization pursues efficiency, be sure to recognize that the competitive protection this provides may not be long lasting. Don't let your role as a big player or market leader make you overly confident that the inefficient and money-losing thing that those *idiots* are doing over there—for example, giving away free Web searching, as Google did early on—has no bearing on your organization and industry. Instead, try to pay attention to what the start-ups are doing, especially if they are doing something in your industry that makes no sense at all from an efficiency perspective. They are doing it for a reason—try to find out why.

Develop New Tests for New Ideas

Consider a product that you've used at one point in time, but then later abandoned in favor of a better alternative. USB thumb drives were substitutes for floppy disks, digital cameras were substitutes for film, and watching television became a substitute for going to plays or to the opera. Substitutes fill a need in a completely different way than the conventional products in an industry do, and as they do so, they change our expectations of how they should perform. For example, when perusing USB drives in the store, customers were likely to look at price and capacity in ways they never did for floppy disks. And as competition arose in the form of online data storage, allowing people to access their data from any computer, the way they thought about price, capacity, and convenience began to change again.

Unfortunately, the changing standards can be devastating. Substitutes will always perform relatively poorly when they first arrive in a new industry. They are too expensive, too big, and too slow as compared to the existing market leader. This poor showing lets incumbent firms become complacent and ignore or ridicule the new approach. Kodak executives and engineers laughed at the poor one-third of a megapixel resolution of the Sony digital Mavica, suggesting that Morita should have been embarrassed to announce the product, not even ready for shipping, in worldwide press releases.

However, they forgot that Sony was driven by competitive pressures just as they were; Pentax showed a prototype of its Nexa video still camera in 1983, Hitachi showed its version in 1984, and Canon launched its RC-701 in 1986. Sony was under great pressure to improve the performance of the camera. Of course it was not as good as Kodak film, but it was good enough for taking a picture. To Kodak, this was still not a threat since the camera didn't perform as well, and people, Kodak felt sure, remained interested in picture quality. If they wanted convenience as well, the ubiquitous one-hour photo-processing machine provided all they would need. Unfortunately for Kodak, customers' preferences were shifting. What was important was not so much resolution, which was Kodak's test of performance, but convenience and instant gratification. Suddenly film's one-hour convenience seemed infinitely long compared to the immediate review provided by a digital camera, even if the picture was relatively mediocre. And as digital cameras improved thanks to new competition, questions of relative picture quality began to recede even as other advantages, such as being able to take as many shots as you want at no additional cost and easily manipulate them with editing software, came to the fore.

Supplier Constraints: No Organization Is an Island

To participate in an industry or sector, organizations typically must negotiate with *suppliers* that control needed resources, such as raw materials, product modules, ideas, capital, or any other input an organization requires to fulfill its mission. Because suppliers make money by providing components essential to the organization's operation, you might assume that the suppliers would have the organization's interest in mind. But this is not necessarily the case. Suppliers may have trouble or be unwilling to provide the resource where the organization needs it; an organization may need your skills, but are you willing to move to Asia to supply them? Suppliers also may balk at helping with innovations they perceive as reducing their importance, or they may have their own bases of power and control, as, for example, skilled labor does through the mechanisms of unions and professional guilds.

Although suppliers to an organization benefit from their relationships with organizations, a number of constraints can arise. Here are three of them.

Suppliers Favoring Their Own Interests

Suppliers of critical goods to an organization—be they raw materials, labor, or even knowledge—have a vested interest in ensuring that there can be no substitute for their contribution to the final product. (Like the organization, they also do not want competition.) This is not a cynical view; it is simply looking at the situation through the lens of economics.

Suppliers therefore have a high incentive to attempt to supply inimitable and otherwise irreplaceable goods and services. These may take the form of highly integrated solutions—for example, supplying the entire dashboard assembly to a car manufacturer. This will make it very difficult for an automobile maker to simply switch to another supplier as a way of lowering prices by driving competition between potential suppliers. While raising the value of the supplier's contribution to the final product, it also reduces the risk that the client organization can or will change.

Obviously, this can be a significant innovation constraint. Highly integrated and embedded systems are going to be more difficult to modify or improve if they have been supplied in essentially turnkey form, because the detailed understanding of the subsystem belongs to the supplier. For innovation to occur, it will have to be driven by the supplier.

These points apply to services and to smaller organizations, not just to large companies making complex products. Consider one family-operated publishing company that decided belatedly to join the Internet age by engaging an old acquaintance to build a Web site to market its regional publications. The acquaintance, who was used to designing for sizable enterprises with marketing budgets to match, created a beautiful but unconventional design whose workings only he understood. When he eventually gave up maintaining the site (the account, after all, was a small one for him), the mom-and-pop company was left with an elaborate Web site and no easy way to change or update it—the kiss of death for anyone trying to attract and retain eyeballs on the Web.

Difficulty Getting the People You Need

Organizations may also need a supply of motive power and knowledge that comes in the form of human labor. The labor supply can also become a constraint in an industry. Particular types of individuals may be needed at a particular time and place. Silicon Valley in California, for example, has an extremely large labor pool of engineers, electronics experts, and computer programmers. This demographic reality suggests that it will be much easier to start a new consumer electronics development company there than it would be in Nashville, Tennessee. However, a health care services start-up would benefit from being in Nashville, given the many dozens of health care service firms that have been founded and operate in the area. Although advances in communication technology have lessened the geographic constraint, it still matters in cases where labor and knowledge really need to be on-site.

Inertia of Powerful Professions, Unions, and Other Guilds

Beyond the problem of availability, the control of the employee labor supply can also affect innovation. There is a common conception that labor unions generally will constrain innovation. Why is that? Union members are generally in a much better position to understand the nature and problems of the work being done and, therefore, to understand the value of innovation in making their own work lives easier and more productive. However, belonging to a union—just like being a member of a profession such as medicine or law—creates mixed loyalties for employees as they go about their jobs adding value to an organization. Like all other suppliers in an economic value chain, employees are concerned with being replaced, so it is only rational for them to act in ways that will prevent their contributions to the final product from being devalued or made expendable.

Consider the difficulty our society currently is having changing public education or the delivery of health care. Creating significant change in such complex and well-established industries would be difficult in the best of circumstances, but the task is even harder because control over these domains is a contest between powerful professions that have far different incentives than do those who demand change. On the one hand, unions and professions can be the source of innovations in the practice of their jobs, because their members can benefit from improvements in the state of the art. On the other hand, they may act to set rigid standards around the performance of particular job duties, thus enforcing the need for particular types of employees to do those duties, even if the standards don't promote the best or most efficient way to perform a task. When these standards are adopted widely in an industry, they make workers more valuable and indispensable. By the same token, in their own self-interest, unions will necessarily oppose the introduction of new techniques or processes if they are perceived to have the potential of making employees less powerful and ultimately more replaceable.

Overcoming Supplier Constraints

Organizations of any size need suppliers of materials, labor, knowledge, and other important components of the value chain. Yet suppliers, by and large, are not under the direct control of their customers. What can you do to ease the constraints that arise from your need for resources from outside the organization?

Don't Outsource the Core

As I noted earlier, a deeply integrated and embedded system provided by an external supplier is more difficult for the client organization to control or to change than one the organization provides for itself. Consequently, it's imperative that your organization understand its value chain and take proactive steps to keep the most critical components in-house whenever possible. Although it is sometimes obvious what these critical components are, like the secret formula for Coke, they can also be obscure early in the development of an industry. IBM learned this hard lesson as competitive pressures from the Apple II computer forced a rushed development of the IBM PC in the early 1980s. Not realizing the core value of the operating system software, IBM licensed PC-DOS software from Microsoft, thus giving the supplier control over the rate of innovation and the dissemination of this critical component.

When your organization is reliant on a particular kind of expertise to fulfill its current or intended strategy, it is time to have a conversation about the costs and advantages of allowing outside experts—who may have divided loyalties—to control your strategic core. Using a lawyer from an outside law firm makes sense when you are in need of customary legal services that organizations require to do business. But when your corporate strategy is to derive income by acquiring and enforcing patents, that expertise should be in-house. Bringing this expertise in-house *and* giving full support to practitioners' efforts at innovating and otherwise improving the "state of the art" in their professions can go a long way in fostering healthy dual loyalties among these important suppliers while helping the professions grow.

Share the Wealth

Although suppliers have an incentive to control their contributions, they also have an interest in helping organizations improve their products and services. After all, gaining increased control in a declining industry is not in the suppliers' long-term interests. By assisting your suppliers to understand industry dynamics and the changing value of different parts of the value chain, you can help them help you while improving their own chances of long-term success.

Walmart, for example, knows that all parts of its distribution system are vital in allowing the company to achieve extremely high levels of efficiency while keeping costs low. For this reason, Walmart proactively engages in improving its suppliers' information technology systems, to enable electronic data interchange. The company will go so far as to send in its own programmers and IT professionals to serve as consultants while manufacturers set up or work to improve production scheduling and inventory tracking systems. By knowing its suppliers' levels of production, inventory location and status, and other important information about the distribution system, Walmart is more efficient. By learning from Walmart's immense expertise in this area, the suppliers become more efficient and productive as well.

Acknowledge the Threat of Your Innovation

Most emotionally healthy people are skeptical of innovation proposals. This is because they have had a lifetime of experience with the dynamic whereby *your* idea means that you get the benefits, but *they* have to endure the risks and costs of change. These costs may not be obvious to you, but they can be substantial. Consider the struggles with changing delivery of health care, an industry populated largely by highly trained professionals. Politicians and policymakers attempting to implement the will of their constituents may have innovative ideas about how health care should be changed. But the suppliers of the labor and expertise needed to do it may have different ideas about the wisdom or value of the change, and for good reason. It can require over a decade of training and hundreds of thousands of dollars of debt before a physician is allowed to practice independently. Doctors have spent that time, money, and effort becoming experts at a particular way of doing things. It's natural for professionals like them to oppose proposals for change when they have made such an investment, and they are even likelier to oppose it when the heavy cost of their investment isn't recognized.

Beyond these investments, there is also the threat to suppliers that the change may portend. I spoke with many small business owners at the National Court Reporters Association, who, while lauding the sophistication of the technology for automatic voice transcription systems, were working to oppose adoption of the new technology. Apparently, some courts were considering adopting this technology as a way to reduce transcription costs. One court reporter and small business owner told me that it was not just a matter of the loss of income but, more important, that court reporting is highly skilled, nuanced work that a machine could never perform in an acceptable way. "Our system requires accurate transcriptions in order for justice to be served!" It's clear that in addition to her income, her identity was under threat by the suggestion that a machine could perform her job.

These more subtle threats, like this one of identity, can be hard to recognize, but the effort is worth it if adoption is your goal. For example, rather than de-skilling or displacing the transcriptionists, the courts might encourage members of the guild to themselves adopt the machines as a way to improve their efficiency and accuracy, which could to lead to the lower prices the court ultimately desired.

Understand the True Costs of Capital

In addition to expert knowledge, an organization may need money to fuel its competition in existing industries or its entry into new ones. Outside capital may be generated from the issuance of stock or through conventional loans, and although there are important differences between these two methods, they share some characteristic constraints. Access to capital is constrained by the general supply in the economy as a whole and by the economic outlook in an industry. The cost of borrowing or using that money varies within an industry depending on the amount of risk an organization represents to returns or repayment of that capital. The more risk to the returns, the more interest you pay. Beyond debt payments, which tie up capital, preventing them to be put to other, more innovative uses, loans may also entail "loan covenants" that stipulate, for instance, your inventory levels or how or when you pay your suppliers.

Stock prices are also set relative to levels of risk. Stock prices increase as a result of high returns delivered at low risk, whereas prices decrease commensurate with low returns delivered at high risk. Of course, low stock prices mean there will be less money available for investment for innovation inside a firm. At Kodak, the management was certainly aware that the company's stock price would have suffered had it gone wholesale into the risky electronic camera business. Not only would the payoff be far off in the future, but also the risk of failure was high because the technology was untested and the market unproven. Why not simply use those funds to increase sales through marketing expenditures instead of putting them at risk?

Be sure to understand these dynamics when using "other people's money" to build and run your organization. The cost of interest payments are obvious, but the other costs of capital may not be.

Market Constraints: Everybody Wants It Cheaper— *and* Faster *and* Better

The third kind of constraint I will consider at the industry level is the constraint represented by the market itself. We normally think of the market as consisting of only the clients and customers, but there is value in a broader definition that includes the product and service producers, along with other stakeholder groups, such as suppliers, regulators, standards associations, and society itself. When we think about markets, it is critical to recognize that different entities (especially customers) are likely to have values, interests, and incentives very different from those of the firms that address that market, and that these differences can represent significant innovation constraints.

Demands for Higher Performance at a Lower Price

Other things being equal, customers prefer lower costs and choose among competing alternatives accordingly. Of course, all other things are never equal, especially when it comes to adopting innovative new products. Even in the case of commodities, customers continue to expect performance increases at the same time that they seek lower prices. With technology products in particular, people have become accustomed to getting more and more performance (higher-capacity disk drives, faster processors, phones with more features, better TV screens) for little, if any, more money than they paid for inferior performance just a few years before. In this context, what can become a significant constraint is the way that performance is assessed.

When companies undertake incremental improvements, their aim is to create new but not revolutionary products or services that will perform better on a market's established performance criteria. If you happen to be a Microsoft Excel user of the past several years, you may have noticed this kind of incremental improvement. The 2007 version offers a spreadsheet that is 1,048,576 rows by 16,384 columns in size, representing an improvement of 1,500% and 6,300% respectively over the 2003 version. This may have affected you or not, but the logic of the improvement is that having more columns and rows is better. Products produced according to this logic are generally easier to sell, as customers know how to assess performance. Competing on this basis, however, shackles innovation in the service of fulfilling a single known need, one that everyone in the market (including competing companies) understands. We may bypass otherwise meaningful innovations because their value is currently unappreciated by customers—that is, the innovations may offer benefits, but only in ways that current performance standards don't measure.

Another difficulty with the way performance is defined is that buyers in a market may have a complex mix of performance needs, some of which are highly subjective and difficult to compare. Is a lighter tablet computer better than one with a bigger screen or one with a longer battery life? Ultimately, producers in a market have to place bets on particular configurations, weighting multiple performance criteria in ways that they hope customers will value. The possibility (and costs) of misstep are great. You may miss an important criterion or overweight an unimportant one. To avoid the risk, many firms simply result to a fast-follower mode, waiting to see what the market leader does and then constraining their own innovation efforts to interpreting and mimicking the weights they believe the market leader actually used.

Legacy Systems and Adoption Costs

In addition to forward-looking performance improvement, customers in a market naturally prefer to have low costs of adoption as they switch to new products. To achieve these low adoption costs, producers must ensure that innovations interoperate with the legacy systems that the customers already have in place. These legacy systems may be technical in terms of how the pieces fit together electrically or mechanically, or they can even take the form of systems of knowledge people may already have—for example, knowing how to operate a Windows PC or a Mac.

Another constraint, one that is easy to overlook, is the maturity of a market. Companies in existing markets meeting demand in conventional ways can compete on bases other than product innovation—for example, by expanding distribution or by lowering price. If lower pricing is achieved by increasing scale, the organization may box itself into a corner because changes to a highly efficient high-volume operation will increase costs. This leads organizations serving large mature markets to be slow in response to competitors' innovation and moves.

In contrast, in immature markets where innovation is driving competition and the speed of competitive response is fast, early adopters may be willing to adopt radical innovations quickly, but the market's mainstream customers will sit out the more volatile periods, waiting for a market leader to emerge before making a final adoption decision. This dynamic can cause innovating organizations to minimize their risk by reducing their discretionary investment in new products. Unfortunately, the self-defeating consequence can be to impede adoption. For example, having overspent on the development of a product, one consumer products company I worked with cut early-stage sales and marketing budgets, virtually ensuring that awareness (and, subsequently, sales) of its innovation would be effectively nil.

It's *Always* the Economy

Economic conditions loom large in shaping the dynamics of innovation in a market. If less capital is available in an industry for organizations to use for the purposes of innovation, organizations may be less likely to use innovation as a basis of competition and may resort to other methods, such as by increasing scale or through mergers or acquisitions. Decreased levels of capital may be due to general economic conditions or to those specific to the industry. During the economic crisis that started in 2008, the automotive industry saw decreased investment and lowered levels of new product development, particularly as gas prices increased and sales slowed. One automaker, GM, reduced the number of brands of cars it produced to reduce the costs of developing and selling a larger variety of cars. In contrast, if an industry is dynamic, with high rates of return generated by rapid innovations delivered to a willing customer base—such as in the portable electronics industry or in the Internet or social media industries—then capital is more generally available, as represented by high stock prices or significant venture capital investment in start-ups in the industry.

The ability and willingness of customers to purchase and adopt new products and services are also subject to economic conditions, and may transcend those within an industry. At an estimated cost of $10,000, Kodak's electronic camera didn't make much sense to its average consumer in normal times, let alone during the economic recession of the early 1980s. In fact, Kodak had seen effects of the recession on its film business: people took fewer pictures as unemployment levels rose and as uncertainty about individuals' personal economic security increased. It is not that they enjoyed taking pictures less; it was simply that it was a luxury they could painlessly cut along with the number and length of vacations they might otherwise have taken, which Kodak knew was a driver in the consumption of film.

Overcoming Market Constraints

Being successful in a market requires you to recognize the constraints that guide the adoption of products and services by customers. These constraints arise when customers, acting in their own interests, behave in ways that reduce the options a firm has for addressing the market need. Once you identify the specific needs of your customers and can pinpoint how the customers' interests diverge from your own, you can use the following strategies to overcome those constraints.

Redefine Performance

Customers use performance criteria or metrics when choosing among alternative products to adopt in a market. It stands to reason, then, that being in control of that definition can generate significant competitive advantage. Performance metrics defined in this way may even provide advantage when the definition of the need has become outdated and is no longer technologically valid. Consider the high-end Rolex mechanical chronograph watches. Although these were once at the top of the watch market in terms of accuracy and durability, now $20 and a visit to your local drug store will net you a quartz-controlled black plastic watch of far greater accuracy and much higher durability (not to mention lower insurance costs). Yet when I ask people why Rolex watches remain popular, the first answer is invariably that they are accurate and durable.

Owning a market's performance criteria is to be in control of the definition of performance. Successfully executed, this strategy allows you to define performance in ways that you can most advantageously satisfy through exploitation of your core capabilities, and in ways that make it difficult for your competitors to meet. However, this strategy can have a significant downside when your organization becomes so enamored of its own performance standards that it loses track of changing needs in the marketplace. You may find yourself investing millions in making film ever better, while your customers are deciding that having it now is better than having it perfect.

Tell Them What's New

Instead of owning the performance standard, you may be trying to break into a market with a decidedly new idea and set of benefits. In that case, you'll find the established criteria to be problematic, as they are unlikely to capture the new kind of value that you are offering. Customers may not understand what criteria to use in evaluating your offering—unless you tell them.

The R&D director of a tool manufacturer told me how the company had put all manner of new technology into a line of hand tools, yet customers failed to appreciate the improvements. The problem was that these tools were sold in retail mass-market home improvement stores. Unfortunately, due to the economics of the product and the demands of the retailer, the packaging of the product was minimal and unobtrusive. That left precious little real estate on the product package to present the information that customers might use to teach themselves about the radical improvements. And although the experts staffing the aisles of the stores understood the advantages, they were too busy to afford the time needed to communicate them to the customers.

Solving this problem can require some additional investment. Traditional marketing is one avenue for building awareness of your products; just make sure you build awareness of the new performance standards in addition to selling your performance in the conventional ones. Another way to educate customers is a result of the explosion in use of social media; it has become a vehicle for getting people to tell and sell their friends. Adele, a thirteen-year-old girl I know, gets samples of the latest makeup and lipstick innovations sent to her from the marketing departments of large cosmetics companies for the low price of an email and the promise of a review. Certainly it costs them in product and in shipping, but it is an ingenious way to sell. Representatives at cosmetic counters in department stores often work on commission and are too busy to fool with mall-trolling gaggles of thirteen-year-old girls with limited allowances. And even when the reps do make the time, a young teenage girl will not find the sales pitch from a thirty-five-year-old woman convincing or compelling. These companies realize that as she reviews them on her blog and demonstrates their use in her video makeup tutorials, Adele will take all the time she needs to convince her friends and fans about their relative merits. Adele has only about seventy-five permanent subscribers, but with over eight thousand hits of her videos, she educates more potential customers in two months than a full-time cosmetic representative will in an entire year.

Grab 'em and Keep 'em

Customers want low adoption costs and the ability to easily find substitutes for your product. The more customers depend on a product or service, the more they would like to be able to substitute it should a problem occur. The lower the adoption cost, the easier it is to implement the switch. They might also like having the ability to use threat of substitution as a means of driving a discounted price.

For the firms in a market, this presents a conundrum. To acquire new customers, you would like to make their switching costs low. This argues for constraining innovation to make the product more like others in the market. But to retain customers, you'd like to set switching costs very high, which argues for a more radical innovation that locks people into what you are selling.

Consider application software for personal computers. When owners of PCs have a significant investment in software that works only in Windows, it's difficult to justify a switch to a Macintosh, which is exactly why Microsoft's Windows platform has enjoyed such a long period of dominance over competitors, such as the Apple's Macintosh platform. Yet as I write this, computer users are switching in record (if still modest) numbers to Apple. Why? Besides redefining performance to include a "cool" factor and experiencing a lower rate of attacks by hackers (turning its lower profile into a competitive advantage), Apple has also made the costs of switching much lower. With the Bootcamp program, all recent Macintosh computers come with the built-in capability of running Windows. This makes the perceived cost of switching quite low—after all, you are not really switching if you can run both. But Apple is really aiming at winning both sides of the "cost of switching" dilemma. The company is betting that once you're on the Apple platform, you'll like it enough to want to stay in that environment—and that means your next computer will be made by Apple. A Mac can run Windows, but there are no legitimate non-Apple machines that are able to run the Apple platform.

Watch the Market, Not the Competition

People don't necessarily know what they want until they see it. That's both the beauty and the curse of innovation. What they do know, however, is whether an innovation they are considering adopting is likely to fit into the larger system of products and services in their lives. In the story of Kodak, the digital camera itself would not have been sufficient to dislodge film from the top of the market. Digital's triumph also required that users have a way to view, print, and store the electronic images the camera produced.

The strategic planners at firms like Sony did not create these other functions through omniscient predictions and brilliant insights; in fact, they didn't create them at all. Instead, necessary innovations such as HP's printer, Conner's hard drive, IBM's PC, Intel's processor, Xerox's network, and Adobe's software were themselves the products of competitive pressures in the industries where they had originated. Once all the pieces were in place, the purchase of a digital camera began to make a lot more sense. As a customer, you didn't have to take the risk of buying all of the parts, because you already owned a computer, a printer, and a hard disk. The only risk, now greatly reduced, was in the camera itself.

The danger of intently watching the competition while ignoring the other weak signals emanating from the far ends of the market and from complementary industries is not only to risk acquiring the expertise needed to develop the core product but also to risk losing out on creating necessary alliances and partnerships that may be needed to enable and then drive full market adoption.

Putting the Framework to Work: Industry Constraints

To aid you in assessing the constraints at this level, use the following diagnostic survey. It is intended to help you assess the extent to which the constraints described in this chapter may be unintentional hindrances to innovation in your organization.

Industry Constraints Diagnostic Survey

The survey lists eighteen statements that describe symptoms that can be caused by the constraints discussed in this chapter. As you read each statement, consider how closely it describes the situation in your industry as it affects those in your organization or business unit. Record your assessment by putting a checkmark in the box that best indicates how accurately the statement describes your situation.

1 = Highly Descriptive; this occurs often or on a routine basis

2 = Moderately Descriptive; this occurs sometimes or occasionally

3 = Not Descriptive; this occurs rarely or not at all

Constraint Level	Constraint Type	Diagnostic Statement
Competition		
1☐ 2☐ 3☐	Strong Competition	Our products are not the most innovative in our industry
1☐ 2☐ 3☐		We are facing a decreasing market for our core products
1☐ 2☐ 3☐	Unwillingness to Innovate	We do not make investments in innovative initiatives without first being sure of the returns
1☐ 2☐ 3☐		Our alliances through mergers or partnerships ease the pressure of competition
1☐ 2☐ 3☐	Disruption or Substitution	Our customers have access to a variety of alternatives to our product or service
1☐ 2☐ 3☐		We do not give detailed attention to our competitors on a regular basis
Suppliers		
1☐ 2☐ 3☐	Suppliers' Self-Interest	We rely on outside experts or vendors for critical components of our products and services
1☐ 2☐ 3☐		Our most important suppliers have an advantaged position in negotiations with us

(Survey continued on next page)

(Survey continued from previous page)

Constraint Level	Constraint Type	Diagnostic Statement
Suppliers		
1 ☐ 2 ☐ 3 ☐	Labor Supply	The skills needed for critical roles in our industry make it difficult to find quality people
1 ☐ 2 ☐ 3 ☐		Experts in our industry are expensive and geographically concentrated in one part of the country
1 ☐ 2 ☐ 3 ☐	Professions, Unions, or Guilds	Our primary value-adding processes are subject to the control of specific professions or unions
1 ☐ 2 ☐ 3 ☐		Critical professional roles must be filled by licensed individuals
Market		
1 ☐ 2 ☐ 3 ☐	Performance Demands	We ignore the needs of our low-end customers when creating or improving our products or services
1 ☐ 2 ☐ 3 ☐		We do not do detailed analysis of our customers on a regular basis
1 ☐ 2 ☐ 3 ☐	Legacy Systems and Adoption Costs	There is a steep learning curve for new customers to get the most from our products
1 ☐ 2 ☐ 3 ☐		Our products or services require customers to abandon their legacy systems
1 ☐ 2 ☐ 3 ☐	General Economic Conditions	Large capital investments are required to deliver new products and services in our industry
1 ☐ 2 ☐ 3 ☐		Our standards for expected financial performance are set by entities outside our company

Using the Results

Note the total number of statements that you rated as "Highly Descriptive." If you have rated more than six of them this way, then working on industry constraints will be a productive effort. Now that you have identified the specific constraints, you can take action. You may wish to turn back and reread the description of the problem and of the specific strategies for addressing that constraint. You may also find that strategies are obvious given the symptom you have identified. For detailed instructions on working with your assessment results, use the steps outlined in Appendix A, Using the Assessment Results, to determine if these constraints are a significant impediment for you in your organization and to develop strategies for overcoming them.

Later, after completing assessment for the other chapters, you will be able to compare constraints and see if one of the other levels poses a greater challenge for you overall than do these industry constraints. Of course you need to recognize that industry constraints are created by interactions among many different participants in that industry and may therefore be difficult to change. Still, this framework can help you understand and anticipate the actions others are likely to take in response to your firm's innovation efforts.

Summary

An industry is a natural grouping of rival organizations and their suppliers around the markets they serve as they produce the goods and services that customers consume. The process of innovation is the primary tool organizations can use to drive the development of products and services that satisfy the needs of customers in that market. However, the three stakeholder groups (that is, rivals, suppliers, and customers) are affected by the competition in different ways, and this can lead them to adopt divergent orientations toward the value of using innovation as the primary tool of competition. As well, even when innovation is the desirable response to tough competition, it can also exact a high cost for those who are charged with producing it. In response to this cost and because of the inherent differences in interests, industries may unintentionally constrain innovation otherwise produced by the firms within. The following chart offers a recap of the constraints discussed in this chapter, along with some strategies for overcoming or living with them.

Competition Constraints: Innovation as a Last Resort	
Competition from strong rivals	Find new ways to compete
Radical innovations by new entrants	Become partners to learn, not to kill innovation
Substitutes for your product	
	Don't overinvest in efficiency
	Develop new tests for new ideas
Supplier Constraints: No Organization Is an Island	
Suppliers favoring their own interests	Don't outsource the core
	Share the wealth
Difficulty getting the people you need	Acknowledge the threat of your innovation
Inertia of powerful professions, unions, and other guilds	Understand the true costs of capital
Market Constraints: Everybody Wants It Cheaper—*and* Faster *and* Better	
Demands for higher performance at a lower price	Redefine performance
	Tell them what's new
Legacy systems and adoption costs	Grab 'em and keep 'em
It's *always* the economy	Watch the market, not the competition

Chapter Reflection: Industry Constraints

It can be helpful to reflect on your insights about industry-level constraints and the process of diagnosing them in your industry. You may wish to consider these questions:

- What evidence is there for the existence of the constraints you named?

- How important are these industry-level factors compared to the individual, group, organizational, societal, and technological constraints you have identified?

- What constraints were overlooked because of your limited view into the industry and the market?

- Would others agree with the need for changing your strategy for competing in the industry?

Why *My* Innovation Means *You* Have to Change

Societal Innovation Constraints

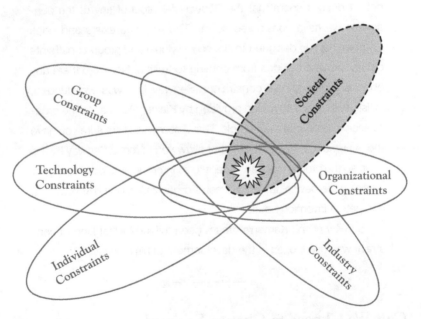

Figure 6.1

At the time he conceived it, Dean Kamen believed that the Segway Personal Transporter would literally change the world. Early specifications said that the machine—code-named *It*—would weigh about eighty pounds, move at a top speed of 12 mph, and have an eleven-mile range. Despite the rather low ceiling on its speed and range, Kamen envisioned the Segway replacing noisy, smelly, polluting automobiles, especially in cities, by providing convenient transportation to all points within its range, and, because it could be driven to mass transit stations and taken aboard buses and trains, to all points beyond. At an expected price of around $9,000 for the commercial version and $5,000 for the consumer model, the invention, Kamen felt sure, would soon have the world beating a path to his door (and leaving on a Segway).

Of course, it never happened. The people who have ridden the Segway will tell you the ride is thrilling and fun. The problem is that there aren't very many such people, certainly nowhere near the forty thousand new riders per month that had once been anticipated. Why not? It doesn't seem that the Segway fell afoul of any of the constraints we have considered so far. The machine exists and does exactly what it is designed to do, so individual and group constraints did not prevent the idea from coming to fruition. Nor were there any obvious organizational constraints. Segway Inc. was well funded, initially with over $80 million provided by Kleiner-Perkins, so the organizational resources were ample. I have seen, and I am sure you have too, a number of tourist outfits that allow you to rent a Segway by the hour, so the problem doesn't seem to lie in producing, distributing, or servicing the device. In fact, Kamen's organization is well known as a competent invention house.

So why hasn't Kamen's dream been fulfilled? What kind of constraint was overlooked in the development of his innovation?

Can We Choose to Change Society?

This chapter, grounded in the perspectives of sociology and anthropology, moves up a level of analysis as we examine how a society—acting through politics, norms, ethics, laws, regulations, and other forms of social control—interprets, values, and ultimately adopts or limits the creative options available to an aspiring innovator.

At times society deliberately, openly thwarts changes it perceives as threatening. For example, the announcement in 2002 by Dr. Brigitte Boisselier of the birth of the first cloned human—which, if true, would certainly represent an innovation—was met first with skepticism and then, more to the point here, with general revulsion. Beyond vilifying Boisselier's company, Clonaid, in the media, the United Nations General Assembly took up the issue and developed a declaration wherein "Member States are called upon to prohibit all forms of human cloning inasmuch as they are incompatible with human dignity and the protection of human life" (United Nations, 2005). The European Union, the U.S. Congress, and a number of states also enacted bans on human cloning.

Societal constraints can also act in more subtle ways to deter the innovation. Witness the ongoing struggles in the digital age around intellectual property and the efforts to devise laws either to liberalize the control of information or to give greater protection to the "owners" of the property.

In days of old, fighting men on the island of Britain used a form of punishment in which the culprit, stripped to the waist, had to run between two rows of men who whipped and beat him as he passed by. Our expression "run the gauntlet" derives from this practice, which provides an apt analogy to the way innovations may be buffeted this way and that by the societal forces surrounding them. In particular, new ideas must run the gauntlet of societal constraints concerning three major areas:

- *Values and identity*: the beliefs that a society holds collectively and uses as a basis for judging its members, and the sense of self that individuals construct from those beliefs

- *Social control*: the formal and informal ways that society guides behavior and holds members accountable for adherence to its values

- *History*: the obligations created by the beliefs and actions of a society in earlier times

Is it possible to survive the gauntlet and change society? Of course. By definition, a new idea requires some level of social change to succeed. But the more societal constraints an innovation challenges, and the more powerful or entrenched they are, the less likely the idea is to make it. This chapter will help you understand the kinds of constraints operating at this level and suggest ways of responding to them.

Values and Identity Constraints: I Like Who I Am

I had occasion to note in the chapter on groups that we experience some kinds of constraints simply because we are social animals. The same truth applies to our participation in a society. We express who we are and what we value through our behaviors and the material objects with which we live our lives, such as our food, dress, cars, homes, and gadgets. We also interpret the behaviors and possessions of others through the lens of our values as we relate to and judge them. To the extent that members of a society seek belonging and esteem, choices of behaviors and possessions will be influenced by societal values. Innovations that conflict with our sense of identity or with the ideals of society will face significant constraints on the path to adoption.

Societal Values and Ideals

The values a society expresses through its laws are usually readily discernible. When governing bodies act to "protect human dignity" and "prevent harm" by human cloning, the values underlying these laws are evident. But it is not always the case that the underlying values are clear. It may be that some important values are not obvious and evident; they may not be formally expressed the way they are in laws. When I discuss the Segway story in my classes, I start by putting a picture of Dean Kamen riding a Segway on the screen. He's wearing a helmet and a huge grin along with his trademark jeans, work shirt, and boots. This causes people to laugh out loud. When I ask them why this is so funny, participants cannot seem to put their finger on it. Finally someone gives voice to the common feeling by offering, "I wouldn't want to ride that thing if it made me look like that!" "What do you mean?" I ask. "Well, I would look like a nerd—I mean, what a dork!"

A short lesson from the older of two young persons in my household taught me that dorks are people who don't share normal social values and who, therefore, don't seem to care what other people think of them. This leads them to engage in behaviors that are considered laughable, embarrassing, and socially reprehensible by those who do adhere to the dominant values. I was also pointedly informed that such socially awkward behaviors might include playing Ping-Pong or being an electronics hobbyist in one's spare time—or riding a Segway.

Of course, becoming overly invested in the ways that others look at the world is problematic; when one is engaged in creative problem solving, ignoring social norms is a smart strategy for getting to new ideas. But people can also become enamored with their own ideas, forgetting that the values they hold, which cause them to judge an idea as great, may not be widely shared. Boisselier, who claimed to have cloned the first human, was also a bishop in the Raelian Movement, an atheist UFO religion. Her immersion in that role and the associated values may have led her to become unaware of the potential backlash against her announcement of a successful cloning attempt. After all, cloning is a central tenet of the Raelian religion's views. This suggests that although individuals may intuitively know what a society holds as ideal, the fact that they are embedded in that society (and in subsocieties within) makes it difficult to develop an actionable understanding of held values.

Conflicting Values

Knowing the values that members of a society hold is helpful, but we may still run into a problem of *conflicting* values. Not only may different segments of society have different value systems, as exemplified by the cloning example; values may conflict within a single value system. Consider our society's grappling with the ecological effects of our consumption behaviors. Such social ideals as sustainability, fair trade, and appropriate technology are based on widely shared ideas of human rights. These ideals have provided broad avenues for new innovations, drawing people both as employees and investors. Companies supporting these ideas also see the value reflected in public measures of their goodwill.

However, there are also people who will oppose these innovations the moment they come into conflict with some other value that these individuals hold more strongly. For example, although the multiple adverse ecological impacts of open-pit coal mining are regrettable and irreversible, you are unlikely to get the support of a fourth-generation coal-mining family for shutting down the coal-fired power plant in their town and switching to wind, solar, or nuclear power instead. Although they may agree in principle that it's a good idea in the long run, there is just too much at stake for them in the here and now.

Tightly Held Social Identity

The ways in which we see ourselves and others see us are based in part on the roles we occupy in society and how society views those who share important characteristics with us. These roles can have a constraining effect, especially when adoption of an innovation means you have to change or abandon a role that is not only deeply internalized but also externally valued and enforced. For example, the court reporter I described in Chapter Five who opposed automated court transcription systems viewed her role as essential to the function of delivering their "day in court" to people who feel wronged in our society. In her eyes, replacing her with a machine not only devalued her skills but also threatened an important value in our society: equal access to justice.

People whose social values contrast with those of the dominant society may not want to change them. They may actually like who they are and revel in being viewed as quirky or as misfits, particularly if they find other like-minded people and band together in subcultures of alternative values. Teenagers, for example, often don't want to feel that others, particularly adults, can share or even understand their values. This leads them to reject many innovations that are designed or marketed to them in clumsy or patronizing ways.

Of course these relationships among values, roles, and identity are difficult to predict or disentangle. But matters only become more complex when members of a pluralistic society hold multiple, potentially divergent roles as they transition from one value system in their society to another. On the one hand, assimilation is desirable, as it creates the identity a person needs to thrive in the new society; on the other hand, assimilation may require a person to let go of a valued role in his or her society of origin. The United States, with its ideal of equality, offers people the opportunity to improve their social status regardless of race, gender, or social class. Yet the same ideal dictates that no special rights be given to a "first born son," this being a highly valued and entitled status in many traditional societies.

Innovators may inadvertently force people into feeling as though they have to make a choice among their multiple identities. Nick Tan (2011) expresses this tension in his review of a video game for the Xbox 360 titled Homefront. This FPS (first-person shooter) game is set in "the American backyard" and built on the premise that a fictional Korean People's Army has invaded the United States; the shooter's (that is, player's) job is "answering the call of resistance to protect humble apple pie from the supposed threat of kimchi." Tan can't get past the characterization of the enemy as being Asian; for him there is tension in "a story of a patriotic Korean-American who experiences the Racial Wars firsthand, defending his family and himself against discrimination [here in the United States], and is then drafted into the military to defend his country." This tension involving identity was also apparent in a controversy about another video game, Medal of Honor, by Electronic Arts. EA came under intense pressure from the public and the military because the game allowed players to assume the role of "the Taliban" to fight against American forces. They changed the name to "the Opposing Force" in response.

Overcoming Values and Identity Constraints

When working on ideas you strongly believe in, it can be easy to forget that your innovation will affect more than you and your intended adopter; there will be other people who, because of their values, care a great deal more than you realize. It is also dangerous to believe that somehow everyone will divine (and embrace) the positive intent that you know is driving you forward. Sometimes they will think you are just a dork. But there are some possible remedies.

Let Values Be Your Guide

Like Dean Kamen and Dr. Boisselier, we may get so excited about the obvious benefits of our idea that we neglect to consider the wider array of values that might come into play on the path to adoption. To correct this potential myopia, there are two well-worn strategies from the world of start-ups and new product development that come to mind. One is to take inventory of all the possible values that might be affected directly or indirectly by your innovation. Do this by casting a wide net, engaging many diverse people, and deliberately seeking out those who represent your target audiences and potential stakeholders. Another strategy is to find ways to involve "customers" in early developmental stages through such means as interviews, focus groups, observations, or letting them try out prototypes and beta versions. As you do this, probe not only for issues of usability—often the explicit target of this kind of research—but for possible underlying values issues.

Understanding the sources and strength of held values can help you judge the potential support you are likely to find for your innovation. Similarly, consider that violations of these values can generate significant constraints as you pursue new ideas. Having access to a wide diversity of opinions can help in this regard. The idea is not to let a poll drive your intentions but to use the findings to understand what you are truly up against.

Look for Clubs That Wouldn't Have You as a Member

The informal nature of social values that you share with your peers and friends in particular strata of society may leave you unaware of the significant constraining potential of those relationships and values. You probably have heard the old axiom about how to make a decision consistent with your values: ask yourself how you would feel if your decision became known to all of society on the front page of the newspaper (or, as we might say nowadays, if it were featured on every wall on Facebook). If you'd be embarrassed that people found out, the axiom dictates, don't do it.

In a study that Damon Phillips and I (2004) conducted examining radical innovation in the early jazz recording industry, we found that the large, dominant firms wanted to profit from the new popular music, but the social context made it difficult for the leaders to choose to do so. The owners and directors of the dominant firms, such as Edison Phonograph, Columbia Phonograph, and Victor Talking Machines, made some successful early recordings, but then came under intense pressure against proliferating this illegitimate music form associated with alcohol, prostitution, blacks, and even illiteracy (because the musicians did not use written music). Although they might have liked to profit from the new jazz music, which ended up constituting about one-third of the market by the 1920s, these leaders, who were connected to the elite class through educational, financial, matrimonial, and political ties, succumbed to the negative pressure that came from these sources. This elite group of people—for example, the founders and leaders of Columbia included influential lawyers, alumni of top universities, and even financiers who had close ties with the U.S. Supreme Court—had a value system to uphold, which meant not participating in the innovation called jazz. Clearly the clubs they were members of had a constraining effect.

The advice here is not to try to overcome this constraint by pulling out of the social networks that form part of your identity. Rather, you should understand the nature of the social ties you have and the effect they might have on your judgments about innovation. You may be tightly tied to advocates for tradition, as in the case of these recording firms, or you may be tied to advocates for radical change, as was Dean Kamen at Segway, whose advisers included venture capital firms and such revolutionaries as Steve Jobs of Apple and Jeff Bezos, founder of Amazon. In either case, knowing the nature and power of these ties creates the opportunity for insight and choice.

In a postscript to the jazz story, the dominant firms still found ways of participating in the emerging industry. One approach was to record the same music played by white musicians, dressing them in tuxedos and requiring them to play from music stands. These derivative recordings did not withstand the test of time in quality, but did provide some amount of profit at the time. Another approach was to found "race records" companies that sold exclusively to blacks and provided a significant degree of social separation between their firms and the music. These firms found success, but the limited market they served also limited the number of records that could be sold.

Do Good Change and Let People Know

The best strategy is probably the same one that your mother or father told you: strive to engage in constantly and continuous unequivocally positive actions; in other words, do the right thing. Sure, that's easy to say for yourself, but how do you do it in a complex organization? Google uses its informal corporate motto to this end. The phrase "Don't be evil" offers people there a test for potential actions and a guide for future ones. Anytime they are considering a product or a change to a product that will affect other people, they should stop and ask themselves: By doing this, am I doing evil? If the answer is yes, then stop. In a letter preceding their IPO (Google, 2004), the founders explained,

> Google users trust our systems to help them with important decisions: medical, financial and many others. Our search results are the best we know how to produce. They are unbiased and objective, and we do not accept payment for them or for inclusion or more frequent updating. We also display advertising, which we work hard to make relevant, and we label it clearly. This is similar to a well-run newspaper, where the advertisements are clear and the articles are not influenced by the advertisers' payments. We believe it is important for everyone to have access to the best information and research, not only to the information people pay for you to see.

If you can build trust enough times and in as many different ways as possible, you'll develop a reputation that allows people to trust you; or at least you will bring them to a point where they will remain open to the possibility that your innovation may, in fact, make the world a better place.

Social Control Constraints: Self-Protection and Regulating Behavior

"Man is born free but everywhere he is in chains," wrote the philosopher Jean Jacques Rousseau ([1762] 1968). Rousseau wondered why people so willingly accepted the chains (that is, took on the yoke of society), accepting the strict limits they set on their personal freedom. In effect he was asking, Of all the things (both creative and wonderful, mean and awful) that we might do to others in our society, why do we refrain from doing most of them?

Explicit Controls: Laws and Regulations

In order for a society to function, it requires a set of *social controls* that put limits on behavior. These controls are meant to deter members of the society from considering forbidden actions and, when deterrence fails, to form the basis of punishment. The most explicit social controls are the laws and regulations that govern so much of our lives, from wearing shoes and shirts when you enter a store to how many milligrams of caffeine can be added to a beverage.

The constraining effect of laws is obvious. No innovation that violates existing law is likely to be widely adopted, and if it were, it would put the innovator at legal risk. Napster is a case in point. Although the service was widely adopted, it was debilitated by a series of legal challenges and injunctions that forced the company to eventually cease operations. The company was resurrected later, but then as a legal subscription-based sharing service.

The more challenging cases are those where there are no current laws that cover the innovation. In the case of the alleged human cloning, it was deemed by most to be unethical, but not necessarily illegal, in early 2000. However, after the birth was claimed, civil law quickly closed in and started the bans. Even religious laws were passed against it. In the "Dignitas Personae," the Roman Catholic Church declared it to be a "grave offense to the dignity of that person as well as to the fundamental equality of all people" (quoted in Stein and Boorstein, 2008); the Islamic Fiqh Academy issued fatwa No. 21582 against the practice, arguing in part, "So it is not permissible to implement something simply because it can be implemented, rather it has to be beneficial knowledge which serves the interests of mankind and protects them from harm" ("Ruling on Cloning of Human Beings," n.d.). According to Clonaid's Web site, as a result of the backlash, and "following visits from U.S.

Government representatives," the company "decided to pursue the human cloning project in another country."

Backlash and illegalization don't arise only with radical propositions like human cloning. In the case of the Segway Personal Transporter, it wasn't just market forces that impeded adoption: the political system imposed constraints as well. In response to the Segway's use and misuse by early adopters, numerous municipalities began to establish rules prohibiting the operation of the transporter on a road with automobile traffic. The Segway's top speed of 12 mph is simply too slow for the road, and they judged it could pose a significant danger both to its rider and to other traffic. But then some of these same municipalities and many others banned the Segway from the sidewalk, where 12 mph is entirely too *fast*. Under the circumstances, it's understandable that Segway users in Internet groups were soon asking, "So where are we supposed to ride it?" Unfortunately for them, this is not a problem that lawmakers see as their business to solve.

Tacit Controls: Morals, Ethics, and Traditions

Social control is not just asserted through formal rules and laws. There are also many tacit "rules" that shape our behavior and our response to new ideas. Morals and ethics are in the category of these kinds of assumed but not necessarily articulated social rules for what it means to be a member of good standing in a society, and for what it means to do no harm. So although certain activities may not be illegal, they can carry a significant negative social stigma. Individuals might not adopt an innovation because it doesn't support their values, but other innovations may conflict so deeply with important values that people want adoption to be stopped. Many parents decry the 1990s fashion innovation known in slang terms as *slabbing*, which means wearing your pants so low below your waist that your underpants show. In addition to being considered indecent, the source of the innovation—rappers who picked up the style from prison inmates prohibited from wearing belts—may irritate as well.

Living for long periods of time in our culture makes us unconscious of its rules and conventions; we have internalized them. But this makes them more powerful and not less so, particularly if we can't articulate why we do not like an innovation, but simply reject it. So, consistent with the philosophy of this book, anything that seems so obvious as to be unnoticeable should draw our attention as being the source of an immense strategic advantage or of a debilitating constraint.

Overcoming Social Control Constraints

Because societies require social controls to function, overcoming the resulting constraints on innovation is not a matter of somehow defeating or overriding these generally beneficial features of society. Rather, we need ways of taking social controls into account, modifying them where that is both desirable and possible, and adapting to them when it is not.

Monitor Impending Rules and Regulations

The unpredictability of the political process means that we can easily be blindsided by new laws, regulations, and court rulings. Consider the example of Virgin Galactic, a space tourism business founded by Sir Richard Branson of Virgin Records and Virgin Airlines fame. The technology certainly posed some difficult constraints—for example, the need to sufficiently reduce the aircraft's weight to enable it to be lifted into space, while also ensuring the fuselage's strength. The market is also a potential constraint, with tickets currently starting at $200,000 per person, not including training. Still, Virgin reports that it has received several hundred $20,000 deposits from aspiring astronauts around the globe.

But what about the safety of those astronauts—how can that be ensured? Certainly the solid-liquid hybrid engine developed for the Virgin spacecraft was designed with safety in mind. However, this was insufficient to satisfy the U.S. Congress, which had begun debating issues of risk and liability in the emerging space tourism business. Many legislators were opposed to a "fly at your own risk" policy for a transportation company, but the economics of a company assuming that risk made the whole business model collapse. The social constraints were moving in a direction that might choke the whole industry, in effect killing any chances that the fledgling industry might have of developing in the United States.

But instead of continuing to fret over rocket fuel formulations and parachute configurations, Branson and others interested in helping and participating in the emerging industry mounted an expensive and significant lobbying effort. A bill in support of the industry was finally passed in December 2004, but not before enduring many near misses. When it finally did pass, one of the space policy consultants working in support of the bill responded with an expletive and then offered, "Never watch sausage or legislation being made, it's been a long and tortuous road" (Boyle, 2004).

Of course most organizations won't have the resources to first detect a pending legislative problem and then to mount a significant lobbying effort the way Virgin did. Still, there are numerous Internet-based sources of information today that make it easier than ever to scan the environment for pending legislation, regulatory hearings, court cases, and other events that can have a direct bearing on your innovation. Know what's on the horizon so as not to be taken by surprise. Early knowledge can help you decide whether you might take your innovation in a slightly different direction or even whether to stop investing in it if you can't change what's coming.

Being well informed will also be the basis for taking positive action to influence the process, which is what the Virgin example demonstrates. Of course you may not be able to act at the federal level, but there are alternatives. For one, you can take an active role in trade, professional, and industry associations that will, through the coordinated efforts of members, have sufficient resources to lobby. You may also work to influence the public debate through newspaper editorials and participation in social groups. In fact, these actions, in addition to aiding your innovation, are those expected of all citizens of a democratic society who would move that society to a better place.

Show Society a Better Way

Beyond the distraction that regulation creates for innovators, it can also constrain them by requiring that new ideas be tested against old standards. Society creates rules and laws based on the situation at one time and place. Although it endeavors to set them in ways that can withstand the test of time, sometimes the situation may change so drastically that the rule no longer makes sense. A premier pharmaceutical researcher I once worked with told me about a dispute she had with the FDA over the protocols being used for a clinical trial. In her company, a group of some of the best and most innovative statisticians in the world had devised a way to set up and analyze clinical trials in a way that made them shorter and that improved the outcomes for subjects by determining sooner whether a drug was working or not. If the drug were found to work as expected, those patients on controls or on placebo drugs would benefit by being moved to the drug sooner. If it wasn't working as expected, the trial could end sooner, and the researchers would remove the subjects from possible harm sooner. Clearly this would be good for the patients and good for the company as well. However, the FDA had very particular rules about how the clinical trials were to be conducted and how the statistics had to be calculated in order to consider a trial as valid.

The work of innovation in this case was clear. Instead of "throwing away" their experiment and walking away, or spending yet more time on the math, the statisticians engaged in a "mutual education campaign" with their counterparts at the FDA, trying to bring them to a "more sophisticated statistical understanding" while allowing the FDA to teach them about the significant implications of allowing additional risk.

Even though the value may seem obvious and evident to an innovator, it may not be quite so obvious to other stakeholders.

Beyond the problems of articulating our ideas to others without error and of providing proof that they work, conflicts based in divergent roles and values may be lurking below the surface. The smart innovator will try to seek them out. As the target of an innovation, the FDA did exactly the right thing. As an important regulator in society, its role is not to accept innovation but to ensure that innovations don't have the potential for generating unacceptable harm. These role differences will affect perceptions of values. Be sure you understand and acknowledge these up front.

Don't Let the Rules Distract You

In the documentary *Triumph of the Nerds*, which details the development of the early personal computer industry, one chapter describes the invention of the first spreadsheet program. Harvard Business School student Dan Bricklin dreamed up the idea of VisiCalc, and he convinced MIT graduate student Bob Frankston to code it. It was one of the killer applications, like email, that drove the PC industry to prominence during the 1980s, in particular because of its effect in the financial industry. Individuals could "run the numbers" at their desks and no longer needed to use their company's mainframes and computer experts to help them make business decisions. VisiCalc enjoyed a great deal of success for a time, but its inventors soon saw their thunder (and profits) stolen when their invention was copied by others, notably Lotus and Microsoft. The obvious question that this brings up is asked so often that Dan Bricklin posted the answer on a page in his Web site, titled "Why didn't we patent the spreadsheet? Were we stupid?"

He points out that whereas software is routinely patented now, software patents were rarely granted in 1979 when VisiCalc was revealed to the public. At the time, the designers consulted with a reputable patent attorney, who gave them, at best, a 10 percent chance of being granted a patent, and only then if they could hide the fact that it was software. Bricklin suggests that although they could have moved forward with the patent, despite the high costs and the low probability of success, it would have caused an immense distraction to creating and running their business. This would have also been exacerbated by an additional distraction: that of being ostracized from the software developer community. Patenting software was not only a legal issue; it was not considered a socially acceptable thing to do. The best software writers of the time all borrowed concepts and ideas from each other; it was part of the culture to give and to receive. To turn around and patent an idea that in all likelihood contained ideas developed by that community would not only have been wrong but also would have killed the sharing, camaraderie, and rapid growth that made VisiCalc possible in the first place.

Of course when society's controls are a direct constraint on your innovation, you need to center your attention on that constraint, as did Richard Branson. However, when the constraint is not critical, binding, or integral to adoption, becoming distracted by it may cause more harm than good. In any innovation there are going to be a number of issues that need to be resolved for the innovation to work. The point here is to focus on the critical ones first; if you don't get past the most critical showstopping constraints, accomplishing the rest will be meaningless anyway.

History Constraints:
The Past Isn't Dead—It Isn't Even Past

The writer William Faulkner famously wrote that the past is never dead. As a native of the American South, Faulkner had an especially keen appreciation of the way yesterday's (and yesteryore's) experiences and decisions continue to shape—that is, constrain—the world of the present.

History's constraints are reflected in words like *standards, conventions, traditions,* and even *infrastructure.* I find it useful to break these down into three general types of constraints. First, there are the constraints of the *things* already in the world. Physical infrastructure, such as highways and copper telephone lines, falls into this category. Second, there are the constraints of existing *skills and practices*, such as using a keyboard or driving a stick-shift car. Finally, there are the constraints of prevalent *understandings*. These are the formal traditions and standards that we inherit and use to assert our identities and to make sense of the world, such as how we honor people who have died, how we decide who pays for a wedding, or even which side of the plate to put the fork.

Working with (or Around) Those Things Already in the World

Technological decisions and subsequent investments made to realize them can come forward from the past, as they require us to make particular design decisions about our innovations. For example, electric cars theoretically could be charged anywhere—you can probably see a number of power outlets from where you sit right now. But you probably would not want to charge your car where you are sitting. In fact, many of the places where you might like to conveniently charge your car, perhaps in front of your house or in your garage, may not have power at all or may have only a relatively low-power source. This lack of basic infrastructure, or the cost of adding it to your home or workplace, will certainly enter the equation if you contemplate buying an electric car.

Similarly, potential adopters of the Segway soon found that the existing infrastructure of roads intended primarily for automobiles and of sidewalks intended primarily for pedestrians left them very few places to ride, and still fewer useful ones.

The Inertia of What People Already Know

Innovations may also run into obstacles in the form of the "infrastructure" of people's existing knowledge and skills. Consider that heinous invention the QWERTY keyboard, which is named after the top row of letters on the left-hand side. There are numerous alternative keyboard arrangements that are easier to learn and much more efficient for entering text into a computer. Yet the keyboards in common use around the globe all display the QWERTY layout, which was first designed by Christopher Sholes in 1868.

Sholes's layout—a definite innovation at the time—was created to address the problem of jamming, a common and frustrating occurrence in the alphabetically arranged mechanical keyboards of the day, which also limited the typing speed that could be achieved. His solution was elegant, and manufacturing rights for the Sholes-Gidden Type Writer were sold to E. Remington & Sons, a well-known sewing machine and armaments company at the time. Remington began production and marketing of its typewriters in 1873.

But even then there were other possible options. In 1893, George Blickensderfer designed a typewriter intended to compete with Remington. His layout had the most commonly used letters in the bottom row, which provided a more efficient typing experience. Further, because he used a ball as the type head (an innovation that reappeared decades later in the IBM Selectric), his typewriter did not have the jamming problem that the Sholes layout had solved. The Blickensderfer design had everything a successful innovation should have. It was faster, lighter, and cheaper. So, with a more effective and efficient solution available, why did people stick with QWERTY? It seems to me that the short twenty-year advantage that the QWERTY design had in the market had created a skill base of sufficient size that there was too much history to overcome. And now, with more than a century of additional experience behind us, the idea of a wholesale change to a more efficient and more ergonomic layout is downright laughable.

The Persistence of Historical Standards

History is also the source of many of the expectations that we bring to new products or services. Traditions about how things should look, how they should be made, or how they should behave can also act as constraints.

Some of these expectations take the form of accepted standards against which new versions of the product or service are judged.

Inventor Thomas Edison worked tirelessly to perfect his phonograph so that recorded music could meet the standard set by live performance—the only way anyone had ever heard music performed in all of history. Ultimately he was able to give demonstrations in which performances by singers on a darkened stage alternated with recordings of themselves, while audiences were challenged to tell the difference ("The History . . .," n.d.). (Decades later, the Memorex company used a similar ploy to market its audiotapes in memorable television commercials that asked, "Is it live or is it Memorex?")

Incidentally, the Great Innovator himself was by no means immune to expectations conditioned by history. Despite his pioneering role in reproducing sound (and also in helping create motion pictures), Edison was dismayed when silent movies began to be replaced by "talkies." "There isn't any more good acting on the screen," he complained. "They concentrate on the voice now; they've forgotten how to act" (Clark, 1977, p. 237).

The Edison and Memorex tales were relived again when CDs made their appearance in the early 1980s. At the time, I happened to be working in a very high-end stereo store. When the first CD players arrived, they were rare and very expensive. Partly because it was fun and partly because it made us feel like experts, my coworkers and I made a game of teaching customers how to hear the "important differences between CDs and vinyl," especially when records were played on one of the excellent but traditional turntables we had in stock. With the lack of true high-performance CD players in that early stage of the technology, people shopping in a store that catered to audiophiles were easily and happily convinced that the technology they already knew and identified with was superior. Twenty years later, the wheel turned again, and the same arguments began to be heard about the relative fidelity of CDs and MP3 recordings.

The ways we cook, eat, and dress, and in fact all the ways we live our lives are potentially subject to being compared or valued through traditional views. When we propose an innovation, our potential adoptees will look at and assess it, not only in functional terms but also in terms of what it signals about their role in society.

Overcoming History Constraints

Not only is the past not dead, but it also continues to create an obligation for innovators. Even when we choose not to conform to the dictates of history, we should acknowledge the power that *what came before* can have on the willingness of society to accept our proposals for change.

Leverage the Existing Infrastructure

Earlier I mentioned the need to supply power to electric cars as an example of an infrastructure constraint. Electric car makers have coined the term "range anxiety" to describe the uneasy feeling people have about adopting electric cars, despite the facts that fewer than 10 percent of people in the United States drive more than one hundred miles a day (the current target range on production electric cars) and that many U.S. families (particularly ones in a position to consider such a purchase) already have at least one other car that can travel farther. Nevertheless, the decision is a hard one because our sense of convenience (and personal safety) is constrained by decisions made long in the past.

Ignoring my proposal of supplying a very long extension cord, one maker of electric cars has been looking for places in the power infrastructure that will favorably support recharging the car. For example, both restaurants and most retail spaces have industrial-strength feeds of the type of three-phase 480-volt power required to charge a car in a relatively short time. These are also the exact kinds of places that people are likely to drive to and where they are likely to spend some time once they are there. Alliances or partnerships with those kinds of establishments can help them become more attractive to the electric car owners while easing the cost of infrastructure development for the car makers. Although the cost of developing and maintaining alliances is certainly not negligible, it is certainly going to be far less than creating the required infrastructure from scratch. As I noted earlier, digital cameras were also able to enjoy spectacular adoption rates as all the ancillary equipment needed to edit, store, and print their photographic output was already present for adopters in the form of personal computers, hard disks, and printers.

Use Knowledge in the World

In his book *The Design of Everyday Things*, Donald Norman (2002) coined the term "knowledge in the world" to signify the kind of intellectual insights, skills, and information that people in a society already have and that they will bring as they use some new thing they have not dealt with before. If you have ever pushed on a door that needed to be pulled or, worse, have stood in front of a door completely perplexed at how to open it, you will know what he means. Even though I, for one, might lament the wide adoption of the inefficient QWERTY keyboard layout, it would be foolish to try to switch the world to a new layout. However, there are alternative approaches that venture somewhere in between.

Palm Computer's Graffiti proprietary handwriting system (Figure 6.2) made it relatively easy for handheld computers to recognize handwriting by getting users to focus on the major gestures that go into writing a letter. Once the lettering was simplified, the recognition problem became easier, allowing these handheld devices to use less complex and expensive processors, bringing the cost of the device to a level that consumers could afford. This new way to write took a little effort to learn, but not nearly as much as it takes to learn one of the many written shorthand systems or as long as it takes to learn to touch-type on a keyboard. Graffiti could be learned in as little as fifteen minutes and mastered in a few hours, because the gestures that stood for the letters corresponded closely to the way they are conventionally drawn.

Although knowledge already in the world can constrain innovation if it requires an innovation to conform to the ways that people currently believe things should be, innovators can also gain advantage in the situation. Allowing people to use skills that they already have can help them be more confident and more competent as they assess (and, you hope, adopt) your proposals for positive change.

Graffiti Reference Card

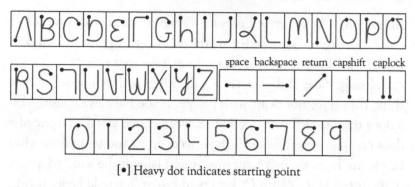

space backspace return capshift caplock

[•] Heavy dot indicates starting point

Figure 6.2

Use Open Standards Unless You Can't

Many of the things we use to get along in life are part of some kind of system and therefore conform to some kind of standard. Your electronic gadgets are powered from a standard outlet with standard levels of voltage, or they use batteries that come in standard sizes. The water that arrives in your house that's connected to the water distribution system comes through a pipe of standard size. The paper you use in a copier or printer also comes in standard sizes that allow you to use it relatively easily in writing and printing devices. Soft drinks are a standard twelve ounces, and the list goes on. In this world of standards, why would anyone want to go against the standard?

At times standards may serve the rest of the world well, but for some reason you find them lacking. The JPEG standard for storing digital photographs, for example, is an imperfect one. If you have ever tried to zoom in on a picture on your computer and watched it become blurry, blocky, and jagged, you know what I mean. That happens because of the way the picture is compressed in a JPEG file; the JPEG standard favors a small file size over retaining the original resolution. Audiophiles make similar complaints about loss of detail in MP3 music files, another space-saving standard that serves most users well by making it possible to store thousands of songs on portable devices. Sometimes innovators will become annoyed or even disgusted or insulted by this kind of "pretty good" solution. But because the standard is a fact of history, this attitude may open them up to a lot of work toward the end of being rejected.

Using the standard has an advantage: you can view that same picture on your camera, on your phone, in your computer, or on your Facebook page, and you can send it instantly to someone else or print out a copy for yourself. For most people, this is the value of the standard. Of course another standard, one that focused on high quality instead of small size, might allow you to zoom in 30× to inspect the nose hairs in a picture of Uncle Ralph; but the cost of lost flexibility in using the picture across the many parts of a person's life systems might simply be too high.

This suggests that for our purposes, you should make a considered choice each time you adopt a standard or reject one in the design of your innovation. Blindly adopting standards means you may be giving up critical features that are essential to your function. Higher resolution than JPEG can provide may be needed for making enlargements of photos for formal portraits or images of a planet's surface. Blindly ignoring standards, or not using them on the grounds that you are offended by their inelegance or illogic, means you may be giving up important leverage over adoption. I'm much more likely to adopt your innovation with open arms if your use of the standard reassures me that your innovation will fit into and even extend the value of the systems around which I've built my life.

Putting the Framework to Work: Societal Constraints

To aid you in assessing the constraints at this level, use the following diagnostic survey. It is intended to help you assess the extent to which the constraints described in this chapter may be unintentional hindrances to innovation in your organization.

Societal Constraints Diagnostic Survey

The survey lists eighteen statements that describe symptoms that can be caused by the constraints discussed in this chapter. As you read each statement, consider how closely it describes the situation in society as it affects those in your organization or business unit. Record your assessment by putting a checkmark in the box that best indicates how accurately the statement describes your situation.

1 = Highly Descriptive; this occurs often or on a routine basis

2 = Moderately Descriptive; this occurs sometimes or occasionally

3 = Not Descriptive; this occurs rarely or not at all

Constraint Level	Constraint Type	Diagnostic Statement
Values		
1☐ 2☐ 3☐	Societal Values	Our products cut against the grain of traditional society
1☐ 2☐ 3☐		Customers use our products to express their personal identity
1☐ 2☐ 3☐	Conflicting Values	The world doesn't understand our innovative ideas
1☐ 2☐ 3☐		Our products are targeted to specific demographic groups (gender, race, age, or economic level)
1☐ 2☐ 3☐	Social Identity	Our products challenge or reinforce ideas that people have about their own identity
1☐ 2☐ 3☐		People use our products or services for political ends
Social Control		
1☐ 2☐ 3☐	Laws and Regulation	Lawyers or top managers stall our innovation efforts for fear of legal risk
1☐ 2☐ 3☐		Our products or services are subject to civic approval or governmental regulation
1☐ 2☐ 3☐		Our innovation efforts are hampered by regulatory concerns

Constraint Level	Constraint Type	Diagnostic Statement
1☐ 2☐ 3☐	Morals and Ethics	We openly discuss the ethical concerns created by our products
1☐ 2☐ 3☐		Society expresses concerns about the ethical impact of our products
1☐ 2☐ 3☐		Our firm has a reputation for conservative but reliable products
History		
1☐ 2☐ 3☐	Current Infrastructure	Our products work best with those the customer already has
1☐ 2☐ 3☐		Our products displace those a customer already has
1☐ 2☐ 3☐	Existing Understandings	Customers have difficulty understanding the proper use of our products or services
1☐ 2☐ 3☐		Using our products requires new ways of thinking and new cognitive maps
1☐ 2☐ 3☐	Historical Standards	Industry standards dominate the design of our products
1☐ 2☐ 3☐		Our customers want our products to look and perform the way they always have

Using the Results

Note the total number of statements that you rated as "Highly Descriptive." If you have rated more than six of them this way, then working on societal constraints will be a productive effort. Now that you have identified the specific constraints, you can take action. You may wish to turn back and reread the description of the problem and of the specific strategies for addressing this constraint. You may also find that strategies are obvious given the symptom you have identified. For detailed instructions on working with your assessment results, use the steps outlined in Appendix A, Using the Assessment Results, to determine if these constraints are a significant impediment for you in your organization and to develop strategies for overcoming them.

Later, after completing assessment for the other chapters, you will be able to compare constraints and see if one of the other levels poses a greater challenge for you overall than do these societal constraints. Of course you need to recognize that societal constraints evolve over long periods of time through a history of interactions of all members of society and may therefore be difficult to change. Still, this framework can help you understand and anticipate the ways others are likely to view your innovation efforts.

Values and Identity Constraints: I Like Who I Am	
Societal values and ideals	Let values be your guide
Conflicting values	Look for clubs that wouldn't have you as a member
Tightly held social identity	
	Do good change and let people know

Social Control Constraints: Self-Protection and Regulating Behavior	
Explicit controls: laws and regulations	Monitor impending rules and regulations
Tacit controls: morals, ethics, and traditions	Show society a better way
	Don't let the rules distract you

History Constraints: The Past Isn't Dead—It Isn't Even Past	
Working with (or around) those things already in the world	Leverage the existing infrastructure
Inertia of what people already know	Use knowledge in the world
Persistence of historical standards	Use open standards unless you can't

Summary

Any innovation that pushes against societal constraints will be perceived as a social innovation, and necessarily a stand against history and against the social structures used to keep us safe and productive. You can, however, envision and create changes to help society move in a direction that makes it better and helps it see itself as better. This starts with understanding how your ideas and actions will be interpreted and then creating strategies for getting those ideas a fair hearing. The chart on page 184 offers a recap of the constraints discussed in this chapter, along with some strategies for overcoming or living with them.

Chapter Reflection: Societal Constraints

It can be helpful to reflect on your insights about societal constraints and the process of diagnosing them in the social group of your most important stakeholders. You may wish to consider these questions:

- What evidence is there for the existence of the constraints you named?
- How important are these societal factors compared to the individual, group, organizational, industry, and technological constraints you have identified?
- What constraints were overlooked because of your own social identity?
- Would others agree with the need to change society to fix these constraints?

How to Take a Really Hard Problem and Make It Completely Impossible

Technological Innovation Constraints

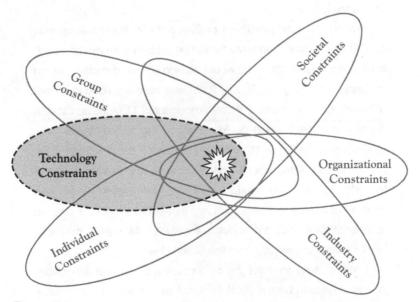

Figure 7.1

In 1960, while conducting a spying mission for the CIA in a U2 aircraft, pilot Francis Gary Powers was shot down over the Soviet Union. This incident demonstrated the immediate need for a new spy plane that could fly higher and faster and that would be less visible to radar. The CIA's specifications for Lockheed were daunting. The new aircraft would be required to fly at more than 2,000 mph, four times faster than the U2; it would need to fly at over 90,000 feet, 20,000 feet higher; and despite being one hundred feet long and weighing over sixty-two tons, it would have to have a far smaller radar cross section to minimize the possibility of detection.

For the designers and engineers in Lockheed's famed skunk works, there were very few of the kinds of constraints I have already discussed in previous chapters. They had ready access to the most knowledgeable experts, an immense amount of funding (over $130 million), and by operating as a skunk works far away from HQ, they faced few organizational barriers. Yet although the initial delivery had been planned for May 1961, the schedule was slipping and the costs were rising.

Among the most significant problems the designers faced was heat. The heat generated by air friction on the skin of an aircraft traveling at speeds up to Mach 3.2 would exceed 500° and in places reach temperatures as high as 1000°. There was no metal used in aircraft design that could withstand those temperatures. Obvious candidates like stainless steel, which could withstand the temperatures, were far too heavy. Eventually titanium was chosen. It could withstand the heat and was half the weight. Unfortunately, it was nearly impossible to work: difficult to form, hard to drill, and excruciating to rivet and weld. What's more, the one company that could supply the needed quantity of titanium could not deliver the quality. As a result, the metal had to be bought secretly from the Soviet Union.

For the plane to meet the performance goals, the J58 turbo-jet would have to be the most powerful aircraft engine ever made. The plane's two engines would need to supply in excess of 320,000 horsepower—each would have more power than the QE2—creating an unprecedented problem of materials, fabrication, and testing. The turbines would have to withstand temperatures of over 2000° but without increasing the weight. These high temperatures also exceeded the capabilities of available lubricating oils, hydraulic fluids, and the eleven thousand gallons of fuel the plane needed. Engine testing was done at night, because the local electricity grid couldn't supply enough power during the day.

Amazingly, solving all these problems—along with innumerable other significant technological difficulties, including accommodation for the pilot in an uninsulated 400° cockpit—would not be enough. The engineers and designers still faced the problem of taking pictures, the whole purpose of the project. The cameras would have to exceed the performance abilities of any camera made to that point in terms of their resolution, coverage, size, weight, and imperviousness to heat. Given temperature differences between the inside and outside of the aircraft reaching up to 400°, the camera's window to the exterior had to be invented to accommodate the thermal distortion such temperature differences would cause. When the quartz window was finally perfected, there was no known way of securing it in the titanium frame.

Once the prototype was built, getting it to the test site was problematic. Too secret to fly and too big to put into another aircraft, it was dismantled and taken by truck. Some parts of the aircraft were so big, however, that during the two-day ride to the test site, parts of the highway had to be shut down, with road signs removed, trees cut back, and bends and curves releveled to accommodate the giant cargo.

After reassembly at the site, flight-testing had to be stopped on account of unpredictable handling caused by errors in reconnecting the navigation controls after transportation, in addition to the general instability inherent in the unconventional design of the aircraft itself. At one point during one of the more successful early test flights, upon reaching three hundred feet in altitude, the plane began shedding numerous titanium skin panels. It took technicians four days to find the pieces and reinstall them.

Finally, on April 26, 1962, a year later than scheduled and tens of millions of dollars over what was planned, the A-12 finally took to the skies. During its first, hourlong flight, the plane reached thirty thousand feet and attained speeds of up to 400 mph. Although it had not flown at the limits of the specifications, the Lockheed lead designer and project manager remarked that the test flight was one of the smoothest he had ever been a part of.

As the story of the A-12 suggests, even without the constraints of adverse group dynamics, a stultifying organizational structure, or a lack of resources, creating an aircraft to fly at three times the speed of sound, sixteen miles above the surface of the earth, evading radar, while taking pictures of the ground to a resolution of eight inches is, to put it simply, really, really hard. Ultimately the designers, engineers, scientists, technicians, pilots, and all the others involved in the project were able to develop the understanding that was required to get matter to behave in exactly the manner they needed it to. If this wasn't easy, then we're left with the question of why it wasn't easy or, more generally, why some things are harder to do than others.

What's Hard About Manipulating Matter, Time, and Space

Although so far I've focused on the constraining effects of the human element of innovation initiatives, technological constraints can be a key factor in innovations that involve the manipulation of matter in time and space. Your own technical challenges may be far more modest than those involved with the A-12 project, but few, if any, innovations can be accomplished with a total disregard for what is physically possible to do given the current state of our understanding of nature and our ability to manipulate it. Of course, it isn't possible to deal comprehensively with such technological constraints even in a small library, let alone a single chapter. Entire sectors of our society, such as those representing schools of science and engineering and R&D labs, are devoted to investigating ways of understanding and manipulating the physical, temporal, and biological world. Consistent with the framework as a whole, my aim here is to offer a way of thinking about innovation efforts that can help you correctly diagnose whether your key constraints would be best overcome by throwing more technological resources at them or by giving greater attention to some other aspect of the problem. I will consider three broad categories of technological constraints:

- *Physical constraints:* the laws of physics, chemistry, and biology, and our ability to understand how they work and how we might manipulate them in desired ways
- *Time constraints:* the amount of time available to accomplish important tasks, and the time lags caused by a need for feedback and learning
- *Natural environment constraints:* the distribution of natural resources and the requirements of maintaining a habitat suitable for human life

Physical Constraints: Knowing What You Know (and What You Don't)

It seems that more and more of the constraints of the natural world are being removed through human efforts to understand physical reality and buffer us against nature's potentially adverse effects. At one end of the spectrum, we've been able to see and manipulate things on a nanometer scale; at the other, we have been able to peer farther and farther into the cosmos far beyond our own galaxy. Yet the more we discover, the more we come to know how much we don't know. Each advance seems to bring even more difficult problems and unintended consequences into view.

In 1966, Abraham Maslow offered a way of characterizing learning skills that seems to fit this description. We begin the task of learning in a state of *unconscious incompetence*; that is, we don't know how to do something, and we don't know that we don't know. Suppose you are watching a teenager do some tricks on a skateboard. After a short time observing her, you come to believe that what she is doing cannot be that hard. It looks easy, and you've just watched her do it. After stepping with both feet onto the skateboard yourself and then landing hard on the ground, you realize that you were unconscious of your incompetence at that task. But all learning is painful, so this act did have some value. It made you realize that balance matters, as does momentum. At this point, in a state of *conscious incompetence*, you begin to know what needs to be done, but you just don't know how to do it. After buying your own skateboard, you begin to practice and get to where you can stay standing on the thing. You've reached *conscious competence*. If you keep riding, you eventually get to the point where you aren't thinking about balance, momentum, foot position, or anything like that. Your mind is somewhere else, and you've reached *unconscious competence*. This skateboard example can serve as a simple model for describing the constraints that create different kinds of technological difficulty.

Unconscious Incompetence: Not Knowing What You Don't Know

Like stepping with both feet on a skateboard, assuming that your understanding is complete—simply because you've been successful in the past, because you have watched it being done, or even because you are an expert in a related field—can be dangerous. History provides numerous examples of innovations being introduced seemingly without a concern on the part of the change agents that they didn't understand how the innovation worked or how it might affect the environment into which it was introduced.

One of the more tragic medical innovation episodes occurred in the late 1950s in Europe. The "wonder drug" thalidomide was first synthesized and then prescribed and sold as a painkiller and tranquilizer and as a remedy for colds, coughs, insomnia, and headaches. It was also found to reduce morning sickness. At the time, medical science held that this kind of drug would not cross the placental barrier between mother and fetus. Unfortunately, medical science was wrong. After several years and the births of more than ten thousand deformed children, doctors realized that it was thalidomide that had caused the horrific birth defects. The adverse impact of the drug in the United States was lessened significantly due to societal constraints in the form of regulation. In a controversial decision, the drug was denied approval by the FDA on the grounds of insufficient study.

Examples like this one demonstrate the first kind of difficulty that makes some things harder than others: things look easy because we don't know *what* we don't know or *that* we don't know, and when the world kicks back, we find we've made the problem worse and not better.

Conscious Incompetence: Knowing What You Don't Know

This next type of difficulty arises when you understand the problem you face, but do not understand how you can address it. In the development of the A-12, for example, the aircraft's designers understood that because of air friction, the fuel temperatures would reach over 350° in the tanks and over 700° on the way into the engine. These temperatures would cause traditional fuels to vaporize or explode. The designers knew they would need a formulation that would burn, but not at normal temperatures. In the end, the A-12 chemists finally concocted a special formulation that burned at 3400°, a temperature so high that the fuel could not be lit by a match. This also meant that the engines could not be fired up in a traditional way and so required liquid explosives to get the engines started.

Innovation of this kind tends to be incremental: through trial-and-error experimentation, we build on what we currently know in order to move just far enough in our understanding to solve the problem. This process is straightforward when the understanding we seek is close to what we already know; the constraint is that it may take immense amounts of time, money, and people to get us there, as it did in the cases of the A-12. But there is also a possibility that the knowledge we need is so far away from what we already know that we will not be able to acquire it using traditional methods or our current understanding.

Conscious Competence: Knowing What You Know

Understanding the type of problem you face and having the tools to solve it is among the less challenging of situations. We use existing methods to solve problems that are exactly the ones those methods were designed to solve. Models and analysis, two tools of engineering and science, work in this way and are powerful for quickly finding solutions. If you were an architect designing a normal house in a normal neighborhood, you could quickly calculate, using models developed in the profession, how thick the beams holding up the roof will need to be. Sometimes it won't even seem as though you are doing an analysis, especially if you are simply looking up the answer in a table based on predefined parameters.

This type of problem is also commonly addressed in business, where "management science" offers defined approaches to solving problems related to product pricing, market segmentation, financing, inventory management, and even employee motivation, among others. Once we have developed an understanding and are clear about the limitations of that understanding, one aspect of the constraint will be that of "doing the math." It may be difficult to find the data you need to be able to apply the analytical model to your problem. Another facet of the constraint is that the solutions you will arrive at are those limited by the models. For example, a problem that airlines face is getting passengers into their seats as quickly as possible before takeoff, because—as the saying goes—the plane makes no money sitting on the ground. One approach to this problem could be to use a mathematical queuing theory model to determine the most efficient order for boarding people. However, this approach will never generate the solution Southwest Airlines used for years: it didn't assign seat numbers. Without assigned seats, people arrived early and then rushed on board to find the best ones. Coming up with such a nonobvious solution requires a wholly different kind of competence, one that you may not have access to.

Unconscious Competence: Not Knowing What You Know

For certain problems, we may intuitively know what needs to happen and why it needs to happen that way. In *Shop Class as Soulcraft*, Matthew Crawford (2010) shares his experience of moving from a job at a think tank to becoming trained as a mechanic of classic motorcycles, and his condition as a mechanic fits this type of technological situation. When someone brings in an old bike for repair, Crawford often doesn't know what's wrong with it, how much it will cost to fix it, or even whether he can repair or restore it. But he takes it in anyway because he is an expert mechanic and has worked on similar bikes before. To effect the repair, he goes through a sophisticated diagnostic process that involves calling on his prior experiences, rules of thumb, traditional understandings, unjustifiable assumptions, ad hoc experimentation, and dumb luck. And in the end, the insights and conclusions of these efforts will have to be actionable; that is, he has to know how he will do what he has decided needs to be done.

Apart from the need to rely on intuition and untested assumptions, a primary constraint inherent in this situation suggests a kind of closure of the circle of Maslow's model. Our success in an unconscious competence mode makes us susceptible to an imperceptible slide toward thinking that we know how to solve problems that we actually don't. This brings us back to the start, in the dangerous place of unconscious incompetence.

Overcoming Physical Constraints

If anything is true about the difficulty of pursuing technological innovation, it is that your chances of success are far lower if you rely on happenstance or luck than they will be if you make significant investments of money, time, and hard work. But as you go about making those investments, you may wish to consider the following strategies.

Determine How Hard the Problem Might Be

The most important strategy for overcoming technological constraints is to start by knowing what you know and what you don't know—that is, to understand how difficult a problem it is that you are trying to solve. With this understanding, you can try to make reasonable estimates of the time, money, and people resources you are likely to need.

Consider the problem of deciding how much money to spend on online versus print advertising. For this problem of *conscious competence*, a person trained in marketing science (or a reasonable facsimile thereof) might be able to analyze your existing expenditures and resulting outcomes and then come to a reasonable conclusion about what to do going forward. Intuitively this problem seems relatively straightforward, should require only small amounts of resources, and could be rapidly achieved. In contrast, a *conscious incompetence* problem like developing the atomic bomb on the basis of the newly developed and still evolving field of quantum physics is obviously going to be terrifically expensive and will take a long time. And the output won't be guaranteed.

To make a first cut, you can use expert opinions, prior experience, and even the patent history in a specific domain to get at least a starting estimate of how difficult the problem is likely to be, given our current state of understanding the world. Of course this is going to be a very rough estimate, but it may serve as a good start for estimating the kinds of time, money, and brains you will need to come up with to tackle the problem.

Next comes the hard work of determining the possible pitfalls associated with being wrong about your estimates of your levels of consciousness and competence with respect to the problem. How much of a setback will you suffer if you have overestimated your ability to implement the state-of-the-art solutions? How much harder or more expensive might it become if you have to develop an entirely new way of thinking if the current methods cannot get you there? And what is the risk that you have misspecified the problem or don't know something important about the problem? Of course this is a difficult line of thinking to engage and an even more difficult conversation to have with others, especially if you are deep in a process, running low on resources, and struggling desperately to keep the project going.

After doing a "reality check" assessment of the difficulty of the problem given your technical approach, the size of the team that you have at your disposal, and the budget you have of time and money, it may be time for a difficult decision. If the project is insurmountable and lies outside too many of the constraints of the type we've discussed in the preceding chapters and especially outside your organization's capabilities, then please stop. Remember, creative people must be stopped when they're going down the wrong path, one that leads them to tackling problems only because the goal is attractive to them and not because solving those problems furthers the strategic aims of the organization. Short of stopping, you might also reframe the problem and rethink your approach in a way that can still yield positive benefits, but that allows them to be achieved in a way that's possible given the people, time, and money that you have.

Hire an Alien

I once had an opportunity to tour the innovation center of a national health insurance company. As we walked around the facility, my guide pointed to two people and said, "Those two were working on the settee when we hired them." I had to ask what "settee" meant, as I was sure he could not possibly mean what I thought I'd heard. He said, "You know, the S-E-T-I project." I'm not sure which would have been more surprising to hear—that they were working on a couch or that an insurance company had hired experts in the search for extraterrestrial intelligence.

My guide explained that the company had realized that its role in the health care industry gave it unique access to immense amounts of data. As the people who handle the bills for a great many health care transactions, they were in a position to see if there were any interesting patterns or "intelligent signals" that might be found in the data.

They would not give me any further details—except to assure me that the data were stripped of all personally identifying information. Still, I could easily imagine learning some interesting things by examining the data. For one, you might look for patterns of treatments and then subsequent recurrences (or lack of recurrences) of the treatment for a particular ailment, giving you some ideas about the efficacy of a particular treatment. Or you might look at patterns of hospitalizations and rehospitalizations based on treatment types or on adherence to medication regimes. I'm sure that the patterns found in the data would have all kinds of potential meanings for people who were actually versed in health care.

What I do know about health care, though, is that analyzing multiple, massive data streams is not a core skill that physicians are trained in or that health care statisticians will commonly use. However, this kind of analysis is *exactly* what SETI researchers do all day and that they probably do in their sleep. My hat goes off to this company that recognizes the need for this kind of analysis, sees the value of bringing that skill in-house, and then finds the people who can perform it. After all, the organization is hiring people who think differently, analyze differently, communicate differently, and—for Pete's sake—look for intelligence in the universe beyond Earth.

Let Other People Do the Hard Part

Beyond the technological development that happens in schools, universities, and R&D labs, a great deal also happens among consumers who have a need to push performance boundaries by modifying and customizing the products they use. Eric von Hipple (1988) calls these people "lead users" and suggests that there is a lot you can learn from them.

Lead users may modify even the highest-end products, not hesitating to void the warranty in their quest for maximum performance. They might be amateur cyclists working to decrease the weight of a bicycle, boy racers fiddling with the software of the engine-control chips in their cars, or even purchasers of an industrial printing machine who, by tweaking the feed rollers just a touch, are able to get the machine to run a lot longer without jams. Some of them even end up starting their own businesses.

Many organizations frown on this kind of activity. And it is worth frowning on when performed by hacks or ignoramuses. But lead users are neither. They are simply people with a real need that a manufacturer has not learned (or bothered) to fill, and an intense motivation to fill it. Honor them by learning from them. They are doing the work anyway; you might as well benefit from it to speed up your own innovation processes. You might take an example from the companies that have legitimized or created online communities where individuals praise or malign their products in public. Users realize that these discussion groups are not controlled or censored by the companies and thus are a place to really tell businesses how you think. Many companies are scared to death of these boards and try to suppress them, building ill will and cutting off an important source of information. A more constructive alternative approach could be to make it the better part of *everybody's* job to monitor, take part in, and, most important, learn from their customers' discussions.

Invest (to a Point)

Technological innovation is, as I suggested at the outset of this chapter, an expensive proposition. R&D tends to require experts, equipment, time, and money, and often more of all of these than we imagine at the start. So if you're going to invest, do what it takes. As one company head said as he approved the biggest project budget he had ever signed off on, "If you're going to jump a chasm, you can't jump halfway."

However, you also need to decide which chasms are worth crossing, or as Maslow (2000, p. 17) observed, "What isn't worth doing, isn't worth doing well." I've already talked about the need to understand how difficult the problem is that you're addressing. If it is too hard (hence costly) relative to your means or the chances of success, don't jump. Maybe you can succeed, and maybe the innovation will genuinely improve things, but you may be at a point of diminishing returns. This is the point where additional improvements come only at the cost of substantially increased investments, and is possibly the point where a completely different technological approach is called for. If achieving the last 20 percent of improvement is likely to cost as much as, or more than, achieving the first 80 percent, then it is definitely time to ask whether it's really worth it to make it 20 percent better using the approach you are currently using. Of course, the answer depends in part on the size of the payoff: if it's big, the cost may well be justified. The key is to ask the question so that you are making a deliberate choice, not simply following the path you were on because you didn't think to question it.

Time Constraints: Having Time and Making Time

"Clock time," that immutable force of nature that has to be dealt with when synchronizing and coordinating the actions of technological innovation, can be a significant constraint. We often treat it in this way, as if it were a completely external constraint, using a phrase like "There isn't time to try that," which can translate as "End of discussion." But our relationship to time is worth discussing because our assumptions about the amount of time we have, about when something needs to get done, or even about how we will use the time we have may create significant yet avoidable constraints that, unlike clock time, can be overcome.

Sequencing and Coordination Requirements

Certain complex projects or tasks require that things be done in a particular order. For example, you would not put the hubcaps on the wheels of a car before attaching the wheels to the axles, just as you would not hire a caterer without first deciding what kind of food you want to serve. There are other kinds of tasks for which the constituent parts can be performed in any order or even in parallel. When digging a ditch, I can start at either end, and additional help from someone starting at the other end can make the job go that much faster. Not recognizing the difference between these two kinds of tasks can be a significant source of constraint.

Using the technical language of operations, we distinguish between *serial interdependence*, whereby one task requires the output of another task as its input, so the tasks must be performed in sequence; and *pooled interdependence*, whereby the tasks don't need to be performed in any particular order. One problem is that we get the tasks out of sequence or mistake the one kind of task for the other.

I was contacted a few years ago by a woman seeking advice for developing a prototype of a device she invented; it was intended for use in a beauty salon during hair washing. She said she needed the prototype to prove the value of the idea to a potential investor. When I recommended several firms that specialized in exactly this kind of model making, she asked, "Do they charge for that?" I told her that of course they charged, that's their business, to which she responded that she "couldn't possibly spend any more money on the project." She then revealed that she had spent more than $20,000 securing a patent for the device that didn't yet exist.

On the one hand, the patent secured her interest and ownership. On the other, the value of that interest had not yet been established. Had she established the value of the device first, which could have been done without a patent (or a physical prototype, for that matter), she would have learned whether a patent was worth pursuing or even whether securing it was the critical task that needed to be performed first. It's as if she had bought a really expensive lock, which left no money for a bike, without first checking if she might store the bike in her locked garage. She also hadn't considered whether the bus might have been the more appropriate vehicle for getting where she wanted to go.

We are vulnerable to this kind of constraint if we become annoyed at the idea of project planning—that is, of diagramming and then disaggregating a hypothetical project in gory detail. We will be annoyed because doing a good project plan is hard, because a good plan has the danger of exposing important weaknesses in the complexity or resource requirements of our pet idea, and because planning requires spending time on the details of a project that we are not even sure is worth doing.

Long Feedback Loops

Another critical aspect of time is that of feedback. The time between when you try a new action and when you get a sense of the success of that action can be critical and difficult to control. In his book *Why Things Bite Back*, Edward Tenner (1997) chronicles a number of landscape-altering examples of people introducing significant innovations on the basis of a thoroughly unconscious and incompetent understanding of how the innovation itself worked or how they would be able to tell whether or not the idea was working and therefore a good idea (or not). Kudzu, for example, is a vine introduced to the United States from Japan in 1876 and promoted not only for use as an ornamental plant but also to feed grazing animals and control erosion. It was widely planted from the 1930s into the 1950s by the Civilian Conservation Corps. Subsequently it was discovered that the conditions in the southeastern United States were *too* ideal for the plant, and it grew out of control, choking out native vegetation and invading cropland, and continues to do so to this day. Estimates of the value of lost cropland and the cost to control the plant exceed $500 million annually; the rate of spread in the southern United States has been estimated at over 150,000 acres per year.

In the case of the drug thalidomide, there was a yearlong lag between when the mothers took the pills and the first affected babies were born. Then there was the time it required to track down the source of the problem; it took four-and-a-half years from the birth of the first affected baby to the identification of thalidomide as the cause.

Time Required for Learning

Besides Maslow's model, there are others describing the progression of learning, one of which bears mentioning here. The *learning curve* (Figure 7.2) represents the amount of learning that we have achieved on the vertical axis, against the progression of time along the horizontal axis. The characteristic S shape is believed to characterize all learning, in that it starts slowly, accelerates rapidly, and finishes in a plateau where it again grows slowly if at all. This is the path we take from our lowest levels of competence to our highest levels of mastery. Given that all new efforts are subject to a learning curve, it is surprising how easily we may fail to consider the rate at which learning will need to occur in organizations to address even relatively simple new problems or innovation initiatives.

The constraint begins to show when we underestimate the time it will take to develop or even acquire sufficient competence in new endeavors. Consider how easy it is to underestimate the time

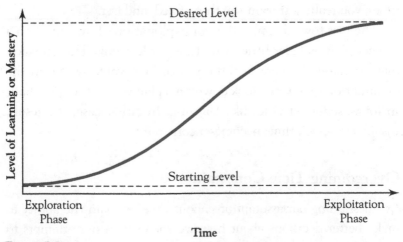

Figure 7.2

it will take to do the things you already know how to do. Overly optimistic views are also vulnerable to the usually faulty assumption that the people being asked to do the learning actually want to learn, or that the people we have engaged to teach us, whether through contract or acquisition, actually want to transfer to us the skills that have made them valuable. If we do our resource and time planning based on systematic underestimates, we can find ourselves in a position where there really is insufficient clock time to do what has to be done at a level that makes it worth doing.

Consulting firms and educational institutions sell learning as their product and are thus able to realize a return on learning, or exploration, which might otherwise be considered wasted. It also helps that the client (or student) is the one paying for the learning. However, organizations that value the application of knowledge exclusively over the generation of knowledge tend to give learning short shrift. Being focused on implementation means you want to get to that point as quickly as possible without investing in any learning that does not have immediate use. You may be in such a mode when, for example, a water pipe breaks under your house. Although it may be of intellectual interest to get a conceptual overview of municipal water distribution systems and to learn the finer points of the materials, diameters, and thread sizes of various pipes, you really just want the thing fixed, and fast.

The bias toward application, or exploitation, shows up when a project plan includes little or no time for learning. This omission may be caused by pure forgetfulness or by a value system in the organization that would look down on a plan with lots of time built in for wasteful activities like learning. In either case, the result, insufficient clock time, becomes a constraint.

Overcoming Time Constraints

By questioning our assumptions about time, we gain the ability to make better decisions about how we spend it in our attempts to overcome technological barriers. We can also gain a much better sense of whether our plans will, in fact, enable us to meet the market need in a meaningful way. What follows are several strategies for overcoming the constraints caused by our assumptions about time.

Leave Time to Learn

Develop a project plan to enable you to surface your assumptions about the tasks involved. Be aware of the tendency to underestimate the overall amount of resources that will be required as well as the amount of time that will be needed for learning.

Project planning is not necessarily a fun task, and you may find, even for simple problems, that you get a feeling along the lines of "It'll take longer to plan this thing out than to actually do it." Ignore the feeling: the analysis will help you develop the optimum way to perform the task. If you don't have time to do this, you probably don't have time to perform the project, either. Consider this to be the necessary work of innovation. Also, if it is a complex project, use a project management software tool.

First consider the time you have allotted to learning, if any. You might check with others who have performed a project with similar learning requirements to see what their experience was. Recently I examined a plan prepared by an outside vendor for the installation of a new accounting system for a business I worked with. There was a great deal of time demarcated as "training" in the plan, but no time denoted as "learning." When I asked if the time estimate was realistic, I was told that it was, "so long as nothing unusual happened." When I asked how often nothing went wrong, the installers eventually confessed that they always ran into some kind of problem, but then reasoned that because the problems were different from customer to customer, they couldn't plan for them in advance. Either it had not occurred to them that they *could* plan for "unforeseen problems" or learning, or they were reluctant to admit to a client that they themselves would also need to learn; after all, as experts, they were supposed to know exactly what they were doing.

Of course experts need to learn. That's how they become experts. Make sure you don't crowd out this legitimate activity in order to make the project appear shorter or cheaper, or yourself appear smarter. If your resources are insufficient (including cognitive resources), it's better to know that up front than three-fourths of the way through.

First Things First

As you break the project down into its likely tasks, figure out how the tasks depend on each other. As noted earlier, some may have to be performed before others; some may not depend on others in any obvious ways. Software tools can automate this process, and some can even suggest an optimum sequencing based on the time estimates, sequencing, and dependencies you have established. You should also consider the possibility of disaggregating and then rearranging the order of the tasks to see whether any tasks can be done in parallel, thus reducing time to finish. A software program can do this for you automatically, but you can do it manually as well.

Once you understand the basic tasks and their dependencies, and believe that you have enough time overall to do the project, you must now try to "pull" the most critical parts of the project toward the beginning of the project. For example, the woman with the hairdresser invention could have moved the task of finding an investor earlier, before the task of applying for a patent. If she couldn't get interest from the investor on the strength of the idea itself, a patent was not likely to make it suddenly interesting. A lack of interest is also a telltale sign that the idea is probably not worth a $20,000 patent. Exploring her project plan further might have suggested that even before pitching the investor, she should canvass some other beauty salons to determine whether there was a general interest in the product or whether it had meaning only for her. If there was interest, she could have documented that interest to convince the investor. If not, she could have used a small part of the $20,000 to have the device built for her to use in her own shop.

Don't avoid building a plan for fear of finding out how hard the project really is going to be; that's the only way you can construct a schedule that won't create a clock-time constraint. And don't be afraid to test the showstopper question; if your idea is not as valuable as you thought it was going to be, the sooner you find out, the better.

Watch the Clock

Estimating the time a project will take can provide an important opportunity to examine the difficulty of the approach being planned. If the timing seems unduly long or puts the innovation beyond an available window of opportunity, probe the assumptions that underlie the estimate. For example, you might ask if there is a simpler and faster path to an acceptable result, or even some way to simplify the innovation itself—for example, by giving up certain features. Aspiring innovators (especially young engineers) are often drawn to more complex solutions than are needed to yield an optimal result, while also underestimating the time that will be required to achieve it. In contrast, more experienced innovators and good managers are able to discern those points of diminishing return beyond which a solution may well be more technically or philosophically correct but where the cost of reaching it is out of proportion to the value. It may be that a 50 percent solution reached on time may be preferable to a 100 percent solution that is arrived at too late. By the same token, there are occasions when an additional cost in time to get to a genuine breakthrough may be worth incurring despite earlier assumptions about the window of opportunity.

Mind the Learning Gap

When we wait for others to innovate first, as Kodak did, we run the risk of finding ourselves in a position from which we cannot catch up. Of course we know that learning takes time, but when it occurs outside our direct gaze—for example, inside our rival organizations—we may not see the length or the difficulty of the learning that was required for competence with the new innovation.

But there are time-based tools we can use to monitor the gaps that exist between the functionality provided by current technology and the functionality that will be needed for future innovations. The *technology roadmap* is a tool to assess the timing and rates of development of technologies that have a potential to impact current products and future innovations. Roadmaps represent the major functions, technologies, or components of the product or service as rows in the vertical axis, while time progresses horizontally in columns from the present to future, from left to right. Each cell indicates the projected state of that particular technology at that point in time. Figure 7.3 illustrates a roadmap for the goal of having a thriving human colony on planet Mars. (This roadmap is adapted from one published by NASA (Kennedy et al., 2010) and has been altered for explanatory purposes.) The columns show time in five-year intervals from now until 2035; each of the six rows indicates a functional requirement that is integral to the success of the project. This roadmap lets NASA forecast and track the level of development of each of the important technology layers needed to fulfill the mission. If the project's managers find that a particular technology is falling behind schedule, they can make additional investments in that area to speed up development.

Develop a roadmap for your intended innovations. It not only disciplines you to pay attention to the rates of development beyond your four walls but also can show you where efficiencies might be gained through selective poaching from other technology domains that may be evolving independently. The story of Kodak shows how the company's executives failed to account for the rapid rate of learning in other domains, such as personal printing, storage, imaging software, and powerful desktop computers. They also failed to see how these innovations, taken in aggregate, might change consumers' ideas about how to measure performance in cameras.

Human Exploration Destination Systems

		2010	2015	2020	2025	2030	2035
In-Situation Resource Utilization	Prospecting and Mapping		• Geotechnical Survey • Gaseous Survey				
	Resource Acquisition		• Atmosphere Acquisition		• High Capacity Atmosphere	• Feedstock Preparation	
	Manufacturing and Infrastructure		• Space Fabrication of Parts and Tools	• Roads, Pads		• Shelters, Tunnels	• Advanced Shelters
Sustainability and Supportability of Human Life	Logistics Systems		• Propellant Servicing	• Roads, Pads	• Consumables Depot		
	Maintenance Systems		• Trash Recycling	• Propellant Scavenging		• Power Production	
	Repair Systems		• Repairable Materials • Repair Processes	• Food Production		• Contamination Control	
Advanced Human Mobility Systems	EVA Mobility		• High Pressure O_2 for Rovers	• Automated Loading			• Consumables Depot Power Production
	Surface Mobility		• Rover Lifetime and Performance	• Propellant Scavenging	• Taxi Subsystem		
	Off-Surface Mobility	• EVA Tools	• Suitport/Suitlock	• Automated Docking Mechanism	• Powered Exoskeleton	• Atmospheric Flyer	
Advanced Human Habitat Systems	Integrated Habitat		• Advanced Fabric Materials	• Internal Systems	• Light Weight Windows		• SMART Habitats
	Habitat Evolution		• Deployable Habitat	• Space Habitat	• AG Flight Test		
	Habitat Components	• Tension Cables, Rotating Joints		• Rotate Joint Power Transfer		• Integrated Artificial Gravity	
Mission Operations and Safety	Crew Training		• Crew Training Ongoing • Thermal Protection		• Virtual Reality Training	• Virtual Reality Training II	
	Environmental Protection		• Radiation Protection	• UV Protection • EMI Protection		• Atomic Oxygen Protection	
	Planetary Safety		• Planetary Contamination Protection: Forward			• Planetary Contamination Protection: Backward	
Other Systems	Modeling and Simulation	• Modeling Tools		• Simulation Tools			
	Construction and Assembly		• Imaging and Data Visualization Tools	• Dust Prevention Basic Construction			• Consumables Depot Power Production • Full Base Construction
	Dust Prevention and Mitigation		• Dust Prevention for Robotic Rover	• Dust Prevention ISRU Prop Plant			• Dust Prevention for Crewed Mars

Figure 7.3

Natural Environment Constraints: Altering Landscapes

We are usually insulated from direct contact with the natural environment by layers of manmade buffering—the walls in our building or the windows in our cars. Nonetheless, we should consider the natural environment as an important facet of the context of our innovation. The natural environment is where we will locate those activities that achieve the transformation of inputs into outputs, such as a mine where rock is turned into ore, a factory where parts are turned into cars, or even a building where human expression is turned into art. To achieve the value-creating transformation, we may need resources (such as raw materials or energy), and we may need a place to direct our products and by-products of the transformation process. It can be easy to forget that our innovation activities ultimately take place within the natural environment. Unanticipated constraints may arise when we fail to consider that the number and location of places that can accommodate the full variety of our environmental needs—for example, access to energy or shelter from weather—are not uniformly distributed throughout the world.

Availability of Necessary Inputs

Any transformation process is going to require inputs. These may take the form of the energy you need to run your machines, light your auditorium, or power your servers. Obviously these inputs may not always be located exactly where you need them. Electric power, itself an amazing innovation, has largely insulated us from the need to consider power as a factor, given that its availability seems ubiquitous. However, as you may recall from the story of the A-12, the testing of the 160,000 horsepower engines had to be conducted at night because the town's electric grid could not supply enough power during the day. This is not an isolated occurrence. An aluminum recycling plant I visited in Kentucky schedules the melting operations of its electric furnaces around the local availability and price of electric power. The newly emerging electric car industry has a related constraint. Even though the electric cars will produce no "tailpipe emissions," the power obviously has to come from somewhere; if the source is going to be an already overloaded electrical system, then the cost of upgrading the system should be accounted for in considerations of the viability of the innovation and the likelihood of adoption.

Although the distribution of electric power may be even more tightly bound by industry constraints than by those of nature, the production of that power is clearly dominated by environmental constraints. Effective locations for wind farms, for example, depend on global weather patterns for their ability to produce power. Meanwhile, nuclear and other large-scale power plants are built at sites near rivers or large bodies of water as a direct result of the cooling needs of the plants. Ironically, though we would like to put them in deserts where there is plenty of sunlight, a large-scale solar farm can require over a billion gallons of water per year for operation.

Besides power, an innovation may need raw materials as inputs, and our ability to transport them to our preferred location may need to be considered as well.

Suitable Site for Transformation

As just discussed, the siting of power plants near bodies of water is driven by input constraints. We will also need to consider the availability of sites suitable for hosting the transformation operations inherent in our innovations. Such issues as weather, humidity, temperature, and even ground stability may affect our ability to generate value in the way we intend. Some activities can be sufficiently buffered from the natural environment by manufactured landscapes—for example, by housing them in built structures. Other transformation activities need to be relatively exposed, as in mining. Though we may try to buffer the activities from the environment, the effort is never fully successful. And sometimes we may not want to buffer them: it is probably obvious to you that more convertible cars are sold in areas with more sunshine and less rain than in others.

We should also classify the biological hosts of our innovations as highly constrained transformation sites as well. Because all forms of life are hard to sustain relative to the ease with which they can be damaged and destroyed, the constraints of interventions in living systems can be significant, not only in larger systems like our ecosystem but also in small-scale systems like human bodies. Keeping the body alive while doing brain surgery is hard. When we further compound the difficult matter of sustaining life with the limitations of our understanding—for instance, knowing exactly what triggers the various kinds of cancers or causes Alzheimer's—the difficulty of innovating within the constraints determined by biological systems becomes uncomfortably clear.

Outlets for Necessary Outputs

The transformation process is intended to create value by converting the inputs into valued outputs. However, there can be constraints inherent in both the desired products and the undesired by-products of the innovation you intend.

Consider the case of "Cowboy City," as the town of Xintang, China, is known. Factories there make many forms of denim, including blue jeans, to the order of two hundred million garments per year. The town is situated near sources of power and water that are used in the dyeing and sewing operations, and it has convenient access to transportation in the form of a navigable river that ultimately flows into the South China Sea. This allows the factories to get their desirable output in the form of denim clothing to the foreign markets they serve using the cheapest form of transportation available. Clearly, a number of important constraints have been overcome by the choice of this locale, as evidenced by the thousands of denim factories that have located there.

Although the factories are situated in a way that supports the valuable part of the output (their product), they do not have a ready outlet for the inconvenient by-product. Residuals of the dyeing process in the form of soaps, bleaches, "acid washes," and blue dye have no ready outlet except a small river that runs through the town. The dye in particular is not easily diluted, and with thousands of factories dumping it in quantity, the river actually runs blue—blue enough that you can see it on an online map (such as Google Maps) at the coordinates [23.129271,113.671975].

Living with Natural Environment Constraints

In the process of gathering inputs, transforming them, and then producing desired (and undesired) outputs, constraints of the types described can limit the universe of effective innovations. Instead of proposing strategies for *overcoming* the natural environment, I offer the following as strategies for living within constraints that can make your innovations more viable and sustainable in the long run.

Use What's Available

In his book *Out of Poverty*, Paul Polack (2008) describes the story of the development of an irrigation pump, one of many innovations his organization, International Development Enterprises, has designed for markets in the developing world. It serves as a great lesson for conforming with the constraints of the environment. The $20 pump allows farmers to irrigate their fields with up to ten times the efficiency of using buckets, the method customarily employed. The pump is human powered, which gives it the advantage of not using expensive and difficult-to-obtain fuel. However, the pump also had a problem to work around concerning the efficiency of the human body. If you have ever used an old-fashioned well pump that requires you to make big arm movements up and down to draw water, you will probably realize that pumping sufficient water to irrigate a one-acre field would require the strength of Popeye, take forever, and likely destroy your arm joints in the process.

Instead, the pump was designed to use the significantly larger muscles and the more natural motions we use to walk. Using a Stairmaster-like motion of the farmer on a set of two treadles, it converts steps into a ready flow of water from an underground well. This design means that arm strength is not required and that even kids can help with the pumping. In an improvement on the original design intended for Myanmar, a group of students at the d.school at Stanford University altered the design of the treadle steps. When the steps were made from metal, the cost and transportation difficulty increased dramatically. However, a material like plastic would make repairs difficult in rural environments. They developed a solution that allowed farmers to use readily available bamboo for the treadle steps and the handholds. This local sourcing option kept the cost down, helped with transportation, and worked well for initial setup and ongoing use.

Look carefully at the locale your innovation is intended for. There may be features of the environment that are not obstacles but in fact resources that can make the innovation much more valuable.

Come in from the Wind and Rain

Whereas societal regulations set limits on the impact you can have on the natural environment, the environment is free to visit all manner of chaos on you. Tornadoes, earthquakes, fires, floods, hurricanes, avalanches, and other forces of nature can constrain your ability to pursue certain kinds of innovation. For example, when fabricating computer chips, the stability of the building is of critical importance, so much so that clean-rooms are often built in "buildings within the buildings" that allow them to be isolated from vibrations from the outside. Chip making is also vulnerable to power outages, as the 2011 tsunami in Japan showed when the resultant power loss rendered unsalvageable the millions of dollars of wafer material that was in process.

As you would for convertible cars, you can seek environmental fit for your innovations. I cannot help but think of the famous San Francisco sourdough bread. In addition to the particular strains of the yeast cultures in the bread, it has been suggested that the moist air around San Francisco generated by the Pacific Ocean on one side and the San Francisco Bay on the other creates a unique environment for that yeast to thrive. Although I'm sure you can get reasonably good sourdough bread anywhere in the country, it is still worth asking if you could or should move your idea to the place where it makes environmental sense.

Mimic Something That Works

The natural environment does not always have to represent something to be worked around or overcome; it can also serve as a source of inspiration for your innovations. In her book *Biomimicry*, Janine Benyus (1997) describes the art of observing and mimicking strategies that other living things have used to sustain their existence in the physical and biological world. By finding examples in the natural environment and then developing analogs to them, you can sometimes solve problems that may elude other analytic approaches.

Jay Harmon, a prolific inventor, developed a propeller based on the shape he observed in a nautilus shell. His impeller is far more efficient at moving fluids than the traditional geometric shapes that have been used for hundreds of years. According to the tenets of biomimicry, the nautilus shell's shape evolved over millions of years within an intricate set of natural forces. The particular shape of the nautilus represents the most efficient response to those forces, much as a water drop's shape is a response to the forces of gravity, water molecule attraction, and air friction, among others. Other examples of successful biomimicry abound, among them the Eastgate office building in Harare, Zimbabwe, where the architect, Mick Pearce, modeled the cooling system on those in termite mounds, with a result of using 90 percent less energy for ventilation than other buildings of similar size.

Get Smart About Your Supply Chain

One example of close work with the infrastructure of the ecosystem is the SmartWood certification system. In work with a major musical instrument manufacturer, Gibson Music, I learned about a problem it had had with the supply of hardwood used in the high-end guitars Gibson hand-makes in Nashville, Tennessee. At times the company experienced a glut of the old-growth hardwood it needed to make its guitars. Although the price was good, Gibson had limited capacity for storing and drying all it could potentially purchase. At other times, there was very little wood available, and the company risked idling the highly skilled craftspeople in its factory.

Some investigation in the rainforests of Honduras pointed to a major source of the problem. In addition to the natural constraint of weather and growth patterns, poachers would steal trees from villagers' forests and sell them discounted on the open market, creating a glut. But later, the missing trees created a potentially debilitating supply-chain issue.

Gibson decided to join a consortium created by the Rainforest Alliance called SmartWood. Companies in the association agree to buy only wood that had been certified by the consortium as having been sustainably and legitimately cultivated. Each tree now had an audit trail, which created some costs, but these were insignificant compared to the threat of idling production of Gibson's high-end guitars. Another benefit was that the customers who bought these guitars valued the fact that they were made from wood that had been fairly and sustainably cultivated.

While on a tour of the factory, I saw a large tractor-trailer being filled with sawdust and the small wood chunks left over from the guitar-making operations. I joked, saying, "I guess you have to audit the sawdust, too!" Completely serious, my host replied, "Yes. And that tractor is heading down to the Jack Daniels distillery, where they use the wood as charcoal to filter their whiskey!"

Find ways to work within the bigger system. Similar to the Jack Daniels example, Starbucks makes bags of used coffee grounds available for customers to take home and use in their gardens. Although coffee grounds are not problematic materials to put into the landfill, giving them to customers who are already at the store anyway saves a bit of transportation energy, saves the customers money, and reinforces to them that Starbucks cares about the environment.

Putting the Framework to Work: Technological Constraints

To aid you in assessing the constraints at this level, use the following diagnostic survey. It is intended to help you assess the extent to which the constraints described in this chapter may be unintentional hindrances on innovation in your organization.

Technological Constraints Diagnostic Survey

The survey lists twenty statements that describe symptoms that can be caused by the constraints discussed in this chapter. As you read each statement, consider how closely it describes the technological context in which your organization operates. Record your assessment by putting a checkmark in the box that best indicates how accurately the statement describes your situation.

1 = Highly Descriptive; this occurs often or on a routine basis

2 = Moderately Descriptive; this occurs sometimes or occasionally

3 = Not Descriptive; this occurs rarely or not at all

Constraint Level	Constraint Type	Diagnostic Statement
Physical		
1 ☐ 2 ☐ 3 ☐	Unconscious Incompetence	Things always look easier when we start than midway through
1 ☐ 2 ☐ 3 ☐		We get caught off guard by things we didn't know starting out
1 ☐ 2 ☐ 3 ☐	Conscious Incompetence	We are in an industry where fundamental scientific breakthroughs are the basis of new product innovations
1 ☐ 2 ☐ 3 ☐		We often have trouble getting our research into production due to the early state of the development
1 ☐ 2 ☐ 3 ☐	Conscious Competence	We use traditional models for solving new problems
1 ☐ 2 ☐ 3 ☐		The analytics we use don't fit the emerging problems we face
1 ☐ 2 ☐ 3 ☐	Conscious Incompetence	We use intuition to make important project decisions
1 ☐ 2 ☐ 3 ☐		We don't test our assumptions when facing new problems
Time		
1 ☐ 2 ☐ 3 ☐	Sequencing and Coordination	We don't prepare detailed schedules and project plans
1 ☐ 2 ☐ 3 ☐		We do not test for the showstopping issues early in a project

Constraint Level	Constraint Type	Diagnostic Statement
1 ☐ 2 ☐ 3 ☐	Long Feedback Loops	Our work does not allow for timely feedback before understanding the success or impact of our actions
1 ☐ 2 ☐ 3 ☐		We do not test our progress as we move through complex innovation projects
1 ☐ 2 ☐ 3 ☐	Reserving Time for Learning	We do not schedule time for necessary learning in our project plans
1 ☐ 2 ☐ 3 ☐		We wait to enter a new market until our competitors have already proven it
	Natural Environment	
1 ☐ 2 ☐ 3 ☐	Available Inputs	We have difficulty getting the raw materials we need to produce our products
1 ☐ 2 ☐ 3 ☐		Our activities require or consume an ecologically limited resource
1 ☐ 2 ☐ 3 ☐	Suitable Sites	The resources we need are difficult to find where we are located
1 ☐ 2 ☐ 3 ☐		Our activities are dependent on specific weather or climate conditions
1 ☐ 2 ☐ 3 ☐	Outlets for Outputs	Our activities require significant mitigating efforts to avoid ecological harm
1 ☐ 2 ☐ 3 ☐		Our products require access to specialized modes of transportation

Using the Results

Note the total number of statements that you rated as "Highly Descriptive." If you have rated more than six of them this way, then working on technological constraints will be a productive effort. Now that you have identified the specific constraints, you can take action. You may wish to turn back and reread the description of the problem and of the specific strategies for addressing this constraint. You may also find that strategies are obvious given the symptom you have identified. For detailed instructions on working with your assessment results, use the steps outlined in Appendix A, Using the Assessment Results, to determine if these constraints are a significant impediment for you in your organization and to develop strategies for overcoming them.

After completing the assessments for the other chapters, you can compare constraints to see if one of the other levels poses a greater challenge for you overall than do these technological constraints. Of course you need to recognize that technological constraints represent among the most difficult to change to the extent that our understanding of the natural world is in any way unclear. Still, this framework can help you understand and anticipate the ways others are likely to view your innovation efforts.

Summary

We are usually quite good at buffering ourselves from the physical world, which makes us susceptible to the illusion that we can operate independently of it. The potentially constraining effect of the technological world should be considered as you explore the universe of possible options available for your innovation. Your needs may be decidedly nontechnical; however, they will still be subject to the demands of physics, time, and the environment they may occupy. Staying aware of what we know (and don't know) about the world, how we think about coordinating our efforts within it, and where we situate those efforts can keep the inadvertent constraints at bay. The following chart offers a recap of the constraints discussed in this chapter, along with some strategies for overcoming or living with them.

Physical Constraints: Knowing What You Know (and What You Don't)	
Unconscious incompetence	Determine how hard the problem might be
Conscious incompetence	Hire an alien
Conscious competence	Let other people do the hard part
Unconscious competence	Invest (to a point)
Time Constraints: Having Time and Making Time	
Sequencing and coordination requirements	Leave time to learn
Long feedback loops	First things first
Time required for learning	Watch the clock
	Mind the learning gap
Natural Environment Constraints: Altering Landscapes	
Availability of necessary inputs	Use what's available
Suitable site for transformation	Come in from the wind and rain
Outlets for necessary outputs	Mimic something that works
	Get smart about your supply chain

Chapter Reflection: Technological Constraints

It can be helpful to reflect on your insights about technological constraints and the process of diagnosing them in your organization and industry. You may wish to consider these questions:

- What evidence is there for the existence of the constraints you named?

- How important are these technological factors compared to the individual, group, organizational, industry, and societal constraints you identified?

- What constraints might get overlooked because of your limited consciousness of the technological issues that govern your problem?

- Would others agree that there is a need to fix these constraints?

8

When Failure Is Not an Option

Leading an Innovation Strategy

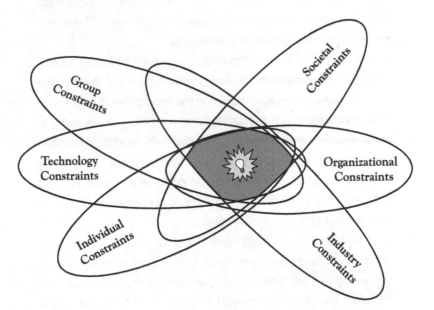

"Houston, we've got a problem." These words open an amazing episode of creativity, leadership, and innovation for NASA, just fifty-six hours into Apollo 13, the third mission to explore the surface of the moon (Krantz, 2000, p. 11). The movie *Apollo 13* (Howard, 1995) dramatizes the scene: chaos erupts as the astronauts report an explosion on board the wildly gyrating spacecraft, amid screeching alarms, with ground controllers listening in disbelief, unsure and mistrustful of the multiple failures their instruments are indicating. In what just moments before had been a normal day at the office, mission director Gene Krantz suddenly has to find some way to bring the group back together and the astronauts back to Earth.

Both the group members' sense of purpose and their emotions explode in the uncertain atmosphere of Mission Control. The astronauts cannot provide the needed understanding of what is happening, nor can the ground-based team rely on its instruments on the ground or in the spacecraft to tell it the nature of the problem it faces. "The instruments have never read this way . . . this can't be right . . . a quadruple failure?" wonders one controller, unsure if the problem is the control panel, on board, or somewhere in between.

As groups do when facing chaos, the group begins to disintegrate as the members of Mission Control retreat into their smaller and safer worlds. Despite remaining in the same physical space, they focus their attention on the displays and headsets they are using to communicate with the members of *their* own support teams outside the room and off-site. But because Krantz cannot solve or even understand this complex problem working as an individual, he must pull them back together as a team by restoring meaning and giving them a focus for their anxious energy.

"Quiet down, quiet down—let's stay cool, people." Getting their attention, he announces the urgent but dispassionate information processing that will need to occur. He then directs the team in how to gather the information needed to understand the nature of the problem and, possibly, to understand the constraints on a meaningful solution. "Wake up anybody you need and get them in here. Let's work the problem, people. Let's not make things worse by guessing." They are empowered to use all the resources at NASA's disposal and are directed to focus on the actual data, not their assumptions about the data.

Later, as the life-support subteam realizes that the CO_2 levels are rising, they learn that there are plenty of scrubbers, or oxygen filters, on board, but these were designed to fit the round hole in the command module, whereas the lunar module requires a square one. Seeing this as an urgent problem, but one that he does not have the detailed knowledge or expertise to fix, Krantz pushes the problem back on the life-support subteam. "Well, I suggest you gentlemen invent a way to fit a square peg in a round hole. Rapidly." Not only does he not have the expertise, but overly detailed involvement in this one problem would distract him from his more important role of keeping the larger group coordinated and focused on information processing and problem solving.

With the responsibility and authority to do what it needs to do, the life-support subteam begins work. The mandate and goal are made clear: "The people upstairs have handed us this one, and we've gotta come through. We gotta find a way to make this [holds up square filter] fit into a hole for this [holds up round filter] using nothing but that [gestures to a table of materials currently on board the spacecraft]." This team has not only a clear and important mission but also access to a duplicate set of the actual materials. This allows the team members to test and refine their solution. Another subteam working to reestablish power in the spacecraft's frozen command module uses a full-size replica simulator to explore and test its options in much the same way.

Again and again, as the film demonstrates, Krantz models the behavior of a successful leader of innovation. Sensing creeping despair and divergence in the group, he pulls them together and reasserts the goal by literally throwing the existing mission plan into the garbage can. "Forget the flight plan; we are improvising a new mission. How do we get our people home?" To search out the best ideas in the team, he starts with an arguable claim about the best way to get them home: "We turn around, direct abort—" Taking the bait, team members immediately interrupt, interject, and begin a loud argument about the various options and their relative chances for success. Instead of stopping the group from engaging in this healthy task conflict, he encourages it, making sure that everyone is heard and every idea considered. Having had their say, they end up committed to the chosen solution.

When the Northrop Grumman contractor is asked if the new reentry plan might work, he replies, "We can't make any guarantees. We designed the [lunar module engine] to land on the moon . . . not to make course corrections." Krantz uses this opportunity masterfully to reinforce the focus of their innovation effort and the strategy, mind-set, and commitment they'll need to achieve it: "Unfortunately we're not landing on the moon. I don't care what anything was *designed* to do; I care about what it *can* do." And, in case anyone had residual doubts about the goal, he offers a compelling reminder: "We've never lost an American in space, and we're sure as hell not gonna lose one on my watch. Failure is not an option."

As the Apollo 13 story suggests, being successful at innovation means identifying and negotiating your way through multiple kinds of constraints. Although I've handled the principal constraints on innovation individually, each of them needs to be kept in mind as you move toward implementation of your innovation. In this final chapter, I offer a way of thinking about the larger, more holistic context within which you will be pursuing your efforts, with particular attention to issues of management and leadership. I'll focus on three main inquiries:

- Up to now we have focused on factors that can constrain efforts to innovate. But what about the people we would have adopt our innovations? What constraints operate on them?

- What are the big-picture issues you need to attend to as you lead a team in an innovation project?

- What is the larger role of innovation within your organization? If your organization wishes to become more strategic about innovation, what steps might you take to help bring this desire to fruition?

Show Me the Money:
Constraints on the Adoption of Innovations

The six general types of innovation constraints refer to those truths of innovation that we know can stop a project cold. The diagnostics and tools in each chapter have offered insight into the general context within which you pursue innovation, and aim to reveal, for example, how the particular behaviors in your group or in the structure of your organization may help or hinder your efforts. Now, with that understanding and a specific problem at hand, the next step is to turn the view outward. You want to understand how the constraints apply not only to you in your context but also to the people you'd like to have adopt your proposal for positive change. Unlike you, these people may have very little invested in the innovation you intend, but they do have a great deal invested in their current way of doing things, a way that they know works. It makes sense that they would want some form of proof that the world will, in fact, be a better place for them if they believe you and adopt your ideas. This means that the obligation is on you to "show me the money" if you want me to change.

To help build a case for the value of your proposal, use the following questions that derive from the insights generated in each of the chapters. The answers will help you diagnose, for a specific innovation that you have in mind, what is likely to get in the way of acceptance and adoption by others. Just as the truths of innovation will apply to you, they will apply to your intended user as well. As you read the questions in the table here, consider your adoptee as the focus of the question and see how well you can answer these kinds of questions that will invariably be generated by your proposal. For help answering the questions, refer back to the relevant chapter to review the strategies you can use to yield an affirmative answer.

Individual Constraints: Do They Understand Your Innovation Proposal?	
Perception	Can they actually see your proposition clearly?
	What perspective are they likely to take on it?
Intellection	Will they believe you, given their sense of how the world works?
	What reasonable questions are they going to ask?
Expression	What language will they be using to gain their understanding?
	How will they talk about your proposal to others?
Group Constraints: Does Your Innovation Create Emotional Risks for Them?	
Emotion	What risk is there that it can, in any way, make them look foolish?
	How might it endanger their social status?
Culture	Why should they change the way they currently do things?
	How does it affect their membership in important social groups?
Process	How will they know how to integrate it in their lives?
	What steps will they need to take to derive the most value?
Environment	Is their environment an appropriate place for this proposal?
	Does the environment reinforce the message you are sending?
Organizational Constraints: Does Your Innovation Support Their Mission and Goals?	
Strategy	Is it consistent with their strategy? Will they recognize that?
	How will it impact their current alignment and priorities?

Organizational Constraints: Does Your Innovation Support Their Mission and Goals? (Continued)	
Structure	Are they in a position to gain value from your proposition?
	Do they have the authority to make the adoption decision?
Resources	What resources will they need to control and provide?
	What additional risks are you creating for those resources?
Industry Constraints: Does the Innovation Account for Their Landscape?	
Competition	Who are their competitors?
	What are the substitutes for them? For you?
Suppliers	Does it threaten occupations or professions?
	Does it devalue any suppliers or resources?
Markets	How many others will be adopting this?
	Will the economic conditions allow them to adopt?
Societal Constraints: Does the Innovation Support Their Values and Identity?	
Values	What does it tell others about them if they adopt?
	Do they actually want to be what it makes them?
Social Control	Which stakeholders will claim that it is likely to cause harm?
	What are the current and future regulations about?
History	Why are they doing things the current way?
	Will your idea work with what they already have and do?
Technological Constraints: Can They Make the Innovation Perform as Promised?	
Physical	Will it actually work in their context?
	Will it increase their control over their world?
Time	Do they have time to learn a new way of being?
	Is the window of opportunity still open?
Natural Environment	Are the inputs and outputs sustainable?
	Are there adverse impacts during the life cycle?

Of course receiving supportive or affirmative answers to all of the questions doesn't guarantee adoption success. However, your innovation will be doomed to rejection and failure if critical questions are left unresolved or unanswered in the minds of those you hope to convince. Consider the situation from their perspective: you are asking them to take on risk and adopt your change without satisfying answers to reasonable questions. You'd have to admit that they would be fools to adopt with a lot of big questions outstanding.

If you have a good sense of the person or people you are aiming at, and know their situation and how they think, you may be able to anticipate the answers to some of these questions in advance. It always helps to start a project with a clear understanding of the goal, and what it will take to reach it, in mind. But as I've discussed numerous times throughout this book, you can easily be biased about your own ideas and how others should embrace them; this means you must actually test the value of your ideas and assumptions with them and other potential stakeholders, on their terms, watching for insights and unanticipated reactions. These tests should also consist of more than simply asking a person if he or she likes it. Simple prototypes or mock-ups of important characteristics of your idea can go a long way in helping you understand how people really feel.

Managing or Leading Innovation?

Business thinkers often draw a distinction between managing and leading. Managing is the work of planning, coordinating, and developing strategy, whereas leading is what must be done in the domains of emotion, motivation, and mission. Although the differences may seem obvious to you, don't make the mistake of thinking that your title as "team *leader*" or "project *manager*" absolves you of the responsibility for the other set of duties. The people who look to you for guidance won't necessarily make the distinction; besides, both types of tasks need to be accomplished anyway. In the next sections, I'll offer some insights into how the work of each of the roles plays into your ability to move your team from idea through implementation.

Managing the Process of Innovation

Think of the process of innovation as simply a set of steps that will need to be accomplished in order to get from the stage of identifying a problem all the way through to implementing a solution. Along this path, there will be a number of management activities that can smooth progress and make for a more efficient effort.

Obviously, an innovation will (and should) have many possible sources of uncertainty. Ideally, all the unpredictable issues will be precisely that: unpredictable. If there are things you can plan or schedule, go ahead and plan for them or schedule them. However, you will also want to keep all the cognitive and other resources of the team focused on the things that cannot be known or determined in advance. For example, a fast-growing consumer products company was having trouble shortening its product development time and fulfilling orders on schedule. I recommended to the president that he consider instituting a "product plan" in the form of a rolling schedule of all the products to be developed over the next six to twelve months. Rejecting the idea, he said, "How am I supposed to know what we'll be doing in six months? This is a fast-moving industry. If you want to know what we need to be doing in six months, just ask me then!"

It is true that we cannot predict the future or fix it into place by writing it in a plan. However, it is also true that we don't need to know exactly *what* we'll be doing, just *that* we'll be doing it. For instance, if you know that for competitive reasons you need to start a big product development project in February, then everyone should probably have taken his or her vacations by the end of January. Or if you know that the retailers need your product on the shelves for the Christmas season, then you should probably reserve manufacturing and shipping capacity, among other things, for use in the months prior. These are the kinds of management activities that can be done in advance, allowing you to drive out needless

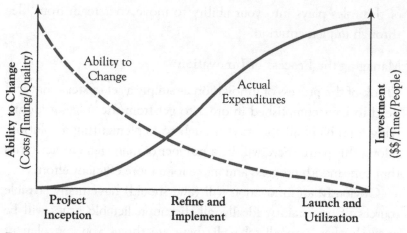

Figure 8.2

Source: Adapted from Blanchard, 1998, figure 1.5, p. 5.

uncertainty. Why spend November scrambling for a manufacturer when you could be using the time refining your marketing plan or analyzing how to set your price?

Another management function is to control which tasks are being performed and the resources and effort being expended in performing them. Consider Figure 8.2, which is based on a study of development projects. It shows how an average project will progress from idea inception on through implementation and launch, as shown from left to right in the chart.

The dotted line represents the actual expenditures that would have been made on a project at that point in time. In the early stages, very little time and money are spent as the work is mostly conceptual and performed by a small number of people. In the later stages, however, investment soars as items are purchased, manufactured, and staged in preparation for utilization. The same pattern holds true for service development, where the later-stage expenditures might take the form of training and advertising in anticipation of launch.

The dashed line traces the ability a team will have to make substantive changes in a project. Such changes might be, for example, lowering the cost of the product being designed, improving its quality or performance, or setting an earlier launch date; they are much harder to make the closer you get to the end.

Taking the two curves together, you should conclude that changes are far easier and far less costly when performed early in the life of a project rather than later. But, as a thought experiment, consider the behaviors you have actually observed in project teams. Are the levels of activity and effort more like the dashed line or the dotted one? Most people see the dotted line as most representative of actual activity. My experience observing and working with teams has led me to refer to the left side of the chart as the *latte phase*, as in "This is fun; we didn't get much done, but that sure was a good latte." I think of the right side as the *inferno phase*, as in "Dear Lord, my hair is on fire and we're going to die!" Is that similar to your experience?

If your answer is yes, this is unfortunate, because that pattern is exactly the opposite of what the chart suggests should happen, and that's a problem of management. Teams should be spending significant amounts of time and resources in the early stages when investment is low and when the possibility for implementing valuable changes based on new insights is high. By considering more possibilities and testing those possibilities in more rigorous ways, a team can identify those ideas and concepts that will be most effective and most easily implemented. If you can develop a plan that enforces committed, vigorous, and critical thinking up front, it's much less likely that you'll be running around looking for a fire extinguisher later. And there's a bonus: if your team's most rigorous efforts indicate early on that a project is a likely dead end, the sooner you know, the better. As a manager of valuable organizational resources, you will have conserved them for use on other, more promising projects.

Without an explicit plan for your team, you have to rely on members' intuitive ideas about how the process of innovation should work. Some have probably always viewed the early stage as the fun and mystical, the part where beanbag chairs and an oxygen bar may help, but they are not really sure why. They may not know what else it is they could be doing besides ruminating on the problem and anxiously watching the deadline approach. A plan, in contrast, could show them explicitly which behaviors need to be performed and when.

Leading the Process of Innovation

One of the most important leadership skills is to discern whether the person standing in front of you is asking for your help as a manager or for your attention as a leader. Sometimes explaining the plan, clarifying a goal, or acquiring a resource is enough management to keep team members moving along the path. At other times, they may need something significantly different. They may want to understand whether this mission is truly meaningful given that they heard otherwise over the office watercooler. Or they may need help staying motivated in the face of seemingly endless late nights and setbacks in the project. Although a detailed discussion of the role of leaders in organizations is beyond the scope of this book, there are some dynamics peculiar to the innovation process that are relevant to the job of leading innovation, and a brief examination of them may help you understand what and when team members are likely to ask you for leadership, and what you might do in response.

Just like the targets of your innovations, team members will also need some important answers as a project proceeds toward completion. Some answers will be in response to unease about the assumptions and justifications on which the project was based. Others may be in response to a desire to understand what the *real* chances are that what you are asking me to do now will lead us toward (and not away from) successfully fulfilling the mission of the project and that of the organization.

My study of groups pursuing innovation and my experience working with and in teams have taught me that there is some regularity to the kinds of questions that will come up. The following table presents those that you can expect to arise at different phases in the process; Figure 8.3 illustrates the corresponding phases.

Phase 0: Identify Problem

What problem are we trying to solve?

Why is this an important problem?

Is this our problem to solve?

How will we know if we've succeeded?

Phase 1: Generate Ideas

Who gets to participate, and why them?

How far will we be allowed to search for a solution?

How will you sanction destructive behaviors?

How will we know we've explored enough?

Phase 2: Assess Concept

What power do you have over our biggest constraints?

Which stakeholders get to have input, and why them?

Do I get to help decide what is the best approach?

Why should I be excited about the concept we've chosen?

Phase 3: Set Direction

Who has to do the hard work of implementation?

Which constraints are most critical to address first?

How will you generate commitment of others to the goal?

Do we still have the problem we set out to solve?

Phase 4: Refine and Resolve

How will you manage risk to our emotions and careers?

What might stop this project dead?

Can I pull the emergency brake if needed?

How can we maintain momentum?

Phase 5: Implement

Who is our most powerful champion?

Can you subdue our most powerful critic?

How do we stop "scope creep" driven by outsiders?

Is the project still valued and valuable?

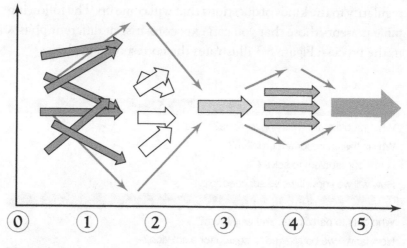

Figure 8.3

Gene Krantz at Mission Control kept reinforcing the answers to these questions to the team, not because the questions were being asked, but because he recognized that they needed to be answered. Your answers will have an effect on the levels of motivation and commitment by team members. Sometimes you don't need a great deal of commitment, as when you invite some nonmembers to participate in a brainstorm session. But most likely you will need it from those you are asking to stay with you instead of working on other projects and to stay for the duration. It's also important to recognize when the question hasn't been asked but the answer should nonetheless be delivered. Everything we know about leadership suggests that people need reasonable answers to be willing to follow. Of course you can choose not to answer them proactively; but then don't be surprised when rumor, gossip, and hearsay gathered from around the office watercooler quickly fill the void you have left.

The Innovative Organization

The primary characteristics of organizations, as pointed out earlier, are their strategy, structure, and resources. In the matter of developing an innovation strategy inside your organization, you will need to pay attention to all three if you are to drive the change you seek. Beyond the basic constraints mentioned in the chapter on organizations, there are some additional considerations when moving toward this new place.

Your Innovation Strategy

Given that innovation is a hot topic these days, with pretty much every magazine and newspaper touting its value, there can be a desire in organizations to rapidly become "innovative" without a great deal of understanding of what it is and without willingness to practice doing it. One of the first things you should think about is the role that innovation will play in your organization's business strategy.

Start Small

I know of several people who have recently been promoted into a role with the word *innovation* in the title, but who are still not sure where they fit within the organizational structure and who are not clear on what being held "accountable for innovation" will actually mean.

This leads me to the blanket bit of advice to start small. Even if you are the director of global innovation for a multinational company, starting small will have a number of significant benefits for the long-term health of the innovation strategy in your organization (and probably your career). First off, starting small allows you to use a smaller budget, which, given most traditional organizational constraints around funding, can help move you out of the crosshairs of those parts of your organization that are really focused on controlling uncertainty and for whom your innovation projects are likely to represent an unacceptable or frivolous risk.

Among other advantages, starting small helps you manage risk. Starting with small initiatives, you can use them to develop and debug a consistent and workable process first, before using it to attack larger problems that have higher resource needs and that will, therefore, undergo much higher levels of scrutiny. Although you will understand that failure (or rather, disconfirmed hypotheses) is par for the innovation course, others in your organization may not. Especially if they are powerful others, you want to make sure you have some level of familiarity with successfully accomplishing innovation projects in a local and controlled organizational context before you start the big expensive and critical projects.

One organization I know well wanted to "reduce its carbon footprint in a big way" and was toying with ideas like moving the administration buildings off the municipal electric grid. It ended up being better served by starting with a small incremental project—namely, putting solar lighting on the path to the parking lot. Not only did the innovators in the organization learn what might work technically, but they also learned that the position of the newly appointed "director of innovation" in the organizational hierarchy gave him insufficient power to get the project implemented without continual intervention by the CEO. Without the trial run, they never would have learned that managers in Administration and those in Facilities have very different ideas of what constitutes a good innovation and of who gets to make decisions about it.

Build a Portfolio

Another advantage of starting small is that it supports the creation of an innovation portfolio. Your portfolio should consist of a variety of projects in various stages of development, which is to say that it will contain not only multiple projects with different goals but also multiple approaches aimed at achieving the same goal. In this way you can also use the portfolio approach to test the components of a larger initiative.

For example, a children's museum seeking ways to increase attendance by its traditional noncustomers, namely older teens, developed a portfolio of approaches—based on hypotheses about new content, different hours, additional services, alternative advertising channels, and siblings—to address the issue. As the innovation team performed experiments to assess the value of each approach in terms of the ease of implementation versus the efficacy of that particular approach, it honed in on the most effective approaches in the portfolio. Even though some approaches were going to require more time and resources than the team had immediately available (for investment in an untested idea), it could still get started. This allowed it to benefit from small gains and to collect the information that would allow the team to assess the wisdom of the risky and gigantic all-or-nothing project it was also considering.

Use Portfolio Maps

A *portfolio map* is a visual tool used to analyze relationships across innovation projects. You can use the maps in Figures 8.4 and 8.5 to conduct a vigorous discussion in your organization of your emerging innovation portfolio.

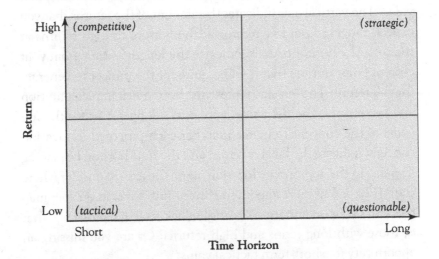

Figure 8.4   Portfolio Map 1: Returns Profile

Source: Developed with James Rosenberg of National Arts Strategies.

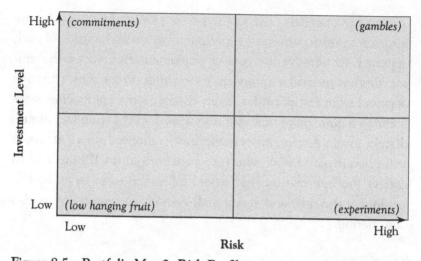

Figure 8.5   Portfolio Map 2: Risk Profile
Source: Developed with James Rosenberg of National Arts Strategies.

Portfolio Map 1 allows you to map out the return profile for your portfolio by comparing the potential return, or overall value, of a concept to the amount of time it will take for you to realize that value. The vertical axis indicates the amount of the returns that you expect, ranging from low returns at the bottom to high returns at the top. The horizontal axis indicates the length of time from your current point in time that it will require for the project to generate the full return. The left side represents short, quick implementation and fast returns; the right side represents a longer wait for the full value of the concept to be realized. For each proposed innovation concept, indicate the level of return and the time horizon by placing its name in the appropriate location along the axes. Consider where your three or four most important current initiatives fit on your map too. Does your organization's portfolio lack strategic projects—that is, those with long terms and high returns? Or are you missing an opportunity for short-term tactical gains?

Portfolio Map 2 allows you to map your portfolio by comparing the risk involved with the level of investment that will be required.

In this map, the vertical axis indicates the level of resources that will have to be invested in order to realize the value of a concept, ranging from a low level of investment at the bottom to higher levels at the top. The horizontal axis indicates the amount of risk the concept presents to your investment should it not succeed. The left side represents low-risk concepts with little likelihood of failing; the right side represents high-risk concepts with important questions left unanswered and significant levels of uncertainty. For each of your proposed concepts, indicate the level of risk and of investment by placing its name in the appropriate location along the axes. Consider where your three or four most important current initiatives fit on your map too. Are you a diehard frugivore, interested in low-hanging fruit, or a compulsive gambler looking for the massive payout? In either case, you should aim for a portfolio that balances returns, risks, your short- and long-term desires, and your resource constraints both within and across your innovation initiatives.

Don't Fear the Reaper!

In an R&D organization I once studied, the research director went to great lengths to ensure that projects in the lab would not continue past the point where they no longer made sense. In his opinion, project managers were a sly and crafty bunch, and what's more, anyone with the word *project* in her job title would not stand idly by and watch her project be canceled, no matter how compelling the reason. He may have also recognized the tendency of people with an emotional investment in a project to prefer to work on in ignorant bliss than to test the most difficult showstopper constraint.

His solution was ingenious. He decreed that membership on any project team was completely voluntary, and that every quarter, all lab employees from junior interns to senior researchers should assign or reassign themselves only to projects that they believed in and that had the highest probability of success. This way projects weren't killed; they simply evaporated as lab employees bailed from loser projects and piled into the good ones that had a significant chance of success.

Although this approach may seem extreme, managers in most organizations are extreme, but in the other direction. They fear playing the role of grim reaper or angel of mercy whose job it is to put the ailing project down. Even when a project is burning precious time and money with no obvious chance of success, there is no appetite to cancel it. If the project manager is well liked and the project relatively benign, the resources being consumed may be considered a small cost to pay in comparison to the pain of the conflict that would be required to put the project out of its misery.

One way I've seen organizations get past this problem is not to use the word *project* when referring to innovation initiatives. Such initiatives can be referred to with terms that describe exactly what they are—namely, *concept development, idea exploration, feasibility studies*, or even *experimentation*. These terms have a built-in sundown clause, meaning that the expiration date is built into the language. That way, initiatives that are working and showing promise can be consciously evaluated for continued investment. Again, starting small with investments in a number of projects of varying risk will go far in getting your innovation strategy under way.

Your Innovation Structure

An innovation structure is one that makes it easy to recognize the opportunities and challenges you face and that lets you move the people, resources, and ideas into the best arrangement for addressing them.

Support Your Innovators

When organizing innovation, a first tendency is to form an innovation group and put it in charge of *all things innovation*. The problem with this approach is the same problem that plagued the R&D megalabs like the mythic Bell Labs and Xerox PARC, and continues to haunt so many university science and engineering labs. The result is an innovation playhouse where lots of ideas and insights are generated, but few of the ideas take root because everyone in a position to help move ideas out of the lab for commercialization is too busy doing his real job to allow himself to be bothered by the crazies in the innovation center. After all, their goofy ideas have nothing to do with what our organization really does or what our society values.

A step in the right direction, however, would be to put a group in charge of *supporting* all things innovation in your organization. This group will have the obligation to help the people who are doing the work to innovate in that work. This assistance may not need to be much more than helping remove constraints, providing motivation and encouragement, and proving to the innovators that the organization is actually serious about supporting their efforts. This kind of arrangement can also provide people with advocates to help them find the places in the structure where they can go to pitch their propositions for positive change.

Reward Both Success and Failure

An innovative organization is also one that rewards the behaviors associated with innovation and not just the positive outcomes. So what does that mean? It means that paying people for simply generating ideas (the easy part), instead of paying them for implementing innovations (the long, hard follow-through) is not the way to go. It also means, in the advice from Robert Sutton (2007) that you may remember from Chapter Three: "reward failure and success equally, but punish inaction" (p. 103), being sure to make the time to let people learn from their successes and intelligent mistakes. Though it may be difficult to solve in your organizational context, another problem arises when organizations don't share the rewards that come as a direct result of a person's hard work and genuine efforts, regardless of which stage of the innovation process he or she contributed to. This will generate deep dissatisfaction among those you most want to encourage to generate and contribute their insightful, hard-earned, invariably controversial, and definitely valuable ideas. These people, who have proven they can take an idea from start to finish and create value, are hardly the ones you want to alienate in your organization.

Ultimately, the most powerful reward may also be the least expensive: simply to let creative people do creative work. You do this by removing barriers and reducing senseless constraints. Consider the comments of Erik Demaine, a professor of computational geometry at MIT, who at the age of twenty when he received his PhD was the youngest professor ever hired there. When asked about leaving elementary school before eventually talking his way into college at age sixteen, he replied, "The main thing I learned was how much time is wasted in school. When you take away lunch, recess and other breaks, the nine-to-three day reduces to about one hour of real instruction. Home schooling is much more efficient" (Nadis, 2003, p. 40). His efficiency in getting the rote, unimaginative learning out of the way is what left him plenty of time for his more imaginative, curiosity-driven pursuits.

Your Innovation Resources

As we saw in Chapter Three, groups can bring unique strengths to the challenge of innovation, provided they are managed well. When groups work well, they drive productivity and efficiency by bringing more capable hands to helping perform a given task. They can be organized to perform specialized functions on a task, thereby ensuring that each part of the task gets done as expertly as possible. By breaking up the task, we can also use a group to tackle a much larger and more complex task than could be completed by an individual. But we have already seen how groups can go wrong if they let social and emotional forces overrule their information processing and retard their progress. What can you do to help optimize the performance of groups?

Intervene in Errant Groups

An important job, albeit a difficult and sometimes distasteful one, of a leader will be to intervene in groups that are clearly having problems. It can be bad enough to have one person working in wholly nonproductive ways, but having a team of six or more people do so should be completely intolerable.

One tool I use in the self-managing student teams I assign is the team contract (see Appendix B). The team contract, drafted by the team and signed by all members, outlines at a high level their goals for the project and their agreements about how they will make decisions and about how they will resolve disagreements. But it also delves into much more mundane issues where much of the potential for conflict seems to reside, such as what constitutes commitment and respectful behavior, or at what time meetings will actually start.

I want to share my experience in implementing this tool, as you may run into the same dynamic. When I assign the completion of the contract to graduate-level MBA students, they moan and groan about this "infantile and patronizing" assignment. Of course they know how to behave, of course they know the goals, of course they can work together—they are adults, after all. However, whenever I have made the assignment optional for teams, I end up with several teams lined up outside my office door ready to complain about the errant members. Of course these are the teams who have not executed a contract specifying what was reasonable behavior and what was not. With a contract, teams are able to resolve these issues themselves. In the spirit of a teachable moment I send them away, seeing as how there is nothing I can do without a contract that specified what the behavior was that was considered so egregious. In my case, this actually improves their learning. However, unless you are in the business of teaching, you will need to intervene. With a contract or other formal written agreement, at least all the team members understand the expectations at the start.

Show Them Your Box

And what about your expectations for the outcomes of the team's innovation efforts? Perhaps you are asking the team members to "think outside the box," but do you really mean that you want them to develop a radical innovation, one that will take ten years for the company to implement, be a great risk for the company, and make you a hero or make us all unemployed? Or maybe you mean that you want a clever but safe adaptation of your current offerings that can be implemented immediately to help ease this quarter's earnings pressure?

I have discussed how being clear about your expectations will allow people to draw their own sense of the constraints around a meaningful solution. Rather than trying to keep them ignorant of the constraints in the hope that they will think of something you didn't, go ahead and tell them the actual constraints (which they probably know or suspect already anyway). Trust them to thoroughly explore the space for possible solutions and trust them enough to believe that if they run across an exciting, radical new idea, even though you asked for a small safe one, they will bring it to you for discussion. Then open your mind and see if maybe you've drawn the constraints in the wrong place.

Once you've set the expectations, start rounding up the resources that the innovation team will need. If you've asked for something radical and you have a mandate from the organization, then turn on the spigot and let the dollars and people flow. If you are aiming small, then you can afford to provide a lower level of resources. At any rate, make sure your organization provides sufficient early-stage resources for both authorized and unauthorized experiments. If there's ever a time to experiment, it's an early cheap stage. By not experimenting, you are pushing off important learning to later in the project, thus delaying your climb up the learning curve. Further, learning (especially where learning from intelligent failures is involved) is going to be much more expensive in terms of time, money, and people in later phases. Put in enough money up front to facilitate the team's significant exploration of the space of possible solutions. And then enforce your expectation that the team search it and search it hard, just as it would if members' hair were on fire.

Creative People Must Be Stopped!

There are clearly times when we need to stop creative ideas—for example, when those ideas have the potential for great harm. But there are also occasions when creative *people* must be stopped. For example, they must be stopped when they sabotage their own creativity by staying stuck in ruts of seeing and thinking. They must be stopped from fearing the consequences of standing up for their ideas, especially ideas that cut against the grain of a group's conventional mind-set. They must be stopped from wandering down paths that take them far from their organization's strategy, paths that can end only in frustration for them and for the organization. They must be stopped when they use only traditional characterizations of the markets they serve as the basis for trying to create value. They must be stopped from judging the desirability of change solely on the basis of their limited self-image and their own values. And they must be stopped when they have become so sure that they know, that they actually don't.

Although there is clearly a great deal that you can do to support, manage, and lead creativity in others by stopping them in these ways, what about your own creativity? I think the famous line from Pogo is most apt here: "We have met the enemy and he is us." If you have problems being creative, it's not going to be because you lack the capability. We are *all* creative; you couldn't last a day on this Earth if you weren't able to solve the innumerable problems that life throws at you every day, like finding food or shelter, or getting around from place to place. Being creative is human and natural, and using it to the ends of positive change, it has power to bring joy and meaning to life. If anyone has the power to facilitate your creativity, it is you. All you need now is the will.

Appendix A

Using the Assessment Results

Working with your results from the assessments in each chapter, you can use the following steps to determine which specific constraints and which types of constraints are likely to be a significant impediment for innovation in your organization.

Which Category of Constraints Is the Primary Problem?

After completing the assessment in each chapter, write down the number of statements that you rated at each of the three rating levels, and then total the number for each constraint category in the worksheet on page 250. If you have rated more than six items in a single assessment as a 1 ("Highly Descriptive"), then working on that category of constraint is likely to be a productive effort. Once you have completed the assessments for all of the chapters, you can compare your ratings across all six constraint categories to gain insight into which of the constraints pose the greatest challenge for you.

After you have completed the assessments for all chapters and transferred the results to the worksheet, use it to identify the one category where you have the most 1's and 2's. You will use your answers there as a guide for where to focus your change efforts.

Constraint Category	Specific Constraint	Number of Statements Assessed as		
		Highly Descriptive (1)	*Moderately Descriptive (2)*	*Not Descriptive (3)*
Individual	Perception			
	Intellection			
	Expression			
	Totals			
Group	Emotion			
	Culture			
	Environment			
	Process			
	Totals			
Organizational	Strategy			
	Structure			
	Resources			
	Totals			
Industry	Competition			
	Suppliers			
	Market			
	Totals			
Societal	Values			
	Social Control			
	History			
	Totals			
Technological	Physical			
	Time			
	Natural Environment			
	Totals			

What Specific Constraints Do You Face?

As you may have already noticed, each assessment consists of several sets of statements that correspond to the constraint categories discussed in that chapter. For example, Chapter Two, on individual constraints, describes three categories of constraints: Perception, Intellection, and Expression. The assessment for each of these categories has two statements describing the specific symptoms of a constraint in that category. Continuing with the example of Chapter Two, the first two statements in the Perception category describe symptoms you're likely to see when *selective perception and stereotyping* is a constraint. The next two statements describe *limiting the universe of "relevant" data*, and so on. This pattern repeats for each of the specific constraints.

At this point you have identified those specific constraints that may be present for you, and you can now develop a strategy for action. You may wish to turn back and reread the description of the constraint and the specific strategies for addressing it in the relevant chapter of the book. You may also find that strategies are obvious given the description of the symptom.

Using Teams in the Assessment Process

If you work as a member of a team or group in your organization, you can use the innovation constraints framework to facilitate a productive session to identify and remedy the innovation constraints in your group and organizational environment. Although the process of identifying constraints is not difficult, differences in people's intuitive definitions of innovation or creativity can quickly derail the conversation in a group. To prevent this problem, you can use the following procedure to manage the process of identifying constraints. This is the first step toward developing a strategy for addressing them. Having more people involved in the diagnosis will lead to deeper investment in the solutions and thus lead to a more effective change.

Working one chapter at a time, start by having each member of the team complete the assessment for that chapter. This should be done individually and without discussion, ideally before the team members meet face-to-face. It is critical to have them work independently to preserve the differences of perception and interpretation that members will have as they make their assessments.

Next, have the team meet to compare ratings. Be sure to meet in a place where you can use a flip chart or whiteboard; this aids communication and encourages all individuals to participate in the discussion. Start by recording each member's rating for *each* item on the assessment on the chart. Then begin an orderly discussion about each item, with the goal of developing a team consensus rating for that item. Give special attention to those items where members' ratings differ significantly from one another. Try to find out why the ratings differ: Is it because members interpret the question differently, because they have differing perspectives depending on where they sit in the organization, or because they differ in their perception of the relative impact of the restraint? Each of these potential differences is worthy of discussion. Gaining an understanding of these issues will be instructive to the team and will build commitment to the team's conclusions about the need for change.

Finally, the team should now try to reach a consensus on the top three constraints that have been discussed in the meeting. Write each of these three on the flip chart along with a specific example of how each one is most commonly manifested in the organization. Now talk about the strategies you can employ to overcome these constraints. Although this book presents a large number of tested strategies that you can use, do not overlook the wisdom of team members who may have experience or contextual knowledge that can impact the potential success of a particular course of action. As you consider the possible strategies, be sure to engage the question of the kind of commitment that each possible approach may require from members of the team or from the organization as a whole. You may wish to review Chapter Eight, which discusses many of issues that are involved with successfully leading innovation in a team and organizational context.

Appendix B

Innovation Team
Contract Guidelines

To create an environment conducive to the success of your team, you can create a team contract using the following process. Complete each of the following steps to help the team conduct an open and honest conversation about the mission, goals, norms, behaviors, and expectations that you will hold for yourself and each other during the course of the team's life. It is important to perform this early in the life of the project because you can hold members accountable only for expectations or responsibilities that were agreed on and clearly communicated.

Before Your First Meeting

- Schedule a one-hour team meeting that *all* members can attend.
- Select a space where the team will not be interrupted and that has a whiteboard or standing easel to facilitate note taking and open sharing. Also have a pad of large Post-it notes and a Sharpie marker for each person in attendance.

During the Meeting

- Start by quickly reviewing the agenda and designating a timekeeper and a facilitator for this process.

- Start with a ten-minute discussion of the types of items that might be included on a contract. These items might include ground rules for conducting discussions, time commitments to the team, online communication rules and standards, how decisions will be made, and more.

- Next, spend ten minutes allowing each and every member to have balanced input. To resist the urge to have one person write the contract for others to vote on, have each member write down her ideas of what needs to be included on her Post-it notes. Make sure all members write at least a few and that they do so in large print.

- Collect the Post-its and position them on the board or easel so that all members can clearly see all of the suggestions.

- Spend fifteen minutes prioritizing, clumping, removing, or adding ideas. With each idea, make sure to discuss the ramification of including it, or not including it, in the team contract. Ensure that everyone participates substantively and has a chance to offer ideas.

- Spend ten minutes discussing how to incorporate the important issues into the contract.

- Next, spend ten minutes pulling together a rough draft of the final agreements that you have reached. At a minimum, make sure there are provisions for attendance at meetings, for participation in discussion, and for addressing violations of established rules.

- Now, have all members sign the contract draft document (*literally* sign it!).

- Assign one member to type up the document and circulate it to all members for approval.

After the Meeting

- Bring a personal copy to all team meetings, and plan to revisit the contract at major phase changes in the life of the project or when new members enter the team.

Appendix C

An Innovation Bookshelf

For an extended version of this list, please visit www.creative
peoplemustbestopped.com and click on the link titled "Innovation
Bookshelf."

Constraint Type	Book Title	Author
Individual	*The Visual Display of Quantitative Information*	Tufte, Edward
Individual	*Conceptual Blockbusting*	Adams, James L.
Individual	*The Design of Everyday Things*	Norman, Donald
Individual	*Flow*	Csikszentmihalyi, Mihaly
Individual	*Decision Traps*	Russo, Edward, and Paul Shoemaker
Group	*Weird Ideas That Work*	Sutton, Robert I.
Group	*The Art of Innovation*	Kelley, Tom
Group	*Seeing Differently*	Brown, John Seely
Group	"The Deep Dive" (video)	*Nightline* (ABC News)
Organizational	*Serious Play*	Schrage, Michael
Organizational	*The Design of Business*	Martin, Roger
Organizational	*Orbiting the Giant Hairball*	MacKenzie, Gordon

(Table continued on next page)

(Table continued from previous page)

Constraint Type	Book Title	Author
Organizational	*Organizing Genius*	Bennis, Warren, and Ward Biederman
Industry	*The Innovator's Dilemma*	Christensen, Clayton M.
Industry	*Managing the Professional Service Firm*	Maister, David
Industry	*Crossing the Chasm*	Moore, Geoffrey
Industry	*Appetite for Self-Destruction*	Knopper, Steve
Societal	*Made to Stick*	Heath, Chip, and Dan Heath
Societal	*How to Change the World*	Bornstein, David
Societal	*The Art of the Long View*	Schwartz, Peter
Societal	*Cradle to Cradle*	McDonough, William, and Michael Braungart
Technological	*Innovation Tournaments*	Terwiesch, Christian, and Karl Ulrich
Technological	*How Breakthroughs Happen*	Hargadon, Andrew
Technological	*Open Innovation*	Chesbrough, Henry William
Technological	*Biomimicry*	Benyus, Janine M.

References

Chapter 2

Electronic Frontier Foundation. "How to Not Get Sued for File Sharing." July 2006. www.eff.org/wp/how-not-get-sued-file-sharing.

Hanks, Kurt, and Larry Belliston. *Rapid Viz: A New Method for the Rapid Visualization of Ideas.* (3rd ed.) Boston: Thomson Course Technology, 2006.

Knapp, Mark L. *Nonverbal Communication in Human Interaction.* (2nd ed.) New York: Holt, Rinehart and Winston, 1978.

Shaw, Mildred L. G., and Brian R. Gaines. "Comparing Conceptual Structures: Consensus, Conflict, Correspondence and Contrast." *Knowledge Acquisition,* Dec. 1989, *1*(4), 341–363.

Taggar, Simon. "Individual Creativity and Group Ability to Utilize Individual Creative Resources: A Mutlilevel Model." *Academy of Management Journal,* 2002, *45*(2), 315–330.

Tufte, Edward R. "PowerPoint Is Evil: Power Corrupts. PowerPoint Corrupts Absolutely." *Wired,* Sept. 2003, *11*(9). www.wired.com/wired /archive/11.09/ppt2.html.

Chapter 3

Adams, James L. *Conceptual Blockbusting: A Guide to Better Ideas.* Cambridge, Mass.: Perseus Publishing, 2001.

Amabile, Teresa M. "Effects of External Evaluation on Artistic Creativity." *Journal of Personality and Social Psychology*, 1979, *37*(2), 221–233.

Ancona, Deborah Gladstein, and David F. Caldwell. "Demography and Design: Predictors of New Product Team Performance." *Organization Science*, Aug. 1992, *3*(3), 321–341.

Knapp, Mark L. *Nonverbal Communication in Human Interaction.* (2nd ed.) New York: Holt, Rinehart and Winston, 1978.

March, James G. "How Decisions Happen in Organizations." *Human-Computer Interaction*, 1991, *6*(2), 95–117.

Newcomb, Theodore M. *The Acquaintance Process.* New York: Holt, Rinehart, Winston, 1961.

Owens, David A., Elizabeth A. Mannix, and Margaret A. Neale. "Strategic Group Formation." In M. A. Neale, E.A. Mannix, and D. H. Gruenfeld (eds.), *Research on Managing in Groups and Teams*, Vol. 1: *Composition*. Greenwich, Conn.: JAI Press, 1998.

Sillars, Alan L., Gary R. Pike, Tricia S. Jones, and Mary A. Murphy. "Communication and Understanding in Marriage." *Human Communication Research*, Mar. 1984, *10*(3), 317–350.

Sutton, Robert I. *Weird Ideas That Work: How to Build a Creative Company.* New York: Free Press, 2007.

Weick, Karl E. *Sensemaking in Organizations.* Thousand Oaks, Calif.: Sage, 1995.

Chapter 4

Abate, Tom. "Digital Pioneers: Xerox PARC Scientists Honored for Groundbreaking Work on Early Computers." *San Francisco Chronicle*, Feb. 25, 2004. www.sfgate.com/cgi-bin/article.cgi?f=/c/a/2004/02/25/BUGDD57F741.DTL.

"Adopting Orphans: How to Stop Overlooked Ideas From Slipping Away." *Economist*, Feb. 18, 1999. www.economist.com/node/186664.

Anderson, Steven M. "Save Energy, Save Our Troops." *New York Times*, Jan. 13, 2011, p. A29.

Cringely, Robert X. *Accidental Empires: How the Boys of Silicon Valley Make Their Millions, Battle Foreign Competition, and Still Can't Get a Date.* New York: HarperCollins, 1996.

Dernbach, Christoph. "Rich Neighbors with Open Doors—Apple and Xerox PARC." Mac History. n.d. www.mac-history.net/the-history-of-the-apple-macintosh/rich-neighbour-with-open-doors-apple-and-xerox-parc.

Hertzfeld, Andy. "A Rich Neighbor Named Xerox." Folklore.Org. 1983. http://folklore.org/StoryView.py?story=A_Rich_Neighbor_Named_Xerox.txt.

Landley, Robert. "How Xerox Forfeited the PC War." *Motley Fool*, Sept. 18, 2000. www.fool.com/news/foth/2000/foth000918.htm.

Mendonca, Lenny T., and Kevin D. Sneader. "Coaching Innovation: An Interview with Intuit's Bill Campbell." *McKinsey Quarterly*, Feb. 2007, pp. 67–75.

Pang, Alex Soojung-Kim, and Wendy Marinaccio. "The Xerox PARC Visit." Making the Macintosh. July 2000. http://library.stanford.edu/mac/parc.html.

Schwartz, Stephen I. (ed.). *The U.S. Nuclear Weapons Cost Study Project*. Aug. 1998. www.brookings.edu/projects/archive/nucweapons/weapons.aspx.

Turner, James. "The Mac at 25: Andy Hertzfeld Looks Back." *O'Reilly*, Aug. 27, 2008. http://news.oreilly.com/2008/08/the-mac-at-25-andy-hertzfeld-1.html.

Victor, Bart. Personal communication, 2009.

Chapter 5

Christensen, Clayton M. *The Innovator's Dilemma*. New York: HarperCollins, 2003.

Doblin Group. "Ten Types of Innovation." 2010. http://doblingroup.com/AboutInno/innotypes.html.

"Has Kodak Missed the Moment?" *Economist*, Dec. 30, 2003. www.economist.com/node/2320143?story_id=2320143.

Sasson, Steve. "We Had No Idea." Plugged In. Oct. 16, 2007. http://pluggedin.kodak.com/pluggedin/post/?id=687843.

Sony Corporation. "Revolutionary Video Still Camera Called 'MAVICA' Disclosed by Sony—Newly Developed Magnetic Disk Called 'MAVIPAK' Used." Aug. 24, 1981. DigiCam History. www.digicamhistory.com/1980_1983.html.

"Sony's New Electronic Wizardry." *Time*, Sept. 7, 1981. www.time.com/time/magazine/article/0,9171,924820,00.html.

Chapter 6

Clark, Ronald W. *Edison: The Man Who Made the Future*. New York: Putnam, 1977.

Boyle, Alan. "Private-Spaceflight Bill Signed into Law." MSNBC. Dec. 23, 2004. www.msnbc.msn.com/id/6682611/ns/technology_and_science-space/.

Google. "'An Owner's Manual' for Google's Shareholders." Aug. 2004. http://investor.google.com/corporate/2004/ipo-founders-letter.html.

"The History of the Edison Disc Phonograph." About.com. n.d. http://inventors.about.com/library/inventors/bledisondiscphpgraph2.htm.

Norman, Donald A. *The Design of Everyday Things*. New York: Basic Books, 2002.

Phillips, Damon J., and David A. Owens. "Incumbents, Innovation, and Competence: The Emergence of Recorded Jazz, 1920 to 1929." *Poetics*, 2004, 32(3), 281–295.

Rousseau, Jean Jacques. *The Social Contract*. New York: Penguin Classics, 1968. (Originally published 1762.)

"Ruling on Cloning of Human Beings." Islam Q&A. n.d. www.islam-qa.com/en/ref/21582/clone.

Stein, Rob, and Michelle Boorstein. "Vatican Ethics Guide Stirs Controversy." *Washington Post*, Dec. 13, 2008. www.washingtonpost.com/wp-dyn/content/article/2008/12/12/AR2008121200774.html.

Tan, Nick. "Homefront—Xbox 360." 2011. www.gamerevolution.com/preview/xbox360/homefront&print=1.

United Nations. "Ad Hoc Committee on an International Convention Against the Reproductive Cloning of Human Beings." May 18, 2005. www.un.org/law/cloning/.

Chapter 7

Benyus, Janine M. *Biomimicry: Innovation Inspired by Nature*. New York: HarperCollins, 1997.

Crawford, Matthew B. *Shop Class as Soulcraft: An Inquiry into the Value of Work*. New York: Penguin, 2010.

Kennedy, Kriss J., and others. *DRAFT Human Exploration Destination Systems Roadmap: Technology Area 07*. National Aeronautics and Space Administration.

Nov. 2010. www.nasa.gov/pdf/501327main_TA07-HEDS-DRAFT-Nov2010-A
.pdf.

Maslow, Abraham H. *The Psychology of Science: A Reconnaissance*. South Bend,
Ind.: Gateway Editions, 1966.

Maslow, Abraham H. *The Maslow Business Reader* (Deborah C. Stephens, ed.).
Hoboken, N.J.: Wiley, 2000.

Polack, Paul. *Out of Poverty: What Works When Traditional Approaches Fail.*
San Francisco: Berrett-Koehler, 2008.

Tenner, Edward. *Why Things Bite Back: Technology and the Revenge of Unintended
Consequences*. New York: Vintage Books, 1997.

von Hippel, Eric. *The Sources of Innovation*. New York: Oxford University Press,
1988.

Chapter 8

Blanchard, Ben. *Systems Engineering Management*. (2nd ed.) Hoboken, N.J.:
Wiley, 1998.

Howard, Ron (Director). *Apollo 13*. Universal City, Calif.: Universal Pictures
and Imagine Entertainment, 1995. Film.

Krantz, Gene. *Failure Is Not an Option*. New York: Simon & Schuster, 2000.

Nadis, Steve. "Computational Origami: Interview with Erik Demaine."
New Scientist, Jan. 18, 2003, pp. 40–43.

Sutton, Robert I. *Weird Ideas That Work: How to Build a Creative Company*.
New York: Free Press, 2007.

Acknowledgments

The ideas in this book build on those of Jim Adams. I had the honor of working with Jim as a graduate student at Stanford, and his book *Conceptual Blockbusting*, the first innovation book I ever read, opened my eyes to a world of possibilities. It was Jim who talked me into trying the life of the mind and who talked Bob Sutton into the absurd idea that it was easier to teach an engineer sociology than the other way around. Bob also continues to inspire me; he is a tireless teacher, a valued mentor, and a true idea man in the best sense of the term.

I continue to channel my prior life at IDEO in my work through the friendships, advice, and insights from amazing design thinkers. It was Tom Kelley who encouraged me to write a book (but not two). Dennis Boyle taught me everything worth knowing about the art of managing creative thinkers. My sporadic design-focused interactions with the generous likes of David Kelley, Bill Moggridge, Jane Fulton Suri, and Barry Katz have proven to me the importance and humanity of design. Nirmal Sethia offered me the much-needed shelter of a research fellowship at Cal Poly Pomona, where he hosted design conferences and where he introduced me to the many influential design thinkers and educators who are his friends.

Jim Rosenberg of National Arts Strategies has been a stead-fast collaborator with great ideas and infectious optimism. A few years ago he helped me craft a rough collection of ideas into a smooth-flowing workshop, and we've been privileged to present it to arts organizations from around the world ever since. I have also benefited from the sage advice and constant encouragement of my close friend Bart Victor, who introduced me to the joys of serious play. After convincing me that my ideas were worth writing down, my mentor Karl Jannasch showed me how to stay focused and motivated through to the finish.

At Vanderbilt, I've found unwavering support for my ideas at every level of the university, including from our current and former chancellors Nick Zeppos and Gordon Gee; my current and former deans, Jim Bradford and Bill Christie; our registrar, Kelly Christie; my friend and associate Jason Reusch, who is also a connoisseur and purveyor of all things shiny and new; and Peter Durand, not only the most talented but also the smartest graphic facilitator in the world.

Key to my ability to finish this book was support from my team at the Vanderbilt Executive Development Institute, consisting of Hermano, Lauren, Maureen, Tim, and Allison; the help I received from the ladies of the third floor, including Linda, Cordy, Betsy, Barbara, Alice, and Rita, who worked on early transcriptions; the indulgence of Sybil L'Heureux, who has suffered through thirteen years of students coming to her and opening with the line, "Hi. I'm in Professor Owens's class, and I need . . ."; and the friendliness of Miss Grace, whose early morning "Good morning, Professor O" never ever fails to lift my spirit.

There are also a number of friends, students, colleagues, and associates who have contributed to this work by sitting through tortured early versions of talks and still found enough kindness to correct me and then urge me on. Most notable among them are Ben Todd, Noah Lidman, Sonya Waitman, Alejandro Corpeno, Joe Boullier, Maria Mendiburo, and Claire Brown. My colleagues Paul King,

Joel Barnett, Germain Boer, David Furse, Michael Burcham, Luke Froeb, Jon Lehman, Tim Vogus, Ranga Ramanujam, Gary Scudder, and Neta Moye provided needed air cover. I got valuable "real world" insights and feedback from Lisa King, Todd McCullough, Joe Thompson, Ed Richter, Pat Lampton, Coy Brown, Chris Knear, Sue Hall, Sam Kirk, Mike Steck, Anish Bajal, Gary Vickan, Stephen Woolverton, Mark Rowan, Bo Roe, Paul Griffin, and Doug Venable, and from so many companies, including TVA, VGT, GTI, Nissan, LEGO, Mars, Alcatel, Newell Rubbermaid, Gibson, NASA MSFC, the Walters Museum, Porter Walker, the Chicago Symphony, and many, many more. There are easily a thousand others whose willingness to engage the topic of innovation has helped push me toward articulating these thoughts in writing. I thank you all.

I owe a gigantic thank you to my agent, Jeffrey Krames, a consummate professional who got me (and others) to believe in the rough set of transcriptions that might one day be a book and who guided me through the proposal process, the first important stage of getting my act together. I also benefited from the thoughtful questioning of Gordon Adler, who helped immensely on an early draft. It has been fabulous to work with Susan Williams, the executive editor at Jossey-Bass, who is a wellspring of ideas and excitement; Byron Schneider, whose patience, wise counsel, and editorial skills were key as the deadlines drew near; Rob Brandt, who managed the implementation masterfully; Nina Kreiden, who managed me masterfully, contributing many great ideas of her own; and Michele Jones, whose deft copyediting work enabled me to better understand what it was that I was actually trying to say. The biggest contributions to the book came from John Bergez, my developmental editor, who made this an unbelievably positive experience by reintroducing me to the joys of writing and the fun of intellectual collaboration. I will also admit that if any errors, omissions, or flat spots remain, they are of my own doing. (John had written me a comment that I should consider fixing each and every one, but I ignored him.)

I also recognize my families. It has been truly humbling to be the recipient of such unqualified support from Arnold and Eva, Sarah and Ruth, Phil and Jean Ann, Dwight and Carolyn, and John and Alanya. My two favorite girls on earth, Charlotte and Adelaide, were inspiring, letting me express my inner geek at home while also forgiving the many weeks of missed dinners and missed games. Finally, I remain forever grateful for the decades of support from my wife, Jennifer, whose humor, wisdom, patience, and love make anything possible and also worth doing.

About the Author

David A. Owens is professor of the practice of management at Vanderbilt's Graduate School of Management, where he also directs the Executive Development Institute. Specializing in innovation and new product development, he is known as a dynamic speaker and is the recipient of numerous teaching awards. He provides consulting services for a wide range of clients around the world, and his work has been featured in the *New York Times*, *Wall Street Journal*, *London Guardian*, and *San Jose Mercury News*, as well as on NPR's *Marketplace*.

Owens has consulted for NASA, the Smithsonian, Nissan LEAF, Gibson Music, American Conservatory Theater, Alcatel, Tetra Pak, Tennessee Valley Authority, Cisco, LEGO, the Henry Ford Museum, and many other organizations. He has done product design work for well-known firms including Daimler Benz, Apple Computer, Dell Computer, Coleman Camping, Corning World Kitchen, Steelcase, and IDEO Product Development. He has also served as CEO of a large consumer electronics firm, Griffin Technology.

Owens earned his PhD in management science and engineering through a joint fellowship program between Stanford's Graduate

School of Business and its School of Engineering. He holds an MS in engineering product design and is a registered professional electrical engineer (PE). In his current work, Owens focuses on concrete strategies for creating positive change in all types of organizations.

He lives in Nashville with his wife and two daughters.

Index

Page references followed by *fig* indicate an illustrated figure.